SPECULATIVE COMMUNITIES

SPECULATIVE COMMUNITIES

Living with Uncertainty in a Financialized World

ARIS KOMPOROZOS-ATHANASIOU

The University of Chicago Press
Chicago and London

The University of Chicago Press, Chicago 60637
The University of Chicago Press, Ltd., London
© 2022 by The University of Chicago
All rights reserved. No part of this book may be used or
reproduced in any manner whatsoever without written
permission, except in the case of brief quotations in critical
articles and reviews. For more information, contact the
University of Chicago Press, 1427 E. 60th St., Chicago, IL 60637.
Published 2022
Printed in the United States of America

31 30 29 28 27 26 25 24 23 22   1 2 3 4 5

ISBN-13: 978-0-226-71327-4 (cloth)
ISBN-13: 978-0-226-81602-9 (paper)
ISBN-13: 978-0-226-81601-2 (e-book)
DOI: https://doi.org/10.7208/chicago/9780226816012.001.0001

Library of Congress Cataloging-in-Publication Data

Names: Komporozos-Athanasiou, Aris, author.
Title: Speculative communities : living with uncertainty in a
financialized world / Aris Komporozos-Athanasiou.
Description: Chicago ; London : The University of Chicago, 2022. |
Includes bibliographical references and index.
Identifiers: LCCN 2021035828 | ISBN 9780226713274 (cloth) |
ISBN 9780226816029 (paperback) | ISBN 9780226816012 (ebook)
Subjects: LCSH: Speculation—Social aspects. | Finance—
Social aspects. | Capitalism—Social aspects. |
Civilization, Modern—21st century.
Classification: LCC HG6015 .K656 2022 | DDC 332.64/5—dc23
LC record available at https://lccn.loc.gov/2021035828

♾ This paper meets the requirements of ANSI/NISO Z39.48-1992
(Permanence of Paper).

Στην αγαπημένη μου αγωνίστρια Σοφία Αθανασίου

CONTENTS

KEY TERMS

Speculation: engagement in investment activities that are inherently uncertain for the purpose of profit. Speculation includes wagers on possible future movements of asset prices, as well as the trading of assets that seeks insurance against such price movements. Speculating is a relational activity, because it relies on a speculator's ongoing anticipations of other traders' expectations and forecasts of the future.

Speculative imagination: a generative, creative (albeit unequally distributed) capacity to imagine under conditions of incalculable uncertainty; to bring forth new collective images of the future, which helps economies, societies, and polities navigate the present's volatile conditions. A social force that is both materially bound (conditional on access to material resources, technologies, and capital) and idealist in nature (dependent on available symbolic resources, ideas, and shared myths). The speculative imagination seeks opportunities to engage constructively (but not to master or eliminate) life's ambiguities and the future's unknowable outcomes.

Homo speculans: the modern hegemonic subject of finance capitalism and successor of the rational *homo economicus*. Its origins lie in the genesis of the nineteenth century's formal futures and derivatives markets, but it resurfaces as a much more salient agent after the 2008 global financial crisis, emboldened by a powerful, resurgent speculative imagination. *Homo speculans* is an economic actor but also a social and political subject, whose struggles, desires, and imagination give shape to our modern speculative communities.

Speculative communities: imagined collectivities that are constituted in the ebbs and flows of the speculative imagination. Their social bonds are defined by a speculative engagement with the future and a connection with others on the basis of shared experiences of volatility and precarity. Speculative communities are based on a collective, mutual recognition of contemporary society's fragility in the face of radical uncertainties across all spheres of life.

Speculative technologies: the commodified digital infrastructures enabling the circulation of speculative imaginations. They are key nodes for the generation of data and images that both represent and occlude the uncertain conditions of everyday social life. Examples of speculative technologies include a growing host of algorithmically powered media, which compete in the markets of the "short-lived experience": from Instagram, TikTok, and YouTube to Tinder, Co-Star, and Airbnb.

Speculative intimacies: the transient type of romantic and intimate bonds formed in the age of speculative communities. Mediated by image-based and location-aware mobile dating apps such as Tinder, Bumble, and Hinge, speculative intimacies reflect the shifting, ephemeral, and uncertain desires of *homo speculans*.

Speculative politics: the politics of sowing chaos to reap power. A political field dominated by actors who draw on speculative technologies in order to benefit (often electorally) from the present's volatile, unstable, and disorienting circumstances. Speculative politics often works to actively generate such chaotic conditions in the first place, and to compound existing uncertainties by, for instance, spreading misinformation and conspiracy.

Counter-speculation: the enactment of a grassroots speculative politics with the express aim of weaponizing existing political volatility in order to counter dominant structures within financialized capitalism. Counter-speculations typically target governments and institutional power holders who oversee uneven distributions of risk and responsibility in society. They often involve solidarities forged in the ephemeral temporality of speculative technologies and wagers on desirable systemic failures, which can lead to reallocation of such risks and responsibilities and thus redress power differentials.

INTRODUCTION

The future is dark, which is the best thing the future can be, I think.

VIRGINIA WOOLF, *DIARY*

Marx and Keynes, both, understood that it was "the animal
spirits," the speculative passions and expectations of the capitalist . . .
that bore the system along, taking it in new directions and into
new spaces (both literal and metaphorical). . . . Until we insurgent
architects know the courage of our minds and are prepared to take
an equally speculative plunge into some unknown, we too will continue
to be the objects of historical geography . . . rather than active
subjects, consciously pushing human possibilities to their limits.

DAVID HARVEY, *SPACES OF HOPE*

Capitalist societies have always relied on their capacity to anticipate, imagine, and speculate on the future in order to navigate its uncertainty and volatility. But what happens to our power of imagination in the era of populist demagogues, "fake news," and "culture wars," when uncertainty becomes radicalized and the boundary between reality and fiction fades away? Deep economic, political, and environmental crises have marked the twenty-first century's first two decades. The world over, trust in public institutions and scientific knowledge is eroding, liberal democracies are becoming hollowed out, and a global tide of nationalist populism is on a precipitous rise. Our era seems to be on a hinge. Time itself feels anxious and unpredictable, while prevailing orthodoxies are shaken in both econ-omy and polity. As societies strive to formulate responses to the volatile conditions wrought by these profound shake-ups, their need for orienting narratives and myths becomes even greater (Beckert 2016; Bottici 2007).[1] And as we anxiously search for cues with which to imagine such narratives and myths, finance becomes the model for society writ large.

This book is an attempt to untangle finance's formidable imagination—to make sense of its impact on the ways we respond to our epoch's profound challenges, not just in the sphere of the economy but across all realms of contemporary life. In doing so, it departs from popular critiques of finance as a source of individuation, social fragmentation, and, of late, a cause of right-wing populist backlash. I argue instead that finance's transformative force is part of a larger story that we need to understand. Contemporary markets have reshaped capitalist societies through mass-scale reconfiguration of credit and debt relations, deepening existing inequalities and spurring new social struggles, which are increasingly fought on markets' turf: speculative fights around individuals' creditworthiness and organizations' asset values substitute for traditional wage-labor conflicts (Feher 2018). I contend, however, that finance's speculative forces are also key levers in the constitution of our modern imagined communities. They mold contemporary societies' collective myths, elicit their nagging anxieties, and suffuse their confused desires and clouded aspirations. We live in the age of *speculative communities*.

"To speculate" means increasingly "to connect," to endorse uncertainty preemptively, and often tactically, as a means of social survival. At the same time, speculating is not just how we relate to the future (by anticipating and imagining it) but how we make it actionable in the present. Futures, securities, bonds—terms once repurposed for the market speculator's lexicon—return to our everyday social and political vernacular to imbue it with finance's own ambition. The narratives this new vernacular pursues are more open ended than those of "security" and "control." If the only certainty in our present is that the future is uncertain, then shorting and hedging the unknowable becomes the zeitgeist of contemporary financialized societies.

In recent years, there has been a noteworthy upsurge of (popular and academic) interest in uncertainty and chaos and, specifically, in how these conditions are being exploited for political gain. Cyber attacks, "fake news mills," "troll farms," and "disinformation warfare" are the order of the day in mainstream politics. Conspiracy theories continue to gather strength, from new antivaccination movements denouncing the coronavirus pandemic as a scam to QAnon's assertions of an anti-Trump "deep state," from Hungary's anti-Soros speculations to Brazil's anticommunist propaganda. This state of affairs reflects a new political unreality, a world rendered more and more opaque by a deliberate sowing of confusion.[2] At the same time, such opacity and confusion become common features of everyday social life. Our routine navigations of image-hungry social media such as Instagram, YouTube, and TikTok teem with disorienting videos unfurling on our smartphones. Screen time and real time collapse in the short-lived experience of Facebook's perpetual scroll and Tinder's left-or-right swipe—a nervous pursuit for ephemeral connection that seems at once compulsive and unyielding. With each scroll and swipe, our notions of truth and observable reality seem to drift further out of our reach.

This book's distinct innovation is to tie these developments to a set of deeper transformations undergirded by modern-day finance, which I consider to be both socially and politically generative. The notion of speculative communities I develop is not just an economic metaphor but a concept that will help me stitch together different repertoires of responses to radical uncertainty and frame the distinct forms of dwelling in the present's queasy volatility. Rather than simply a critique of finance, then, the contribution I endeavor to offer in what follows is a broader conceptual framing of modern capitalist society as a whole.

RE-IMAGINING FINANCIALIZATION: FROM *HOMO ECONOMICUS* TO *HOMO SPECULANS*

Ever since George Simmel's authoritative *Philosophy of Money*, and over the course of the long twentieth century, sociologists have richly cataloged the myriad entanglements between finance and society. We know how economic exchanges, promises, and interests entrench themselves into life's social fabric, not merely to corrode but also to shape capitalism's intimate bonds.[3] We also know how finance's tempestuous dynamics comes alive in the modern world of derivatives and high-frequency trading, where algorithms and screens connect (and disconnect) imagined communities of traders (Beunza 2019; Borch 2020; LiPuma 2017; Miyazaki 2013; Ho 2009; Zaloom 2006). At the same time, studies abound on the powerful political rationality of our time's finance-driven neoliberalism (e.g., Gago 2017; de Goede 2005; Brown 2015), as well as the alternative rationalities emerging against globalized finance—from self-reflexive cosmopolitanism (Beck 2008) and populist reason (Laclau 2007) to the subaltern rationalities of postcolonial polities (Chakrabarty 2009; Chatterjee 2004; Guha and Spivak 1988).[4] There are still, however, very few sociological works dealing with the intensified struggles of imagination *within* finance capitalism. This book redresses this lacuna by drawing together groundbreaking theorizing of the imagination from a diverse range of fields including social theory, history, philosophy, and technology studies, which have not been previously considered systematically in the study of finance—most notably the works of Benedict Anderson and Cornelius Castoriadis.

My argument is that, as we are increasingly impatient with capitalism's future promises, our imagination becomes more and more speculative in nature, ranging from our choices of partners to our choices of government. At the same time, speculative imagination determines our capacity to hedge ourselves against future uncertainty and broken promises surrounding work security, home ownership, and life fulfillment. Speculative communities, in that sense, are formed around neither calculating reason nor irrational passions—they are propped up by the spirit of finance, which fuses logic and feeling into a generative speculative imagination. The proposal I advance, then, is not about reclaiming a positive social imagination of finance, from which it has strayed because of its unhinged speculative impulse.[5] My framing aims to illuminate conceptually broader circuits of power that have not yet been adequately studied—most vitally, the capacity of finance not only to cleave, fragment, and oppress but also to generate connections among marginalized dwellers of speculative communities and, in doing so, to unwittingly afford new political possibilities.

▲

Contemporary capitalism sees the risk-taking, entrepreneurial agent of the post–Bretton Woods era being refashioned as a politically disoriented, speculative subject who accepts rather than averts the future's radical uncertainty. *Homo economicus* is no longer. But although much has been said about its pronounced death, we still know remarkably little about the social and political subject that has succeeded it. Over the course of this book, I conceptualize the ascendancy of what we may call *homo speculans* and the consequences of this development for contemporary societies. My core interest is in this most recent stage of financialization: the explosive expansion of high-risk speculation in and around financial markets that culminated in the 2008 financial crisis and the tumultuous 2010s. However, I trace the origins of this subject to the birth of the world's first formal futures exchanges in late nineteenth-century Chicago—a time and place characterized by fierce political conflicts around speculation, which involved unprecedentedly large swaths of society beyond the market pits in both urban and rural communities (as well as greatly influential populist and labor movements auguring new radical forms of political speculation). This, I suggest, is a period when the imaginative capacities of the new economic and political actor of a nascent finance capitalism find new expressions, so that those functions could be no longer concealed behind the cloak of a dominant rationality.

I understand financialization to be the driving force behind this momentous historical shift from a rationality-driven *homo economicus* to an imagination-fueled *homo speculans*. The transition I document here, however, is neither a rupture nor a serialized shift.[6] As Giovanni Arrighi's and Fernand Braudel's magisterial histories have shown, the development from earlier industrial forms of capitalism to modern finance has been nonlinear. De Goede (2005) has demonstrated that finance has in fact been "ambiguously located in religious symbolism, colonial conquest, sexual imaginations, gambling, superstition, and discourses of moral obligation, which still underpin the ways we make sense of money, credit, and investment" (14). Importantly, moreover, "the history of modern credit practices is inextricably bound up with the violent histories of European state formation, colonial conquest, and slave trading" (21).[7] In spite of this, the history of finance has often been told in a progressive narrative. Its complex contradictions are often written out of dominant rationalist accounts. In my previous work (Komporozos-Athanasiou 2020), I have shown, following the trail of many scholars (e.g., Bourne et al. 2018; Gago 2017; Hoang 2015; van der Zwan 2014), that financialization is a global but not universal or homogeneous process. Its development has been greatly uneven in different countries, most notably between the Global North and the Global South.

Thus, I do not intend to declare a "new man" in the figure of *homo speculans*. All *homines* are, after all, imaginary species rarely found in their pure form. They are limited and thus often problematic portrayals of economic actors, caricatures used by critical (as well as uncritical) thinkers as models to understand the nest of those actors' behaviors. As such, they reflect the inherent limitations and flaws of such categorizations. *Homo economicus*, a term first coined by John Stuart Mill in the early nineteenth century, has typically sought to capture dominant characteristics of capitalism's economic subjectivity. It has been social scientists' prevailing explanatory model, used to describe dominant views of the archetypal economic agent, rather than a description of the person itself. *Homo economicus* has long been a creature "fantasized about and fulfilled by the liberal imagination and its doctrinaires," as Verónica Gago (2017, 235) puts it—a universalized ruse despite being accessible only to a small minority (Haiven 2020, 139). It is also a gendered figure, inherently masculine and sexist, free of the so-called pathologies, irrationalities, and vulnerabilities historically associated with women (Brown 2015; de Goede 2005).

I therefore remain alert to the peril of flattening differences and inequalities by occluding the profound contradictions of *homo speculans*. I use the concept precisely to probe the great prominence of *homo economicus* not only as a model of rational economic behavior but also as the locus of critical theories of capitalism to date, which have dominated appraisals of capitalist rationality in all its forms. Thus, my use of the term suggests a loose taxonomy for framing finance capitalism's contemporary subject in ways that are more sensitive to its imaginative capacities. Relatedly, I do not wish to idealize this new subject or to suggest that the spaces it pries open are necessarily positive. Vast swaths of the global population have in fact no choice today but to occupy a speculative position. But the experiences of *homo speculans* are collective experiences, situated within speculative communities; its imperatives are universal, yet its struggles are profoundly uneven. Hence the path of critique I take in this book scrutinizes the imaginative motor at the heart of finance as a force with devastating consequences for capitalism's excluded populations in both the Global North and the Global South. I contend, however, that a great deal of this violent power stems from finance's capacity to blend myths and facts, to both obfuscate and spectacularize—a power found not in some kind of mighty rationality but in finance's own vivid imagination, which is what ultimately makes modern capitalism work, and what affords its resilience.

Lastly, I want to be clear from the outset that *homo speculans* should not be confused with a gambler. A long-standing view of financialized capitalism as "casino capitalism" is often translated into depicting modern capitalist societies as "poker nations." The most sophisticated relevant argument that I am aware of is proposed by LiPuma's (2017) and LiPuma and Lee's (2012) prescient studies of financialization, which contend that emerging global imagined communities of poker players are driven by a sanitized speculative ethos and an ill-placed belief in "having a good hand" against all odds. Poker nations indulge in gambling tournaments and online betting of all sorts and are prone to "individualistic wagering against others" (LiPuma 2017, 260). As I show, however, this view ultimately contributes to the legitimacy of the rational *homo economicus* by setting it up against the immoral and irrational caricature of the gambler. This language complements the argument of a fragmented, anxious, and narcissistic (collecting ego-boosting likes and swipes) political subject, which this book seeks to debunk.

OVERVIEW OF THE BOOK

The first part of this book presents the rationale behind the project and situates it within current debates. I argue that the theoretical reinstatement of the imagination is today more urgent than ever, at a time when dramatic political and economic transformations—broadly captured in debates around financialization, neoliberalism, and ethno-nationalist populism—call into question previously "settled" relations between reality, fiction, reason, and feeling. I contend that what threads such contemporary transformations is the emergence of *speculative communities*, whose unique types of speculative imagination represent a new mode of engagement with capitalism's radical uncertainty. The contribution is a distinctly sociological enterprise, which charts the multifarious impact of finance across the spheres of capitalist economy (speculation—part 1), society (spectacle—part 2), and politics (specter—part 3).

Chapter 1 develops the theoretical edifice represented in the idea of speculative communities, introducing the key conceptual tools that underpin it. I map out the transformations of capitalism in the post-Bretton Woods era, from nation-statist capitalism to the neoliberal order of the 1970s–2000s, and the twenty-first century's speculative capitalism. I trace the evolution of the core escalating contradictions guiding the future-oriented dynamics of capitalist society. I locate the rise of speculative communities in the culminating tension between the speculative imagination of finance on the one hand and the entrepreneurial logic of neoliberal reason on the other, which leads to a radical reordering of capitalism's promissory legitimacy. To demonstrate the book's key proposed concept, I turn to Benedict Anderson, whose groundbreaking work *Imagined Communities* has rarely found a place in the study of finance capitalism. I analyze the great relevance of this work for the present study by unpacking the increasingly complexified links between imagination, temporality, and materiality. I discuss specifically how Anderson's innovative focus on the standardizing and synchronizing role of early capitalist commodities can be applied to identify the new, contingent practices of speculative imagination at a time when we are routinely overloaded with digital images but also befuddled about how to imagine a collective future (Bottici 2014).

The second chapter historicizes these important transformations by trailing the evolution of the historical forerunner of *homo speculans*. I provide an in-depth genealogy of the distinct speculative imagination that emerged in (and around) the first formal futures markets of global capitalism's new hegemon, the US economy of the fin de siècle. This is not a history of finance or of speculation, both of which predate the events that I review here by hundreds of years.[8] My historical focus is the second half of the nineteenth century and the early years of the twentieth, a period that augurs unprecedented political conflicts around speculative finance, leading to a widespread moral legitimation of speculation in modern societies.[9] During that period, debates around the morality of speculation were also rife in many other countries, most notably in Europe's financial epicenters and in colonial South Asia's market capitals. However, I argue that the depth and breadth of political conflict (involving governments and courts, traders and farmers, populists and urban workers) around history's first standardized futures markets in Chicago were a catalyst for tectonic global shifts in the distribution of risk, credit, and social insurance and therefore a salient precursor of finance's more recent transformations.[10] My particular emphasis on that time's surging populist movement, and specifically on the ambivalent position of that movement toward finance's most speculative constituents, offers a more historically complete and accurate representation of the original *homo speculans*, which goes well beyond the suave figure of the financier or the working-class urban gambler. In doing so, I also set the stage for a discussion in chapter 5 of current developments such as the new emerging alliances between regressive populism and speculative finance.

But, as I contend, we also need to trace imagination's historical role in theories of political economy. Major works in capitalism studies have been at pains to conceptualize the contradictory function of speculation, yet they have by and large neglected the multivaried significance of its unique imagination. I track this oversight in the history of Western philosophical thought, which has traditionally considered imagination as an epiphenomenon, leading to a general lack of deeper grounding of imagination within social theory. Too often such accounts position imagination as equivalent to fantasy—or, more alarmingly, pay lip service to the imagination as an individualized, psychological faculty (embodied in the figure of the heroic entrepreneur) or, further still, as the steam engine of capitalism's "creative destruction." Importantly, the social nature of the speculative imagination has been underdeveloped, which is even more damning at a time when speculation relies increasingly on the relational capacity of the imagination (to imagine, as it were, what others speculate, and in doing so to relate to them).

Through this genealogy, chapter 2 offers a deconstructive reading of the foregoing dichotomies and plants the seeds of a constructivist (rather than imitative, reflective, fictitious, or irrational) view of the speculative imagination. I inquire into the cultural and historical variability of the concept, and I demonstrate comparatively how Marxist and Weberian political economies approach the speculative imagination with a mixture of wonder, neglect, and dismissal. In response, I propose a theory that redresses materialist determinism and its dogmatic closed dialectics (which leaves little room for incalculably creative acts and politically radical agents) without however relapsing into the universalism of Kantian idealism. To do so, I draw on the underexplored political philosophy of Cornelius Castoriadis to develop a more open-ended framing of capitalist dynamics.

Having established the importance of the speculative imagination in political economy and how it intervenes in the contradictory impulses of *homo speculans*, part 2 delves into finance capitalism's contemporary transformations. Speculative imagination permeates struggles old and new, yet it appears with extraordinary intensity in our current moment, which is marked by talk of "fake news" and "alternative facts" and is compounded by a sense of confusion in our everyday digital lives. Scholarly attention is increasingly focused on the dominant role of Silicon Valley in the rise of digital, algorithmic, and surveillance forms of capitalism and disciplinary control (e.g., Zuboff 2019; Bucher 2018). Yet, as I argue, we still lack a conceptual understanding of the links between the proliferation of such digital technologies on the one hand, and everyday life's deepening financialization on the other. The book's second part proposes that social media's incendiary growth and the ascent of new financial technologies share a deeper and more profound affinity. I analyze, in particular, the technologies through which speculative communities are formed: the ways in which their fragile social morphologies are represented, yet at the same time occluded, in our new spectacle society.

Chapter 3 argues, specifically, that in the years following the 2008 crisis, we have gained unprecedented (yet stratified and asymmetrical) access to the social vernacular of speculation. Today, capitalism's commodified microtechnologies tap into the desires, myths, and imaginative labor of quotidian life to produce a precarious subject. Drawing on a range of examples of *speculative technologies* (from social media and video-sharing platforms to popular astrology apps), I show how our ritual use of image, video, self-presentation, and techniques of rapid valuation becomes a way of collective coping with uncertainty. I am particularly concerned with speculative technologies' capacity to both hypervisualize and obfuscate; to continually represent a vertiginous reality in our smartphone screens, and at the same time conceal the complexity of such a reality. Proprietary algorithms and computational code fulfill this role by ceaselessly arbitrating what is shown and what is hidden, as we scroll through lip-synching videos on TikTok, or as we swipe on images of possible partners on Tinder. I claim that such technologies nurse a speculative mode of being "in the present," a disbelief in capitalism's future promises, and an invitation of the unknown into all aspects of life. I thus offer a corrective to dominant theories of surveillance capitalism and "digital governmentality," arguing that their neglect of the complex, speculative sociality undergirding such technologies is a significant blind spot.

Chapter 4, in turn, focuses on how speculative technologies reshape intimacy and desire in the contemporary moment. I examine the staggering growth of mobile dating apps, in particular, as an overlooked but powerful manifestation of the growing convergence of spectral and affective political economies under financialization. I contend that such platforms afford underexplored spaces for the exercise of the speculative imagination, expanding its sway on our emotional and sexual lives. I critically review sociological framings of modern intimacy that project a neoliberal romantic subject, haunted by the hyperrational figure of *homo economicus*. I challenge the view that contemporary intimate bonds are upended by the financialization of sex and intimacy and the ascendancy of an entrepreneurial logic of choice. I argue instead that the more transient intimacies forged in the ephemeral space of the digital swipe are part of a rite of passage into speculative communities: an uncertain and anxious pursuit that may not chase after security but is nonetheless productive of new social connections and even political possibilities.

Finally, part 3 discusses the ways in which speculative imagination foments new (and often unexpected) political realignments in finance capitalism. Synthesizing insights from the preceding discussions, I examine the ostensibly paradoxical conjunction of global finance and the advent of a nationalist populism that has taken capitalist economies by storm. I critically review proposals (especially in the wake of Trump's presidency and the Brexit vote) that suggest a causal link between financialization and populism. Such perspectives, I argue, see new populist disillusionment as an "outcome" of financialized society—driving what Wendy Brown (2017) has called the "anxious authoritarians" of an "apocalyptic populism." Instead, through a close reading of influential theoretical works on populism and empirical studies of grassroots nativism, I trace the role of speculative imagination in the formation of this new alliance. Too often we think of markets as natural proponents of economic and political stability, much as we associate the parochialism of regressive nationalism with a nostalgic craving for the (imagined) security of an earlier era. But what if markets and publics now coalesce around a shared yearning for uncertainty?

I propose an alternative interpretation of what is typically considered a paradox: the apparent contradiction of communities opposing government interventions that might credibly improve their economic wellbeing, endorsing instead finance's destructive forces—a choice that has been described by some as an act of collective self-harm.[11] My argument is that, just as market speculators bet against the movements of the market to profit from fluctuations in the prices of securities, today's speculative communities do not merely "misjudge" the populist promise (nor do they necessarily place [blind] hope in a coming nationalist utopia). By contrast, they are intent on speculating on the promise's possible, yet uncertain, outcomes. Nationalism, in that sense, is the symbolic insurance taken out by resourceless speculators, allowing them to wager on political chaos. Put crudely, what is at stake here is not the promise itself ("take back control," "make America great again," etc.), but the volatility that the promise is likely to trigger—that is, the distance between the promise and its likely breakdown.

Through this analysis, I illuminate what is often studied as a crisis offering fertile ground for right-wing populism's resurgence. My proposal, however, is that what defines the modus operandi of such speculative politics is not merely the exploitation of crisis but the cultivation of specific conditions of volatility that merit closer examination. Moreover, the framing I suggest is more sensitive to the myths undergirding neopopulism's moral bonds and interdependencies under such conditions. Myths, I argue, are not mere lies, but complex, imaginative narratives allowing people to respond to uncertainty much more effectively than is often acknowledged.

Chapter 6 further develops these insights into the political implications of the speculative imagination. I consider the radical and transformative possibilities embodied in speculative communities by posing a seemingly paradoxical question: can "alternative facts" spur on progressive alternatives to capitalism? Returning to some of the key theoretical arguments developed in previous chapters, I identify possible routes for such reimaginings that include practices of more inclusive myth-making and collective action that seeks new ways to exploit the politics of ambivalence and unsettledness. I offer evidence that speculative communities of the post-Trump, post-Brexit era develop methods of *counter-speculation*: a speculative politics that does not simply resist the all-encompassing specter of finance but wields it against oppressing structures in all realms of social, political, and even intimate life. This final chapter discusses emerging political practices such as "hashtag hijacking"—the coordinated obfuscation attacks deployed in the 2020 Black Lives Matter protests—as well as the activism of movements like France's Gilets Jaunes (Yellow Vests) and political events such as Greece's 2015 debt-bailout referendum. It explores the questions How can we envision resistance in the sense of genuinely alternative life patterns, capable of defeating the oppressive forces of finance capitalism? What are forms of struggle and subjectivity that exceed the set menus of political choices offered by neoliberal risk management? How can the communities formed under the fog enveloping *homo speculans* nurture such alternatives? And, finally, how can the necessity of imagining the future without access to adequate resources become an instrument for overturning the conditions producing financialization in the first place?

I argue that the immersive attunement of *homo speculans* to the present contains underexplored political capital. Speculative communities' dwelling with the unknown—called into being by our routine digital rambles (what I term the "infinite scroll" and the "infinite swipe")—has made people both more aware of the "here and now" and, relatedly, more open to the future's unpredictability. While this state of affairs has undoubtedly sparked new anxieties (and a worrying surge of regressive conspiracies), it has also made societies better equipped to navigate what we may call the "real fake" of the present speculative politics: a political reality that relentlessly blends myth with facts, yet is no less real for it. These developments have profound political ramifications, opening up new possibilities for contemplating as well as, importantly, for pursuing alternatives to capitalism. But, in the same manner, a critique of financialization resting on my framing of speculative communities must itself be open ended. Departing from the persisting emphasis on self-reflexivity and the Kantian idea of freedom inherited from Western modernity, I contend that counter-speculations point to a more decentered speculative imagination at work, which accounts for more diverse social and political experiences of financialization.

I conclude with a plea for illuminating the overlooked affinities between the speculative imagination of financial markets and the radical potential of counter-speculation in society. I argue that understanding these affinities requires a departure from monolithic accounts of negative speculation, as well as myths of risk-taking and risk control, acknowledging instead the complex sociality of speculative communities both within and beyond financial markets. Such an integrated approach points to the unexpected ways in which the speculative imagination can empower the project of collective autonomy and offer the political grammar for a more radical engagement with the future's indeterminacy. Harnessing the transformative forces of speculative communities for progressive political purposes means fighting financialization on its own ground—while acknowledging that this ground is shifting in unforeseeable ways.

Correspondingly, formulating critique in the face of financialization requires more conceptual sensitivity to the power of the imagination. Contemporary theorizing of capitalism, focused as it is on the conflict between hegemonic and "counter" rationalities, has to a large extent overlooked discussing the conditions for imagination. A shift of interest is needed if we are to avoid the risk of losing control of the speculative imagination. Exposing the inherent uncertainties, complexities, and opacities of the present conjuncture is a crucial step toward forming such a critique. Orienting our speculative imaginations toward a more progressive and equitable politics can happen only through recognizing the irreducible contingency of the present moment in ways that embrace its darkness, but without reproducing the exclusionary violence of speculative finance. For Castoriadis, doing so is bound up with the project of taking ownership of our communal indeterminacy by giving a form to chaos and "a meaning to the incongruences of life," or, to paraphrase David Harvey, with taking "a speculative plunge" into our own collective unknown.

PART I: SPECULATION

FINANCE AND CAPITALISM

In common language, speculation is associated with the fancies of global stock markets and the whims of Wall Street's bulls and bears. But what exactly is the role of speculation in modern capitalist life? Why, after decades of rampant financialization throughout the world, do markets and publics remain today so closely aligned? And how do we account for the paradox of a political economy where debilitating uncertainty about the future brings growing yields for financiers and politicians alike? This first part of the book disentangles these paradoxes by proposing a theory of speculative communities. I argue that, ever since the transition from industrial to finance capitalism, a sweeping speculative imagination has been integrated into everyday life: a profoundly generative social force, whose important role has remained neglected to this day, despite its great influence in shaping capitalist societies and their uneven abilities to cope with the future's radical uncertainties.

The first chapter sets up the core argument of the book, offering an overview of key concepts underpinning my theory of speculative communities, and situating them vis-à-vis Benedict Anderson's prominent study of the capitalist nation-state, *Imagined Communities*. The second chapter traces the historical evolution of these concepts, in order to provide a genealogical account of the speculative imagination. My analysis is both historical and theoretical. I engage the ideas of thinkers including Marx, Weber, and Castoriadis to show how *homo speculans*—the new political and economic subject of fin de siècle finance capitalism—arrives on the scene to usurp *homo economicus* from its throne. Unlike its rationality-driven forebear, *homo speculans* is a more relational and imaginative agent that throws itself in the whirlpool of life's chaos without the desire to master its contingencies. My intention, specifically, is to illuminate the implications of this momentous development for the historical relationship between markets and publics, as they became imbricated in intense struggles for power from the early days of finance capitalism. I suggest that, although fraught with conflicts between passions and interests, these struggles must be understood in their essence as collective bids to harness the forces of speculative imagination.

Recognizing that some readers may be more interested in contemporary finance and its recent social and political transformations, I provide summaries of these key arguments, so that interested readers can return to this chapter to clarify how I arrive in my analysis of specific examples of speculative communities in parts 2 and 3, from Instagram and TikTok virtual enclaves to the neopopulist movements of Trump's United States.

1: THE RISE OF SPECULATIVE COMMUNITIES

Speculation is . . . the genius of discovery . . . that invents,
innovates . . . that creates something from nothing.

PIERRE-JOSEPH PROUDHON,
MANUEL DU SPÉCULATEUR À LA BOURSE, 1857

Every asset class deserves its own volatility index,
including volatility itself.

CHICAGO BOARD OPTIONS EXCHANGE
VOLATILITY INDEX WEBSITE

THE PUZZLE OF SPECULATION

Historically, speculators have been seen as both insurers of and gamblers on financial systems. On the one hand, they correct misvaluations, taking on risks others avoid and thus preventing markets from overheating, while on the other hand mastering short-selling games and betting on volatility. From Weber's "unscrupulous speculators" to Marx's "commodity fetishizers" and Polanyi's "fictitious value-dealers," the function of speculative finance as a motor for capitalist dynamics has long fascinated students of capitalism.[1] Pierre-Joseph Proudhon (1857) memorably distinguished between productive speculation (a formidable force driving economic futures, able to "create something from nothing") and unproductive speculation (the immoral and unjust trading that plays the stock market like a lottery, leading to inequality and exploitation of some classes by others).[2] But at its core, the art of speculating always encompasses an imperfect knowledge of the future and the acceptance of high risk; it combines the Lutheran fatalism of an inexhaustible human desire for accumulation with the ingenuity that Adam Smith believed speculation fosters.

In the aftermath of the 2008 financial crisis, accounts of speculation again seized the public imagination. Mainstream media and a series of Hollywood films called out financiers' greedy trading practices as the main ill of modern capitalism and a key cause of its spectacular demise.[3] Speculation came to symbolize a promise that lacks proper foundation—a world of fiction that has taken over reality. Indeed, speculation seems to be a perfect metaphor for capitalism itself: at once loved and hated, daring and creative yet destructive, it is rational in its inventive search for profit opportunities but also just as irrational in its quixotic pursuit of endless wealth. But in the literal sense, speculation is "the forming of a theory or conjecture without firm evidence" or "investment in stocks, property, etc. in the hope of gain but with the risk of loss" (*Oxford English Dictionary*). Oxford's *Dictionary of Finance and Banking* provides more nuance, distinguishing speculation from "investment" in that the former is carried out "for the sole purpose of making a capital gain."

To a certain extent, our ongoing fascination with the highs and lows of speculative frenzies comes from conflating speculation with "betting"— that is, with risk-taking "for its own sake" and without ambition to generate substantive value. Yet as economists from David Ricardo and Frank Knight to Hyman Minsky and John Maynard Keynes have long demonstrated, reducing speculation to gambling is a mistake because it overlooks the fundamental difference between risk and uncertainty in the behavior of economic agents. Knight's classic work *Risk, Uncertainty and Profit* (1921) posits that (unpredictable) uncertainty characterizes much more economic activity than does (probabilistic) risk. Risk is the concern of gamblers, but most economic and social actors are faced with decisions that are in fact conditioned by uncertainty—that is, by incalculable "outcome probability" (everyday life decisions, the outcomes of which are simply impossible to accurately predict). Harvard economist Richard Zeckhauser (2014, 3) illustrates this inescapability of uncertainty in some of the most important decisions that could possibly be made—those concerning life or death in the medical field: "Terms such as relative risk ratios and survival risk pepper the literature. But a patient who presses a physician will learn that aggregate statistics do not apply to the individual's case, that the physician and delivery institution can significantly affect risk levels, and that no data are so finely parsed as to predict individual outcomes. Uncertainty rules."[4]

With this important distinction between risk and uncertainty in mind, speculation can be seen as a complex response to the immeasurable unpredictability of economic life: *an imaginative act* that confronts uncertainty by way of both hedging and wagering. This function of speculation first came into sharp relief with the dawn of formalized derivatives trading in Chicago's grain, hog, and cattle markets during the 1870s. Based on a financial technology (the *futures contract*) that allowed for nonprobabilistic engagement with uncertainty (Lambert 2010), speculating was then—and still is now—much more than calculative risk-taking. In those early days of speculative fever, brokers could see and smell the goods (underlying assets) whose prices they were speculating on. Yet even during that time, traders were selling wheat that had *not yet* been grown, livestock that had not yet been (and likely never would be) produced. No material commodities were exchanging hands in what were essentially "fictitious dealings." The distance between the world of trading and the realities of agriculture and farming was growing fast in the pits. Market observers were soon wondering, "Was the practice of setting off a form of productive financial speculation with real benefits for society or were dealers playing with 'imagined differences' in their own minds—engaging in an unproductive form of gambling?" (Levy 2006, 245–46).

Meanwhile, in the shadow market of makeshift "bucket shops" that were set up adjacent to the formal futures markets, speculation was breaking away from the elite trading pits to become a game for the many. Bucketshop trading focused the public imagination on the sensationalist aspect of speculation—what Stäheli (2013) calls "spectacular speculation," for, unlike consumption, work, and production, speculation abstracted from "real" values intentionally. Yet, just as the fin de siècle explosion of grassroots speculation was met with a mixture of contempt and alarm, the trading activities of those with privileged access to derivatives markets (such as those inside Chicago's futures market) represented, in the famous words of Supreme Court Justice Oliver Wendell Holmes, "the self-adjustment of society to the probable."[5] Some decades later, Friedrich Hayek echoed this sentiment, seeing in the uncertainty and unknowability undergirding speculative finance the preconditions of a "spontaneous order"—inherent in human agents' striving for converting contingency into stability and fictions into reality.

I will examine this important early history of speculation and its moral vicissitudes in the next chapter, but the point I would like to stress for now is this: debates surrounding the market crashes of 1893 and 1907 in the United States, the Great Depression of the 1930s, and the real-estate debacle that led to the 2008 global financial crisis, centered markedly on the difficulty of differentiating sober (thus rational) and reckless (thus irrational) speculation (Banner 2017).

▲

At the center of the speculative imagination is an instrument that binds together present and future, thought and action, the desire for stability and the openness to the unknown. From its inception, the *derivative* epitomized speculation's inherent conflict, capturing both its investment and its insurance sides. A contract whose value is derived from the performance of an underlying entity (whether rice and hogs or interest rates and market indices), the derivative is capital's security form. It aims to provide offsetting compensation (insurance) for an undesired event or, conversely, to take a bet on such an undesired event by speculating that the party seeking insurance will be wrong about the future value of the underlying asset.

The derivative product that emerged in the second half of the twentieth century offers a fruitful terrain on which to explore the speculative mode of today's political economy because it captures the development of a particularly complex and opaque type of speculation. In their most speculative use, modern-day derivatives are used to *increase* rather than limit exposure to future volatility, with the hope of profiting from underlying asset price movements.[6] Volatility, in that sense, now becomes the means of ensuring all-important finance liquidity. To put it more blandly: if prices don't move, speculators will induce price movement for gain.[7] It was this calamitous exposure, through the trading of collateralized debt obligations and credit default swaps in the 1990s and 2000s, that precipitated the collapse of financial institutions in 2007–8. As Warren Buffet cautioned in his famous 2002 statement, "The derivatives genie is now well out of the bottle, and these instruments will almost certainly multiply in variety and number until some event makes their toxicity clear."[8]

Wish-granting genies have spectral, ghostlike properties, including the ability to swiftly disappear from their own masters' vision. *Opacity* is a core feature of financial instruments in contemporary markets (and, as I will argue in subsequent chapters, a central tenet of the commoditized technologies permeating modern-day social and political life). In the days of algorithmic high-frequency trading, and the emergence of "dark pools" (the exclusive forums of block trading of securities evading the transparency requirements of exchange markets), the intricate workings of computational bundling of securities and alternative trading systems remain inaccessible not only to the public but to the majority of traders themselves.

A recent stream of critical studies of finance (e.g., LiPuma 2017; Ascher 2016; Appadurai 2016; Martin 2015; Ayache 2010; Bryan and Rafferty 2006) has focused on this technologically augmented form of the derivative as a logic that is deeply implicated in the reordering of economy, politics, and culture. Derivatives can be especially insightful sociologically, because they open a window onto the relationship economic subjects have with their own imagined futures, through (rather than against or despite) the broader dynamics of financialized capitalism. Crucially, the speculative imagination that derivatives facilitate relies on some of capitalism's most volatile aspects. The derivative is in essence a *promissory instru-ment*—a contract that is based on promises about the future, capturing a conscious anticipation of the latter's unpredictability and of nonquantifi-able unknowns. As such, the derivative foregrounds rather than averts life's radical contingencies—or, according to Elie Ayache's (2010) well-known account, it breaks out of the prison of probabilistic thinking and enters into the wilderness of contingency.

In that sense, the derivative stands for a particularly interesting way in which financial volatility appears as internalized opportunities for capital-ist subjects, unready to question the logic of capital but willing to leap to its speculative far limits. One of the most important transformations repre-sented by the derivative form is thus the "reversal" of neoliberalism's own promissory logic. In politics and in lucrative derivatives markets alike, the future often no longer harbors the promise of redemption that justifies sac-rifice in the present (the logic of austerity)—rather, it signifies increasingly a time-space of repudiation. Speculation, then, can be understood as the very act of endorsing a failed promise or, put another way, the act of know-ingly entering into a broken contract. Much like speculating on the degree of volatility prices (regardless of their fall or increase), political speculation centers not on *whether* a promise will be kept or broken, but on the *distance* between the promise made and that promise's likely forswearing.

If all this seems nonsensical, that is because at the heart of this logic lies a paradox. What do speculative agents stand to gain from their whole-hearted acceptance of failed promises if not their inclusion in capital-ism's reward system? In what follows, I suggest that while the speculative imagination leaves a set of political promises unfulfilled, it does nonethe-less project those broken promises onto a collective realm that is conjured around new political myths and shared narratives of the future. In doing so, speculation pries open possibilities that swell over social and political life. As I will show in part 3, this radically different understanding of speculating subjects and their motivations can lead to both regressive and progressive "collectivizations" of uncertainty—and to different corresponding types of *speculative communities*. Speculation absolves uncertainty by breathing new life into social groups that have suffered loss of certainty, security, and sta-bility, thus re-enchanting collectivities. But, first, it is important to see how speculation—understood as endorsing a failed promise—tightens the link between the economic and the political in ways we can no longer ignore.

▲

In the days and years after the 2008 global financial crisis, a range of Nobel laureate economists and central bankers grew increasingly concerned with a strange re-alignment between markets and politics. Stretching beyond the realm of secondary markets, speculation was also coming to be what made a new type of populist politics tick. Akerlof and Shiller (2010) wrote, in their acclaimed *Animal Spirits*, that post-2008 recovery had been inhibited by two key factors: the future's rising uncertainty and the public's anger. Shiller (2015), in his earlier best-selling *Irrational Exuberance*, had singled out the public's irrationality as the cause of speculative bubbles and thus a key threat to healthy economies. Alan Greenspan, who first coined the term *irrational exuberance* in the 1990s, now appeared further alarmed by "irrational populism" at the ten-year anniversary of the 2008 crisis.[9] These positions all appear to share a seemingly critical view of speculation's irrationalities and passions, not merely because of their adverse effects on the economy but because of the way they appear to recalibrate the relationship between political institutions, experts, and publics. As Shiller (2015, 255) puts it,

> The high stock market levels did not, as so many imagine, represent the consensus judgment of experts who have carefully weighted the long-term evidence. The markets have been high because of the combined effect of indifferent thinking by millions of people, very few of whom have felt the need to perform careful research[,] . . . who are motivated substantially by their own emotions, random attentions, and perceptions of conventional wisdom. Their all too human behaviour has been heavily influenced by news media that are interested in attracting viewers or readers.

Hayek's own radical endorsement of the irrational and his stress on the generative force of the unknowable in capitalist dynamics appear all but lost in these accounts. More than a decade after the latest crisis, the tension between rationality and irrationality (and between reality and fiction) that is embodied in speculation seems to define the fault lines of dominant conflicts such as those between experts and publics or between liberal elites and neopopulist insurgents. Speculation, then, is at the heart of today's political economy and, as we will see, the ground on which capitalism's new struggles for power are fought.

THE ESCALATING TENSION BETWEEN NEOLIBERALISM AND FINANCE

History's dialectic plays out between what is proximate and certain and what is undetermined and uncertain. Capitalism's longevity and its ideological purchase owes much to the successful functioning of this dialectic, at least in theory and in the minds of those who endorse it. Yet our financialized times see the forces of these struggles intensifying, as speculation itself becomes the primary terrain of power conflicts. Those engaged in speculation are in that sense vying for power, with winners and losers decided by their capacity to deploy imaginative resources, in order to speculate with any hope of success about the future. The new divisions fan the flames of older ones between speculators and those who are speculated on. This shift originates in the growing unequal distribution of risk and debt dependencies in financialized society. As anthropologist Laura Bear (2020, 7) notes, "our ability to accumulate capital from speculation is unevenly distributed in relation to intersecting inequalities of class, race, ethnicity and gender."

Yet, under conditions where speculation *is* the norm in all financial transactions, the very distinctions between speculating and investing become themselves blurred. Joseph Vogl (2014, 67) describes a present situation in which "the criterion for distinguishing between real and imaginary value no longer applies, and where hedging (or trade with financial derivatives) requires investment in risk (and thus more trade with financial derivatives)" such that "not only does investment become indistinguishable from speculation but both gain a new lease of life as matching sides of one and the same operation." As a consequence, traders "who 'speculate' on the risky difference between present and future prices—now appear to be those who avoid all hedging and thus all speculative trade." The hard work of finance, then, falls on the shoulders of a new class of laborer-speculators: ordinary people residing outside the world of exchange markets who don't enjoy access to the resources required for successful hedging.[10] These laborer-speculators become increasingly absorbed in the process of speculating on their future—and they do so ever more intensely, ever more desperately.

As chaos swirls through all aspects of everyday life, the arch-villain of finance capitalism is no longer Leonardo DiCaprio's handsome "wolf of Wall Street" but the obscured, algorithm-cracking trader quietly speculating on what others might fear, on how their own fears may be speculated by others—or even speculating on fear itself.[11] Today's markets have their very own fear gauge: the Chicago Board Options Exchange's Volatility Index—commonly called the VIX—is a measure of future volatility expectations as indicated by the S&P options market. The more active the index is, the wilder the market swings that are likely to appear in the near future. A wide range of VIX futures and options products (forward contracts on the index itself) mean that lucrative wagers on volatility as an asset no longer "track" actual stock-market volatility. VIX may be called "the fear index," but speculators are far from fearful of volatility. They knowingly descend into chaos while savvy entrepreneurs who ably navigated uncertainty in the past (by mastering the forces of creative destruction) seem to be fading away.

Michel Feher (2018) has put forward a bold thesis on the political role of finance in these recent developments: capital's increased fixation on "asset value" speculation has "backfired," so that neoliberalism now generates its own resistance—a spin on Marx's "inherent contradiction" thesis. According to Feher, financialized economies now compete more intensely than ever for investment in perceived (that is, in "reputational") value, while the rapid proliferation of social media-based evaluation technologies fires up mass speculation conflicts in wider society. Neoliberal capitalism's unintended consequence thus becomes a threat to its own dominance. But even if openness to the unknown poses a threat to the status quo, it can also coexist with the regressive instincts of "order" that ultimately reaffirm neoliberalism's legitimacy. Therefore, as a first step in understanding what fuels these new speculative conflicts, we need to look more closely at the recent history of neoliberalism, from the years following the collapse of Bretton Woods and the optimism of the 1990s–2000s to the financial crash of 2008 and the recent days of "populist backlash."

▲

Recent decades have been characterized by the escalation of tension between ongoing financialization and the failed promises of neoliberal reason. As the world emerged from the oil crisis of 1973, the defeat of Keynesian economics (and the corresponding dominance of the neoclassical model) was resounding on both sides of the Atlantic. The story is more or less familiar. As national and international controls over the flow of financial capital were gradually lifted, financial activities expanded exponentially: in the United States, the total financial sector share of gross domestic product increased at a faster rate between 1980 and 2007 (13 basis points of GDP per annum) than it had done in the prior thirty years (7 basis points of GDP per annum) and more than doubled between 1970 (4% of GDP) and 2007 (9% of GDP). The growth rate of financial securities (activities typically associated with investment banks and asset management firms) was even more staggering: from just over 1 percent of GDP in 1980 to just under 5 percent in 2007. Broadly cited as a central event in this chronology is the repeal of the Glass-Steagall Act (which had kept commercial and investment banking separate since the fallback from the Great Depression) in 1999, which broadened the government safety net under the trading of securities, in effect unleashing the full force of "reckless" institutional speculation during the following decade. Through these developments, the relationship between industry, state, and finance shifted further toward its current form, with markets acquiring greater power over economy and society. This new hegemony has been often described as "the dictatorship of creditors" (Chesnais 1996) or "rentier capitalism" (Christophers 2020).

During these final decades of the long twentieth century, the ultimate victory of financialization lay in furnishing an ideological dominance "of the individual over the collective, and of private profit over public interests" (Lapavitsas 2013, 793). Or as LiPuma and Lee (2004, 23) put it, a dominance of "a huge, not production-directed, and continually expanding pool of mobile, nomadic, and opportunistic capital that resides in the hands of private hedge funds, leading investment banks, ... and the financial divisions of major corporations." At the same time, as we have already seen, with the breakdown of Bretton Woods uncertainty became an even more salient feature of finance capitalism, initially in the form of interest-rate instability and subsequently across broader social and political life. In the political sphere, these dramatic developments sparked heated discussions about the advent of the "neoliberal subject": a financialized social agent, who is defined, (self-)governed (and by many accounts imprisoned) by neoliberal reason—a form of suffocating capitalist rationality on everyday life. As argued by Wendy Brown (2015, 79), a key proponent of this view, "economic values have not simply supersaturated the political or become predominant over the political. Rather, a neoliberal iteration of the *homo oeconomicus* is extinguishing the agent, the idiom, and the domains through which democracy ... materializes."

This greatly influential portrayal—the neoliberal iteration of *homo economicus*—is rooted in two (not necessarily compatible) theoretical traditions: on one hand, the Aristotelian distinction between "the political" and "the economic," which underpins much of Hannah Arendt's political theory; on the other hand, Foucault's influential analysis of governmentality and of the biopolitically controlled, neoliberal economic subject, which has influenced some of the most widely cited critiques of financialization.[12] For Brown, under late neoliberalism this becomes a full-blown conflict between the modern *homo economicus* and *homo politicus*, with the latter having been "vanquished" by the former.[13] Above all, the alleged growing dominance of neoliberalism's economic rationality reflects a change in the ways capitalism derives and renews what Beckert (2020) defines as its "promissory legitimacy": the perceived (that is, *imagined*) credibility of promises of the future through which political authority gains support. To put it plainly: according to these critiques, the modern *homo politicus* has not only been ensnared by the *homo economicus*, but it has also "bought into" the imagined futures promised by neoliberal reason.

The function of this promise relies in the systematic and wholesale transfer of risk and responsibility from the powerful to the powerless, where debt (from student loans to mortgages) operates as a "promise machine" (Appadurai 2016), following the motto "sacrifice today and hope for a reward in the (distant) future." In the United States, governments over the last thirty years recast the family unit as the natural home of finance-driven and risk-taking agents of neoliberalism (Cooper 2017). In the system of so-called democratized finance that they fostered, the powerful promise of future home ownership on the one hand and the reliance on family bonds on the other worked to sustain the legitimacy of neoliberal order in the face of continuing marketization. But when faced with surging economic uncertainty, the debt investors of new social conservatism became increasingly disillusioned. This state of affairs entered a whole new phase after the 2008 financial crisis, when the failures of financial markets and the subsequent "adjustment" of their host economies around the world exacerbated a climate of generalized anxiety and worldwide impatience. These events culminated in a "fed-up-ness" both with incumbent global political elites and with their technocratic reasoning (Davies 2018).[14] At the outset, then, these mounting conflicts between "experts" and "publics" seem to suggest a global withering of neoliberalism's promissory legitimacy.

Yet it can be suggested that some of these tensions have in fact been successfully contained by neoliberal politics all along. The aftermath of the global financial crisis of 2008 saw an amplification of the conservative ethics of individual responsibility, as well as a discourse of sacrifice and "tightening the belt," which helped justify years of austerity politics (Konings 2018). According to this view, ordinary people did not so much involuntarily adopt the ascetic logic of austerity as willingly embrace it. Neoliberal reason thus bolstered (rather than undermined) a renewal of the Protestant ethic of "asceticism," with paradoxically reverse effects on the legitimacy of experts (who were rejected for their duplicitous espousal of marketization policies) and that of markets (which were respected for their upfront, if unapologetic, pursuits of capital accumulation). Thus, even as experts, political elites, and publics entered into new conflicts around neoliberalism's broken promises, markets and publics did not part ways. One explanation for this riddle is that traders and citizens alike were bound by the "auto-finality" of the Weberian capitalist spirit: the ability of economic and social agents alike to relate to their own futures in an autotelic way (Stimilli 2017). In other words, promises (fulfilled or unfulfilled) did not matter to them as much as "the pursuit" itself. But what exactly *was* this pursuit? To draw out Weber's formulation further, "ascetic" faith embodies a permanent restlessness that is channeled into an irrational pursuit of wealth. The contradiction between the capitalist subject's chimeric quests and its existential anxiety dissipates as instrumental reason advances triumphantly, until we are left with *The Protestant Ethic*'s famous "specialists without spirit, sensualists without heart."[15]

Political economist Martijn Konings (2015) has argued that this coexistence of neoliberal reason and austerity with irrational markets and publics has not confirmed Weber's prediction of the dilution of capitalism's spirit. He calls the new spirit of the finance capitalism era "speculative austerity"—a state of affairs characterized by a novel type of faith in the redemptive power of speculation, which combines an iconoclastic belief in markets with an iconophile endorsement of the promise of austerity.[16] Yet as we enter a new era when even conservative neoliberals appear to be inclined toward neo-Keynesian approaches to the allocation of debt and credit, the post-2008 austerity consensus is patently on the wane.[17] The logic of financialization now appears to grow more and more at odds with the neoliberal rationality of redemption, both in its ascetic and in its risk-based forms.[18]

Correspondingly, people's faith in capitalism becomes more focused on the present and less on the future. It no longer follows Weber's sacrificial paradigm, which is embodied in the "deferred gratification" principle (see, for instance, Straus 1962). Relations and transactions alike are underpinned by a compulsion for instant gratification in an economy that rewards speed, reveres immersion in the present, and endorses volatility. What is more, with the contraction of mortgage credit, average households are today less tightly involved in the risk and debt imaginaries of home ownership and more conscious of their own present precarity in the face of uncontrollable uncertainty. It is against this background that finance's speculative dynamics emerges triumphant over neoliberal reason. The reenchantment of capitalist ideology and its secular rituals continues apace, but economic agents now espouse the capitalist spirit by adopting finance's insatiable speculative imagination.

A POLITICAL THEOLOGY OF SPECULATION

The foregoing discussion delineates what we may call a political theology of speculation, tracing the outlines of a political subject that is quite different from the neoliberal iteration of the *homo economicus*. Markets have always paralleled religious cosmologies, but their secular, "connecting" role becomes more important in periods of heightened uncertainty and restlessness. If faith in neoliberal promises dwindled during the latter phases of marketization and austerity after 2008, finance continued to provide a powerful platform for navigating the wreckage of volatility that ensued. As a result, the tentative pursuits of accumulation, risk-taking, and redemption were outpaced by the speculative celebration of uncertainty itself.

That is, the speculative imagination intervenes in how faith and promises are linked together in finance capitalism. In doing so, it renews capitalism's legitimacy through the vehicle of the "broken" rather than the "redemptive" promise. In the long run, we will all be dead, as Keynes's celebrated dictum goes, but speculation emerges as an answer to the contingencies of human existence in the *here and now*.

Importantly, as we have seen from the outset, speculation cannot be considered as merely reflective of autotelic action (Stimilli 2017)—that is, as "speculating for its own sake." Today's economic and political subject—to which I will refer from here on as *homo speculans*—throws itself into the swirl of our speculative moment with the hope of connectivity. It seeks not mere instant gratification but new secular mythologies. This contingent link between present and future that sets the tenor of current financialized life orients *homo speculans* and in turn emboldens its distinct imagination. As political economy steers investment and labor toward a chaotic—yet immersive—present, the spirit of capitalism undergoes a qualitative change: from the entrepreneurial animus of risk-taking to the uncertainty-endorsing speculative imagination. This incipient speculative mode of being throws further light on the so-far-discussed changing relation between markets and publics. Even in the neoliberal economics inspired by Hayek's belief in a "fluid," spontaneous order, economic subjects are expected to "translate" fictions into "facts" when devising practices of self-governance (Spieker 2013). Faced with the perpetual domino of collapsing promises, from housing and healthcare to work security and family, the translation from fiction to facts is now all but sidestepped. More and more, *homo speculans* lingers in the space of fictions, not irrationally, but because fictions become the most reliable ordering principle in a protean reality.

A core argument of this book is that radical uncertainty is no longer the exclusive purview of economics—all aspects of life now revolve around collective experiences of uncertainty in the form of labor precariousness, rent dependency, indebtedness, emotional insecurity, and political instability. And when it comes to formulating responses to uncertainty, finance becomes the model for society writ large. The divergence of neoliberal reason from finance's speculative imagination has meant that present struggles of speculation and insurance are experienced more intensely *but also more collectively*.

Traditional institutions such as political parties and expert bodies provided some insurance against uncertainty during past decades, but today they are distrusted, when not altogether collapsed. Meanwhile, the speculative imagination seeking to capitalize on such uncertainty continues to gain currency. In the wake of these developments, it is essential to re-examine the very categories of conflict: for speculative, opportunistic "shorting" of uncertainty and for "hedging" against the profound instability defining financialized capitalism. Somewhat paradoxically, the new struggles for speculation and insurance I have examined so far have not turned financialized societies away from the phantom of Hayekian "natural order." Conspiracy, nativism, nationalism, and a resurgence of anti-gender ideology (Butler 2019) become increasingly the redoubt of their collective experiences of uncertainty. Against this backdrop, the need for "stabilizing" narratives (Beckert and Bronk 2018) and reassuring "political myths" (Bottici 2007) accrues renewed importance, reconfiguring the relationship between finance and polity—an issue that part 3 of this book explores in depth.

It is therefore important to understand *how* today's speculative communities draw on their imaginations to respond to uncertainty—concretely, how the temporal and material conditions of capitalism shape financialized societies' collective identities and their shared futures. To do so, I now turn to the first key theoretical inspiration behind my proposed concept of speculative communities, which, at its root, represents an attempt to unravel the generative role of capitalism's imagination in the genesis of the modern nation-state.

IMAGINED COMMUNITIES

Benedict Anderson (1991) may not immediately strike us as the most relevant thinker when it comes to understanding the productive function of imagination in our speculative moment. His *Imagined Communities* was written in 1983, a decade after the major oil crisis of 1973, in a climate characterized by the rise of political and economic conservatism (and the "final defeat" of postwar Keynesianism) and fast-pace financialization taking hold worldwide. Against the current of contemporaneous analyses, *Imagined Communities* offered a powerful theory of nationalism, showing how the imaginary forms it takes are intrinsically connected to capitalism's brick-and-mortar reality. First, Anderson developed his thinking to analyze the historical birth of nationalist movements in the colonized Americas, which, as he argued compellingly, emerged out of the development of a nascent, print-based capitalist economy. Class, ideology, and material grievances of course mattered in the anticolonial struggle. But, for Anderson, the germinating nation-state was first and foremost *imagined* through shared national narratives circulated in print media, novels, and newspapers. In his famous words, the nation was thus imagined as a community by people who never knew, met, or heard of each other. Imagination is here not to be confused with "fancy" or "fantasy." Imagining is instead seen as a generative force that brings forth new social forms, relations, and ways of thinking, all of which would have otherwise been unthinkable. In short, imagining, for Anderson, is the process of both producing and relating to the world around us.

Imagined Communities had a great impact on a range of disciplines, from political science and sociology to anthropology, geography, literature, and history, and it was particularly influential on nationalism studies. Reflecting Anderson's own training, the work emerged from the interdisciplinary field of area studies, putting forward a highly original approach to the study of national identity and community. The intellectual innovation of *Imagined Communities* lay in diverging from the Marxist dismissal of nationalism and at the same time offering a "hard-headed" analytical framing that at least partially relied on Marxist categories of capitalist forces (Calhoun 2016). Anderson's dual emphasis on the modularity *and* on the material conditions of the reproduction of national communities offers his theory an enduring strength, which has survived the setbacks of "cosmopolitan critiques" in vogue during the 1990s and 2000s. In the post-2008 crisis world of nativist politics and nationalist upheaval, *Imagined Communities* is once again becoming a natural source of interest.

Yet there have been only scattered attempts to apply insights from *Imagined Communities* systematically to critically examine financialized capitalism. There is indeed great scope for deploying Anderson's framework to understand today's imagined communities, their collective beliefs, desires, and myths. The relevance of *Imagined Communities* is evidenced in the rising importance of questions of collective identity, self-image, and collective representations in our mediatized societies. Anderson's interpretive premise is uniquely placed to illuminate the productive role of everyday routine practices in the imaginary construction of contemporary nation-states. *Imagined Communities* can thus be used as a sociological device for teasing out the intersubjective processes through which contemporary collectivities are formed and sustained. But imagining, as I have already shown, is now inexorably linked with speculation, a defining feature of economic, social, and political life. The concern of *Imagined Communities* with the contingent, materially grounded routines of national imagining invites a Durkheimian reading of the new collective enactments of the speculative imagination, one that stresses "close interrelation between symbolic classifications, ritual processes and the formation of social solidarities" (Alexander 1990, 2).

Such emphasis speaks to the need to bring the material and the imaginary onto one analytical plane when examining the rituals binding modern communities together: on the one hand the tools, infrastructures, and technologies we use to navigate everyday social life and on the other the shared images that such tools help us conjure. As already discussed, well-versed critiques of financialization have tended to afford primacy to the abstract over the material, overlooking the intrinsic entanglements of the two. According to such critiques, finance tightens the grip of the neoliberal *homo economicus* on everyday life and colonizes our collective imagination. I am, however, less interested in the power of finance to control, to tame, or to co-opt the social imagination and more in the specific type of imagined communities that produce (and are produced by) financialized capitalism. Though we now know a lot about the myriad ways in which finance hollows out contemporary social life, we understand far less about its own way of imagining—not just the future but our puzzlingly uncertain present too.

To develop my argument, I take my cue from Craig Calhoun and Arjun Appadurai, two of the few scholars to explicitly deploy concepts from *Imagined Communities* in their studies of global political and economic transformations in the 1990s and 2000s. Appadurai (1990) draws on Anderson to flesh out the complex interlinkages and disjunctures between the global imagined worlds of finance, politics, and culture, which led to the new "uncertain landscapes" emerging on the eve of 1990s globalized capitalism. Calhoun (1991, 111) shows how new technologies and media "offer extraordinary potential for furthering the concept of imagined communities" beyond the terrain of "traditional nationalism" to wider social and economic constellations—"both as object of identification and as objects of antagonism."

▲

The particular nationalist imagination of the movements that Anderson studied in South America, in Haiti, and in Indonesia was propped up by the development of a newly shared vernacular—an unprecedented sense of synchronicity made possible by the widespread availability of newspapers and novels. Capitalism lurked behind these first nationalist revolutions, but not quite in the way that had previously been imagined. Mass commodity printing, rather than coal mines and sugar plantations, shaped our first notion of a "nation-state." Colonization itself designated a togetherness that fashioned a "territorially specific imagined reality" for local "inlanders" through its educational policies and administrative systems and its deployment of maps, censuses, and museums.[19] In doing so, colonial capitalism had the unintended consequence of contributing to the "sedimentation" of the first nationalist, anticolonialist movements in the "New World." In what was then called the "Dutch East Indies," such sedimentation through capitalism's administrative and print technologies continued "until, like a ripe larva, [the people were] suddenly transmogrified into the *spectacular* butterfly called 'Indonesian'" (Anderson 1991, 123, my emphasis).

Language, through its forces of standardization and simultaneity, was a vital scaffolder of the imagined community. It was, however, not just an "emblem of nation-ness, like flags, costumes, folk dances and the rest" (Anderson 1991, 133); that is to say, language did not merely reflect nation-ness—it helped *conjure* it. Print capitalism, in turn, afforded a new "fixity to language," helping it build the "image" of the nation. The idea of simultaneity, or the notion that nationhood is experienced by members of a given nation in a particularizing, homogenizing way, was "transverse, marked not by prefiguring and fulfillment, but by temporal coincidence, and measured by clock and calendar"; it embodied a "homogeneous, empty time" (24).[20] The role of the newspaper, in particular, is key here as a medium that enabled such "fixity." Anderson (1991) writes of "an American" who will never meet "more than a handful of his 240,000,000-odd fellow Americans" but nonetheless "has complete confidence in their steady, anonymous, simultaneous activity." (26) This togetherness was largely realized in the quotidian ritual of reading the morning newspaper, which imbued a national image through "the refraction of even 'world events' into a specific imagined world of vernacular readers" (63), performing effectively a sociospatial reordering. Consumed simultaneously by otherwise spatially isolated individuals, commoditized newspapers thus mark the momentous transition from simultaneity across time (history) to simultaneity across space—a mass ceremony substituting for that of daily prayer.

SPECULATIVE COMMUNITIES

What rituals do our late capitalist societies draw on to imagine their own collective futures in financialized times? Today's convergence of markets and publics, passions and interests, financial and political futures marks the emergence of *speculative communities*. If publishing novels and reading newspapers were the tools by which Anderson's proto-national imaginaries materialized, then posting "stories" online and scrolling through streams of social media content is how speculative communities come to life.[21] The everyday use of speculative technologies is capitalism's new vernacular: cloud computing, proprietary algorithms, image- and video-sharing platforms, social media, and location-aware dating apps are the commodified tools of connectivity animating such speculative communities.[22] The "mass ceremony" that refracts "world events" into the imagined world of speculative communities is arbitrated more than ever before by *screens*. The new stage of media commodification centers on "appearing" ("image") rather than on "having" ("possession"), and, importantly, on how relating to others is mediated by appearing.

Manuel Castells argued more than twenty years ago that meaning making in "informational capitalism" does not rely on what people do but on the basis of what they "are, or believe they are" (Castells 2009, 3). Today, such collective meaning making is conditioned by what people, and the collectivities they form, *appear* to be. In order to "believe" in the legitimacy of institutions, parties, and organizations (or in the promise of capitalism itself), we need images that represent them. Speculative communities are defined by overabundance and ultrafast circulation of such images, and so the role of imagination, and particularly of the speculative imagination, becomes even more important.

The decline of the textual and rise of the visual in the collective imagination of nationalism was anticipated by Anderson. *Imagined Communities* described the transition to the importance of modern technological media that rely on image in addition to print language: "advances in communications technology, especially radio and television, give print allies unavailable a century ago" (1991, 135). Beyond the pivotal role of newspapers and novels, imagined communities have relied on hegemonic tools of representation such as maps but also on the emotionally loaded spectrality of cenotaphs, tombs, and monuments to the Unknown Soldier. In speculative communities, it is through incessant flows of image that power circulates in the compressed time-space of the digital cloud and the seamlessly interconnected apps on our smartphone screens. But at the same time, traditional tools for scaffolding the image of the modern nation continue to reflect retrograde instincts and nativist mythologies. Sociologist Michael Rodríguez-Muñiz (2021), for instance, has shown how recent demographic representations of the US have mobilized racialized ideas to generate a collective sense of trauma and in turn offer valences to xenophobic and exclusionary futures. He calls such regressive visual representations "demographobia": a nagging anxiety about dystopian demographic futures. The instrumental role of the census as a demographic tool (for measuring how many "we" are) is afforded here new spectacular visibility. Or think of how risk speculation in the contemporary mining industry generates an exclusionary spectrality through its risk assessments of "developing economies" by producing images of "politically risky" and unstable territories on the one hand and Europeanized or pro-Western ones on the other (Gilbert 2020).

In *Imagined Communities*, the iniquitous aspect of spectrality, beyond forming collective identity and "shared fatality," lay in obscuring the "actual inequality and exploitation that may prevail" within the nation (Anderson 1991, 7). Speculative communities draw their own veil over power asymmetries in the vast networks of computational code, sensors, and backend analytics. Consider, for instance, how the deployment of algorithmic technologies (from Google's search code, to Apple's virtual assistant program Siri), which purport to redress discriminatory "human systems," often deepen existing racial inequalities, not by erasing racialized bodies but by making them more "visible"—a process that sociologist Ruha Benjamin (2019) calls "The New Jim Code." At the same time, today's communications media afford a sense of simultaneity at the level of the screen, which engenders a more opaque, and hence less well understood, copresence. The underlying mechanism is here hidden code rather than the newspaper's visible ordering of text (via the display of calendrical day). The complex algorithms driving, mining, and controlling the traffic of commodified personal data are often not fully legible even by data miners themselves.

Hence, the transition to image-based standardization and simultaneity presents important new questions around the temporality of speculative communities. The commodified technologies of connectivity of financialized capitalism combine speed and impermanence with *visual movements*. In the physical swiping, tapping, and scrolling and the virtual repetitive motions of TikTok memes, image now blends with text in novel ways. The backlog of Facebook's or Instagram's feed remains "there," in the background, but it is the short-lived "story" format that thrives in the contracted time span of a vertiginous present. Instagram Stories, used by more than one billion accounts globally as of summer 2020, are fast becoming the most popular mode of "sharing" content online. Their duration corresponds to the twenty-four-hour bracket that was once covered by print newspapers, though of course Stories do not offer top-down national/local "news" but rather an algorithmically generated blend of user-generated representations (of their current experiences) and targeted business advertising (which constitutes about a third of the total uploaded content). "Speculative simultaneity" thus differs from "imagined simultaneity" in the importance it places on speed, movement, and impermanence.

▲

Before outlining the origins and infrastructures of the first national imagined communities, Anderson (1991) described the temporal circumstances that prepared the ground for their emergence. Of fundamental importance was the loss of a temporality "in which cosmology and history are indistinguishable" (36), unsettling previous certainties around temporal continuity and "simultaneity across time."[23] The newly arrived type of social time gave a new, sociospatially defined, "horizontal" meaning to existential questions of life, death, loss, and servitude. The great achievements of print capitalism, most notable among them the commodification and acceleration of communications, "drove a harsh wedge between cosmology and history" and impelled people "to think about themselves, and to relate themselves to others, in profoundly new ways" (36). It was against the backdrop of this heightened existential uncertainty that the "revolutionary vernacularizing thrust of capitalism" (39) originally developed, generating a new sense of simultaneity among members of imagined communities. For Anderson, therefore, the collapse of *precapitalist* certainties was just as crucial as material political economy in this process.

Today, capitalism's new media commodities have undoubtedly renewed its vernacularizing thrust, but the breakdown of pre-2008 certainties has been no less spectacular. As I write these lines at the end of 2020, the optimism of the 1990s and 2000s could not feel more distant. A sense of generalized anxiety is becoming a condition that makes societies no longer able to "look the future in the eye" (Berardi 2017). What I described earlier as a radicalization of pervasive uncertainty in the aftermath of the global financial crisis of 2008 has cleared the way for the circulation of new "standardizing" vernaculars, around which speculative communities now coalesce. Luc Boltanski (2009, 2011) argued some time ago that such radical uncertainty, deeply embedded in modern capitalism, can be thought of as the very distance between the "world" (*monde*) and "reality" (*réalité*). Blokker (2012) emphasizes the implications of this proposition: "The world is normally in the background but comes to the fore in instances of 'radical uncertainty'—that is, when our existing modes of giving meaning to the world seem inadequate. 'Reality' is then exactly that which is 'orientated towards permanence' or the 'preservation of order,' providing a closed set of meanings of the world, in an attempt to eradicate radical uncertainty" (25).

But speculative communities no longer strive toward the "order" of permanence. We have seen how speculation emerged as a powerful vernacular in response to the growing tension between neoliberalism's enfeebled promises and finance's accelerated temporality. The distance between reality and our experiences of radical uncertainty defines our sense of time in speculative communities. Acceleration, as I have shown, is the order of the day for financial markets. High-frequency trading not only conceals a dark world of its own but also widens existing, visible inequalities in the "real world." Political and social time too—the time it takes to "slot in" the everyday-life tasks of remote work, caring responsibilities, or social reproduction—are compressed in ways that exacerbate our uneven experiences of the present. Carrying out this vital work requires resources that, under today's precarious circumstances, are unavailable to most. Thus, not only does time feel accelerated, but its acceleration reorders and masks power relations among those investing and trading, as well as among those merely consuming and desiring. And as the propensity to speculate expands rapidly in society, greater numbers of ordinary people become embroiled in—often unwinnable—fights for time, value, visibility, and *imagination*.

Against this backdrop, the new forms of standardization and simultaneity in speculative communities reflect a changing relationship between economy, society, and politics under financialized capitalism. Our collective exposure to fluctuating housing and mortgage values, the everyday engagement with the abstracting algorithms of social search platforms, image- and video-sharing interfaces, and the data-driven intimacy of dating apps has nursed a more speculative mode of being, of appearing, and thus of *relating* to others. Our routine experiences of this computational techno-world are not only a new strategic commodity for financial markets but also powerful conveyors of feelings and imaginings, as Anderson would put it. Imagined communities have not quite dissolved. It could be argued that they are formed instead around different types of "awareness," which may appear to be "detached from the limitations of particular places, neighborhoods, and experiences" (Day 2006, 20), or in groupings that take the form of "virtual communities" (Holmes 2005). But much like late Dutch colonialism's "unintended consequence" of the Indonesian imagination, financialized capitalism's own unintended consequence is the triggering of a new shared vernacular. This is a uniquely important insight, and foregrounds one of this book's central tenets: the socially and politically generative operation of finance; its productive, rather than merely destructive, role in shaping new speculative communities.

Even though the emergence and "sedimentation" of imagined communities was colonial capitalism's unwitting effect, the impassionate investments of people such as Latin America's middle-class Creole groups in nationalism presented Anderson with a riddle: why were such groups willing to sacrifice for an idea going against their own interests?[24] In tackling this question, *Imagined Communities* moved beyond class-oriented theories of nationalism, arguing that they cannot explain sufficiently how anti-Spanish Creole sentiment was "emotionally plausible" in the "separate zones" of Venezuela, Mexico, Chile, and Peru during the early nineteenth century (Anderson 1991, 51). Drawing on Victor Turner, Anderson argued that imagined communities require meaning-making experiences like the "secular pilgrimage": the shared journey made by Creole functionaries toward colonial administrative centers to take up their assigned posts. Religious pilgrimages under preprint capitalism bound otherwise isolated pilgrims to God. By contrast, succeeding secular pilgrimages bound individuals to government bureaucracies, such that the administrative hierarchy between the

Old World and the New was made plain: "the Creole was always laden with the knowledge that someone from the Old World would always be above him" (Ullock 1996, 431). Today's advance of a speculative populist politics presents us with a similar riddle: why do constituencies most affected by years of continuing market deregulation come to endorse finance-driven populists such as Donald Trump, Jair Bolsonaro, and Narendra Modi? Why are people seemingly voting "against their interests"? Reading Hochschild's (2016) influential ethnographic account of Tea Party activists in the years leading to Trump's rise to power, we can see parallels between the Creole sentiment of unjust treatment and post-2008 Louisianans' remorse for Americans who are "cutting the line."[25]

Imagined and speculative communities each have their own "narrative readerships," their own collective ways of using the capitalist vernaculars of their time to create meaning, from the seventeenth century's collective reciting of Bible passages and the reading of Balzac's and Dickens's narrative novels, all the way to our current impulsive scrolling of Instagram Stories and Facebook posts.[26] With the rise of "reading classes" during early print capitalism, imagined communities saw a readership that not only broadened (starting with the expansion from the "working father" to the rest of the family) but also became more clearly designated geographically.[27] The explosion of new media and the commodification of complex digital technologies have continued to help expand the narrative readership of speculative communities in a much similar way. "Connectivity" may have grown exponentially, yet it rarely exceeds national borders for the majority of spectator-speculators, who remain bound to the local or national level through a myriad of area-specific technologies such as location-aware Google searches, virtual short-term rental networks, geosocial networking services, and location-based dating apps.

Such speculative technologies often circulate images of a life that their narrative audience cannot have. The space between representations of reality (fantasy) and reality shrinks as these images come closer to us (through our smartphone screens), yet at the same time swells as the resources with which we could reach out to those images become scanter. Thus, the new denizens of speculative communities "sediment" around imagined collectivities that transcend traditional class politics while often remaining anchored within national boundaries. They exist in the accelerated simultaneity of the TikTok feed or the Tinder partner stream (which are increasingly just as popular in finance's metropoles as they are in their rural hinterlands) but also in the formation of political movements as diverse as the Gilets Jaunes, the Tea Party, or Black Lives Matter.

▲

In a new concluding chapter that was added to *Imagined Communities* in 1991, eight years after its original publication, Anderson argued that if print provided the *language* of imagined communities, then infrastructures such as the census, maps, and museums afforded the *grammar* for this new shared language. Revealingly, he used the metaphor of the glass house to describe the distinct way in which the colonial state imagined its own "domain": "a total classificatory grid . . . which could be applied with endless flexibility to anything under the state's real or contemplated control: peoples, regions, religions, languages, products, monuments" (184). The effect of the grid, Anderson continues, "was always to be able to say of anything that it was this, not that; it belonged here, not there. It was bounded, determinate, and therefore—in principle—countable . . . The 'weft' was what one could call serialization: the assumption that the world was made up of replicable plurals . . . This is why the colonial state imagined a Chinese series before any Chinese, and a nationalist series before the appearance of any nationalists" (184). Hence the *total visibility* of the glass house depended on the condition that all its dwellers could be grouped together by their unique serial numbers. The force of the collective nationalist imagination that sprang forth in anticolonial struggles rested on the very shoulders of this transparent—yet controlling—administrative imagination. In part 2 of this book, I return to the metaphor of the glass house, as a more translucent "social container" than the Weberian iron cage, to discuss how finance works to construct the spectacles demarcating our epoch's social and political morphologies.

Let me now summarize the key propositions emerging from the concept of speculative communities that I have put forward. Nationalism continues to influence how power circulates in today's social and political collectivities, even if the latter now seem more evanescent than ever. But, at the same time, speculative communities are suffused by the capacity of finance's own imagination to both represent and occlude uneven power relations. This important two-pronged contribution underscores the enduring relevance of Anderson's work. The three core elements of imagined communities were capitalist relations of production, print technologies, and the radical uncertainty bequeathed by collapsing global certitudes such as those reflected by linguistic diversity across geographical space.[28] Speculative communities, as the subsequent chapters of the book will show, can be understood through the evolution of *each of these* three core elements: financialized relations between speculative subjects, digital and computational media technologies, and new radical uncertainties precipitated by the stagnation of neoliberal promises.

The sociotemporal horizon of our speculative communities has shifted in ways that have surprised and confused us, dramatically refashioning how notions of collectivity are experienced and represented in everyday life. But we have only begun to scratch the surface of the processes propelling these shifts. A more systematic theory of the speculative imagination and its role in political economy is required in order to fully account for the generative, relational, and moral dimensions of speculative communities. This is where the book begins to part ways with Anderson's analysis. For all its great strengths, and despite its pioneering coupling of time-space experiences with political connectivity and social organization, *Imagined Communities* never explicitly theorizes either of the two constitutive terms of its title.

A relevant critique raised by Partha Chatterjee (1991) is that although *Imagined Communities* highlights the outside domain, the "material" of the imagined community, it ignores the inside domain, the "spiritual" aspect of nation-state capitalism. Anderson does not follow Max Weber's judiciousness in illustrating not only the constitution but also the *transformation* of the capitalist spirit. While the imagined community is "modular," it appears fixed once formed—a static outcome of people's shared imaginings. Crucially for the critique I will develop over the course of this book, although a focus on language and text can be helpful in "pinning down" symbolic collectivities, it also reflects a key limitation of *Imagined Communities*: its inflexibility to account for the dynamics of change over time and space. By contrast, imagination is an act from which new meanings, rationalities, myths, narratives, and images of capitalism may always spring forth. As I have shown in my previous work, imagination's complex role has to be understood both as a process (that is, open ended, ongoing, and therefore elusive) and as an outcome (that is, fixed, temporally distinct, and hence more easily legible) (Komporozos-Athanasiou 2020; Komporozos-Athanasiou and Fotaki 2015, 2020).

Anderson acknowledges uncertainty—a core aspect of our time's particular speculative imagination—as constitutive of the historic circumstances within which imagined communities emerge, but he does not engage it in sufficient depth. If the latest phase of twenty-first-century financialization has accelerated and compressed our experiences of present-future constellations, then the impact of radicalized uncertainty on our collective imaginings has to be brought right to the fore of our analysis. We need a more detailed account of exactly *how* imagination works to construct collective meanings under extraordinarily turbulent conditions—how collectivities are anchored, sedimented, and reassembled through this ongoing and contradictory construction. The legacy of the 2008 global financial crisis reverberates in contemporary life, reminding us that capitalism's glass house is fragile and precarious and that the struggles for power within it are also struggles for imagining the future. The question of imagination, then, requires recentering in order to understand these volatile dynamics. As I will demonstrate in the next chapter, the so-far-discussed shortcomings of *Imagined Communities* reflect a surprising theoretical neglect of the imagination across the disciplines of political economy, philosophy, and social theory. To address these issues, I turn to important studies of capitalism, with the intention of systematizing their tentative insights into finance's unique speculative imagination and thus demystifying its contested (yet elusive) role. In doing so, I intend to offer a more comprehensive sociological account of today's speculative communities and their historical origins.

On the last page of the concluding chapter of *Imagined Communities*, Anderson (1991, 162) quotes a well-known passage from Walter Benjamin on the angel of history: "His face is turned towards the past. Where we perceive a chain of events, he sees one single catastrophe which keeps piling wreckage upon wreckage and hurls it in front of his feet. . . . [T]his storm irresistibly propels him into the future to which his back is turned, while the pile of debris before him grows skyward. This storm is what we call progress." And he adds his own words as an epilogue to the book: "But the Angel is immortal, and our faces are turned towards the obscurity ahead." Anderson's comment is telling of the importance the future plays in his analysis of imagined communities. In spite of the concept's limitations, his unique emphasis on our shared uncertain futures offers a timeless insight into capitalism's speculative dynamics, opening a window into "the obscurity" that lies ahead. It is the historical evolution of this speculative dynamics that we must therefore explore now.

2: A GENEALOGY OF SPECULATIVE IMAGINATION

OLD SPIRITS OF CAPITALISM

The bell has rung the close at last,
The sound of conflict is ebbing fast,
The settlement price is posted too,
It cannot suit each one of you.

Now one by one they trickle out,
Some are sure, some are in doubt,
Some will gain, and some will pay,
Ah, well, tomorrow's another day.[1]

Capitalist relations of production, commodity printing, and the bureaucracies of major colonial powers gave Westphalian nation-states their unique form. With Benedict Anderson, we considered the genesis of a national imagination in the eighteenth and early nineteenth centuries before fast-forwarding to the emergence of today's speculative communities. But how did the forbearers of speculative communities evolve into their current form during the intervening nineteenth and twentieth centuries—notably in birthplaces of formal speculative markets such as Chicago, New York, and London? How did markets and publics respond to the divisive moral dilemmas thrown up by the early outburst of organized speculative activities?

The power of imagination has been at the core of capitalism's ideology, binding people together in vastly unequal destinies throughout capitalism's history. But while unfettered markets concealed labor value and exploitative relations of dependence, they also produced social bonds and suffused imagined communities with their distinctive moral codes. Imagination indexes the form of such bonds and summons desires; it inspires faith (and instills doubt) in uncertain futures. In doing so, it offers a "providential paradigm" of freedom, even if such freedom consigns people to destructive or sacrificial fates.[2] Still, the role of imagination has been surprisingly undertheorized, especially in the fields of economic sociology and capitalism studies. This chapter remedies this issue by trailing capitalism's most recent transformations in the so-far-untold history of its speculative imagination.

A speculative type of imagination has become especially salient in modern life, but it has been a major force in capitalist economy and society for some time. In this sense, the arrival of today's speculative communities is far from a rupture with the past. As we have seen, scholarly interest in financialization has most often centered on the importance of the post-Keynesian era and the tumult that ensued from the collapse of the Bretton Woods system in the 1970s. However, as I will now argue, the rise of speculative communities must be located in a *longer arc of historical changes* originating in the dawn of modern finance capitalism and, specifically, in the second half of the nineteenth century, when the first formal futures markets were established in North America and Western Europe. It was the time when speculative markets were hurled to the fore of capitalist life and the fictitious trading of options, futures, and derivatives grew intemperately, upending industrial economies' social contract. These first and unprecedented heights of speculative activity shaped markets' relationship with publics for years to come. They caused tremors that shook up fin de siècle politics and portended new power conflicts. In the heartlands of global finance, financiers, farmers, industrial workers, and populist movements became steeped in wars of speculation and gambling: around the future prices of hog and grain, the wages of urban laborers, and the state's own monetary and regulatory interventions. In the United States, a speculative fever spread fast beyond the pits of the newly inaugurated futures exchanges, sowing new tensions in farms, factories, and fraternal societies.

But, beyond the new enmities, unexpected alliances also began to form among the vanquished of these battles of speculation. My contention in the present chapter is that agrarians and lay speculators of that time developed a shared speculative imagination that came to define modern capitalism's history of financial inclusion (and exclusion): a willingness to take a stake in the future's uncertainty for economic and political benefit, despite a dearth of available resources and limited access to "expert knowledge." This distinct speculative imagination heralded a new moral order that dampened ethical objections to speculation and became firmly embedded in finance capitalism by the end of World War II and the New Deal era. Importantly, as I will argue, these developments shifted the ways in which tensions between what Albert Hirschman (2013) famously called "passions and interests" are negotiated. As fin de siècle societies gradually succumbed to the speculative fancies of finance, the contested figure of *homo economicus* started to give way to a new subject, around which both markets and publics gravitated. The advance of *homo speculans* began in earnest.

In the following pages, I first offer a potted history of this important period, whose consequences for the speculative imagination go deep yet remain unexplored. I then chart a genealogy of corresponding conceptual attempts to account for the speculative imagination in the study of capitalism and propose a new theoretical framework inspired by the philosophy of Cornelius Castoriadis.[3]

CROWDS, BUCKET SHOPS, AND THE EMERGENCE OF *HOMO SPECULANS*

It has uncovered resources[;] . . . it has created values; it has quickened industry[,] . . . awakened ambition, augmented the comfort of life; it has introduced delicacies and luxuries, it has brought refinement and development to human character, built churches, constructed railroads, discovered continents, and brought together in bonds of fellowship the nations of the world; it is aggressive, courageous, intelligent, and belongs to the strongest and ablest of the race; it grapples undismayed with possibilities; it founded Chicago; it rebuilt a great city upon smouldering ruins, and impels it in the march of progress. Whenever this kind of speculation is denounced it is mis-understood, and it is often decried by those who unconsciously share its benefactions.

CHARLES HAMILL, PRESIDENT OF THE
CHICAGO BOARD OF TRADE (1892)

The city of Chicago offers a critical historical backdrop to the early struggles to harness and contain the speculative imagination.[4] Home to the first and largest futures and derivatives markets in the world, Chicago was also an epicenter of the intense conflict between agrarian populism and laissez-faire economics that shaped the path of US politics after the Civil War. Moreover, the city has a unique place in the history of the labor movement, forming the dramatic setting of workers' struggles for an eight-hour workday, which culminated in the 1879 Haymarket massacre. During the Gilded Age, it emerges as a key nerve center of both US and global financial capitalism, alongside New York and London: a symbol of the country's move from a "capitalism of the cotton fields" to financialized capitalism. It is in Chicago that, for the first time in history, formal futures exchanges begin to set prices of underlying asset products, leading to trading in amounts of produce that far exceed farmers' annual crops and therefore radically reconfigure the relationship between markets and publics. It is also, finally, in Chicago that the first "bucket shops" are established in the 1870s, forcing the speculative imagination to burst out of the pits and swell dramatically in society at large. But just as finance's distinct speculative imagination emerges triumphant in this fin de siècle tumult, the colonialist expansion that sought new surplus capital (with which to feed the Global North's insatiable markets) also reaches its peak. The city's futures markets, like any form of financial trading, continued to rely on exclusion and segregation, most notably of women, migrants, and people of color. This violence is not a "backdrop" to the speculative wars I catalog in this chapter but an ever-present reality that cannot be disentangled from the history of the speculative imagination.

Historian William Cronon (2009) memorably called Chicago "nature's metropolis" because of its role as a getaway to "the Great West," spearheading new connections between financial markets and their surrounding communities—most notably those working the land in the vast crop fields of Iowa and Missouri. Although a formal exchange had been operating since the late eighteenth century, the opening of the city's futures market, the Chicago Board of Trade (CBOT), in 1848 was an event of major importance. Cronon (2009) captures adeptly the profound, transformative effect that CBOT was to have on its surrounding rural and urban landscape in the ensuing decades: "By the end of the 19th century, Chicago was filled with temples of commerce that were also, less obviously, mausoleums of landscapes vanishing from the city's hinterlands. The grain elevators and Board of Trade celebrated the new speculative furor of the futures markets while simultaneously commemorating the tallgrass prairies being ploughed and fenced into oblivion. . . . Behind each urban structure were the ghost landscapes that had given it birth. In sinking roots into the western soil, the city was remaking the countryside after its own image" (263).

Before the CBOT's arrival, speculation in Chicago, much as it was in the rest of the country, had been staged around future land values and rent prices. Real estate had been an outlet for the over-accumulated gains made in the early years of frantic industrial growth, railway construction, and commercialized agriculture. Booms like the great Chicago real-estate bubble of 1836–37 raised the first serious public concerns around the vagaries of irrational speculation. But the heightened political uncertainty in the aftermath of the Civil War (1861–65) laid the foundation for a more incendiary and hotly contested surge of speculation originating in the CBOT. At first, this new game of financial speculation appeared to be open to far fewer participants than was land speculation (which had been widespread among farmers, bankers, and merchants alike during the seventeenth and eighteenth centuries). In the 1870s, public access to financial markets was extremely difficult, especially so in the formal futures exchanges. In Chicago, the CBOT's architecture specifically aimed to convey the exclusive nature of futures trading. Its pit featured an octagonal design, so as to punctuate the distinction of the formal market order from the crowd dynamics of the city's more chaotic urban life (Borch 2020; also see Cowing 2015).

While the Civil War had brought great uncertainty in the city's markets, the newly arrived options trading opened entirely new trading opportunities, which not only sought to deliberately expand existing uncertainties but also to *create* new ones. CBOT speculators with "large purses" were now responsible for new waves of volatility reverberating throughout the city's hinterlands, making crop prices so unpredictable that they shook up even age-old trust in the crop's redeeming promise. In the face of unprecedented volatility, farmers increasingly lost faith in long-held providential beliefs about divine intervention and "God's will." With this move away from providential explanations, they turned to methods of "market forecasting" (Levy 2012, 181), crop production estimates, and weather forecasting. It was a time when meteorology became the new common sense for navigating uncertainty in farming communities, and actuarial science the trusted model for hedging unknown futures. More farmers now chased after an elusive "probabilistic certainty" in the hope of regaining some control over their futures.

But the specter of uncertainty continued to engulf the rural hinterlands and, as a result, such determinist worldviews never fully took root. In steering financial and weather volatility, the growing agricultural risks were to be borne by individual farmers, who ultimately found little solace in forecasters' promise of probabilistic certainty. The new "actuarial theology" delivered no more often than not and, in the end, the commodified risk that underpinned it left farmers exposed to the whims of financiers. In response, collective practices of risk mutualization began to emerge: fraternities, cooperative associations, and the first coordinated agrarian movements offered much-needed social insurance against the violent swings of speculative markets. At the same time, farmer culture sought ways to accommodate rather than control the "forces of chance and contingency" (Pietruska 2017, 2).

It is against this backdrop of popular thirst for speculation that a new shadow market opened up. A vast web of unincorporated "bucket shops," which popped up in every corner of the city, permitted anyone with a few pennies in their pocket to participate in the "mass communion" of speculation.[5] This was possible thanks to a transformative technological innovation: the rollout of the first national telegraph networks. These networks were instrumental in the growth of formal exchanges in Chicago and New York City and also in the establishment of their surrounding bucket shops, whose mushrooming in the 1890s brought futures trading to the masses on an unparalleled scale—making it a "national sensation."[6] Telegraph cables connected such bucket shops with formal exchanges like the CBOT, allowing for a constant feed of "real prices," displayed on ticker tapes, to be viewed in-house by their clients. At the same time, the cables linked Chicago's bigger urban bucket shops with new extensive grids of satellite shops in the city's farthermost rural heartlands. Much like print technology and the proliferation of nationalist imagination a century before, the invention of the telegraph was thus central to the spread of the speculative imagination outside established futures markets. Meanwhile, the introduction of the stock ticker sensationalized the performance of speculation, dramatically changing how speculators were initiated in the trading rituals of both pits and bucket shops. A device that made it possible for the first time to display price movements in real time outside the exchanges' walls, the stock ticker created a mysterious, often confusing, yet almost mystical atmosphere around itself. In doing so, it summoned not so much the economic rationalities of speculators as their "collective sentiment" (Stäheli 2013).

Important for our discussion is the fact that bucket-shop speculation offered an extraordinary opportunity to those who had so far fallen prey to financiers' opportunistic wagers. Agrarians could now hedge their own physical products against market-price volatility, while everyone else was given a chance to gamble on the radical uncertainties of the time. Hence lay speculation, thanks to the ticker innovation and the proliferation of bucket shops, became a mechanism of inclusion in the fray of early finance capitalism, thrusting a new imagined community to center stage.

▲

This history of the speculative imagination is important because it is a history of vexed division around the moral legitimacy of speculative activities.[7] Right from the outset, what came to be accepted as legitimate speculation diverged markedly for formal incorporated exchanges such as the CBOT on the one hand and informal bucket shops on the other. Whether speculation is rational or irrational became a key battleground in the conflict between markets and publics during the nineteenth century's concluding decade. Public discourse was rampant: What makes speculation ethical, and thus legitimate? And, contrarily, what makes it morally dubious, and ultimately irrational? To answer these questions, traders, regulators, and even legal experts centered specifically on the types of imagination underpinning speculative activities in and out of the pits. For speculating in formal exchanges and bucket shops alike was imagined: no underlying assets were ever delivered; not even contracts exchanged hands. Nonetheless, as formal exchanges alleged during these feuds, the bucket-shop "mimicry of speculation" (Stäheli 2013, 89) was *even more* fictitious than speculation in the CBOT, because no "actual prices" were "set off" there—hence such speculative transactions had no *real* effect on market prices of stocks and commodities.[8] But did this "fictitiousness" of bucket-shop speculations also make them more "irrational"? And how could their moral legitimacy be arbitrated anyway?

Grassroots speculation had to be distinguished from pit trading (rather haphazardly and hence quite controversially) as a gambling activity. Probability theory and the law of large numbers see gambling as the very embodiment of irrationality—speculating on the future is nothing less than a denial of progress along the trajectory of Enlightenment rationalism. For their part, agrarian movements of the time (especially in the United States and Germany) railed against traders' grain and hog speculation, deploring it as entirely "imaginary," "unreal" and hence no different from mere gambling. In Chicago and the United States in general, this upheaval became an important cause for the rising populist opposition and revolt. Stäheli (2013) calls the conflict between professional and lay speculators a war between competing forms of "economic fictionality"—or, in the terms introduced in this book, between different types of speculative imagination. He writes, "Speculation relied on fictions of the future, fictions that could be derailed by investors with speculative fantasies. Precisely this *articulation of fictionality as a mode for imagining the future became a central site of conflict* in discourses of speculation at the end of the nineteenth and beginning of the twentieth century. Educating the speculator required producing an individual by means of disciplinary mechanisms, and thus also required *normalizing the speculative imagination*" (107, my emphases).

The passage is worth scrutinizing more closely. "Fictions of the future" alert us here to the transformative power of stories to create orienting narratives, as opposed to deceptive lies or mere fantasies (Beckert 2016; also see La Berge 2014). In market speculation, specifically, fictions were the very means by which traders deciphered the messages contained in the stock ticker's representation of price movements in order to formulate their insights into the future. Yet not all "articulations of fictionality" were (considered) equal. Formal exchanges were eager to propagate the notion that "uneducated" and amateur speculator fictions naturally drift toward unruly fantasies that trigger cycles of exuberance and even mania (Borch 2012; also see de Goede 2005; Fabian 1999). Their speculative imaginations were cast not only as naive but also as perilous and hence had to be "disciplined"—for instance, by means of "stock reading guides" and manuals, which delivered "crowd psychology" techniques for navigating crowd irrationalities (Stäheli 2013). Normalizing the speculative imagination, then, involved *taming the passions* that risked steering it away from the somber (though still intuitive) speculation of experienced traders.

In Gilded Age Chicago, the speculative imagination of "markets" such as the CBOT's futures traders battled against the speculative imagination of "publics" (the broader classes of lay speculators and bucket-shop punters). We can see this fight most clearly in the 1892 Hatch Bill—a flat tax proposal of 10 percent on futures trading that nearly posed an existential threat to the CBOT's activities. What at first sight appeared to be a fight over taxation was in fact a turning point in the conflict about the moral legitimacy of speculation itself. Much of the fierce criticism of the bill defended professional speculators on moral grounds, praising their service as the "nation's insurers" against risk. The CBOT's president extolled the stabilizing effects of future traders' fictitious dealings on the city of Chicago. In the meantime, the Supreme Court of Illinois played its own important role in cementing formal speculation's legal legitimacy—its decisions in a series of cases offered enough moral loopholes for futures trading to continue uninterrupted. By contrast, the CBOT and other formal exchanges argued, the "undisciplined" speculative imagination of the shadow economy made markets susceptible to panic, and it was therefore morally repugnant.

By the time of the Panic of 1907, the speculative imagination of market pits had triumphed over that of grassroots publics. That year's tumultuous events seemed to conclusively settle the issue of speculation's moral legitimacy, marking the death of unincorporated bucket shops in Chicago, and in the rest of the country as well. The sole concession of futures traders had been a modest acceptance to inject some rationality into their dealings with uncertainty—which would have to be arbitrarily evidenced by showing they had at least "contemplated" a corporeal delivery of underlying assets "in their minds," even if that delivery actually never happened (Levy 2006).

Around the same time as the Chicago speculation wars, a rising antigambling movement led to the total prohibition of all betting among the wider population on the other side of the Atlantic too. In Berlin, stronger agrarian opposition and stricter legal provisions (such as the 1896 German Stock Exchange Act [*Börsengesetz*]) forced a mass exodus of elite speculators to London, where financial speculation was animated by a flourishing bookmaking culture. The United Kingdom shut its own bucket shops with the Street Betting Act of 1906, although gambling itself continued unabated in the country's exclusive racing courts.[9] The pattern here, as in the United States, is familiar: as the speculative imagination of the masses was disparaged, inside traders' own speculative imagination was elevated to a "heightened fictionality"—a more knowledgeable and considerate use of the market's fictions, which were put in the service of the greater good (and were thus dissociated from the gambling crowds' vagaries). Similar developments could be observed in major colonial centers of early formalized speculative activity. In India, during the decades after the Indian Rebellion of 1857 and the dissolution of the East India Company, the British unleashed "an imperial financial machine" (Bhattacharyya 2019) on local lay speculators. As historian Ritu Birla (2009) shows, the imperial establishment mobilized criminal law swiftly in order to quash indigenous commercial practices and "vernacular forms of hedging and speculation" (144) in the country's major financial markets. After 1895 (just as the conflict between agrarians and futures markets came to a head in the United States), colonial regulation of indigenous futures trading intensified in India. A set of formal demarcations of "legitimate speculative activity" were pushed forward in a concerted attempt to police what was denigrated as "recreational gambling" in local colonial bazaars (Bhattacharyya 2019; Goswami 1991).

This vexed division between gambling and speculation was thus drawn along class, gender, and race lines. Historian Ann Fabian (1999) has documented the links between the antigambling crusades of early financial capitalism and successive US administrations' racist attempts to defend economic liberalism's political rationality from "a logical revolt" (137). Fabian illustrates this most deftly in her discussion of "policy shops"—lottery betting establishments, whose primarily African American clients were commonly portrayed as "idle, indolent and thriftless" (127), not least because their speculative activities "reappropriated the extravagance that the rich had reserved for themselves" (125), thus instilling fear in the heart of "White middle class political economy." But just as the denunciation of gambling helped to pathologize vernacular speculations (the wagers made by workers, immigrants, and people of color), indictments of populists' "mob irrationality" were used as a lever for buttressing the government's "elite coalition" with the formal exchanges. Historian Richard Hofstadter (1956) famously posited that early American populism was a form of "paranoid" politics, while James Turner (1980) painted a vivid picture of that era's populist farmers, whose "foggy and partial understanding of the political system, vague and uncertain gropings toward reform, a nagging fear of being hoodwinked, and a prickly defensiveness about their own naivete" made them vulnerable to "retreating in confusion and distrust, apt on occasion to stray into irrationality" (357).

Hence, while agrarian movements challenged the moral legitimacy of financial speculators, populists' own political subjectivities were often cast as inherently irrational. The broad populist coalition of farmers, wage earners, and vectors of the urban middle class represented a threat to prevailing political rationality at the time. My contention is this: by treating grassroots speculators and populist farmers alike as "irrational crowds," it was possible for the formal future exchanges and their institutional allies (in the courts and in the legislatures) to isolate the pathological characteristics of *homo economicus* and thus preserve its virtuous spirit—*without*, however, necessarily casting it as a calculating rational subject. During that important period's battles of speculation, the burgeoning field of crowd psychology offered significant support to the project of upholding the moral integrity of *homo economicus.*[10] A legacy of the nineteenth century's bitter class conflicts and fears of irrational and unruly crowds centered on the threat of popular insurrection: mini-revolutions, demonstrations, union struggles, riots, and workers' strikes. True enough, a threat of popular insurgency came closer to materialization in the century's twilight, with the Populist Party's dramatic entry onto the stage of US politics.

▲

I would like to draw a parallel here between the historical fates of Chicago's lay speculators, the fates of the farmers in its hinterlands, and those of the populist agitators among them. As we saw, the masses that were drawn to bucket shops during the tumultuous 1890s found themselves on the losing side of intense legitimacy battles over speculation, and they were ultimately excluded from expanding formal exchanges such as the CBOT. Meanwhile, farmers and those allied groups that joined the agrarian movement's rising tide failed to make inroads into their radical financial reform agendas (including, prominently, the abolition of formalized futures trading, as well as an agenda of broader class and racial political inclusion). On the face of it, the Democratic Party's assimilation of the populist movement in 1896, and its subsequent defeat in that year's presidential election, brought an abrupt end to such ambitions. But, besides their apparent shared decline in power, farmers and lay speculators had deeper affinities. Most importantly, they shared a speculative imagination that lived on in debates around financial inclusion and exclusion in US politics well into the twentieth century.

Sociologist Sarah Quinn (2019) notes that farmers of that period included "property owners, product sellers, *and speculators*" (51–52, my emphases) and thus they "generally identified as profit-seeking businessmen," but, "in their indebtedness, [they] could also identify with laborers as fellow producers similarly subordinate to a more powerful class." I adopt here Charles Postel's (2007) approach to populism "as a national movement, focusing on farmers but also including wage earners" (viii), labor organizations, women groups, "urban radicals, tax and currency reformers, prohibitionists, middle class utopians, spiritual innovators, and miscellaneous iconoclasts" (13).[11] It is crucial to note that this broad constituency often overlapped with the denizens of bucket shops—who were themselves drawn from a widely diverse demographic that included not only the urban middle class but rural and farming constituencies too (Levy 2012). As Postel argued, populist movements did not represent "premodern" values (family, community, church)—far from it—or resistance to the coming market revolution on the basis of Protestant morality. They had a "distinctly modernising" sensibility (Postel 2007, 9) and a special interest in the function of the economy. Arguably, then, ordinary agrarian populists did not so much begrudge speculation itself but the lack of access to insurance that would enable them to hedge their own radical uncertainties as effectively as CBOT speculators. Yet, as historian Jonathan Levy (2012) suggests in his account of that period, with access to a telegraph and a broker blocked, and without "enough cash or credit for the margin requirement" (250), such a speculative impulse had now little chance of materializing.

My argument, contrary to the "atavistic crowd" explanations of the Gilded Age, is that farmers, outcasts, and grassroots speculators deeply understood the importance of modern financial fictions. Their incipient shared speculative imagination did not seek a return to the previous status quo of either providential or actuarian risk control, but strove instead for new forms of insurance that would allow them to benefit from the (economic as well as political) possibilities arising from speculation. Most notably, the populist movement challenged the personal assumption of risk and competed for guarantors and forms of socialized risk that would allow it some access to the gains of speculative markets. Meanwhile, despite their spectacular demise, bucket shops became important levers in the formation of the dominant financial culture of the twentieth century (see Hochfelder 2006). As new responses to the logic of risk mutualization and social insurance began to crystallize in the lead-up to World War I, the normalization of speculation in the US economy continued apace.[12]

These developments laid the groundwork for a new phase in the modern history of speculation. The interwar era saw US administrations pursuing an ambitious project of "stakeholder democracy" (Ott 2011), which opened up the financial securities markets to a "national community" of federal debt holders and mortgage bonds investment. The first two decades of the twentieth century marked a concerted rehabilitation of speculation, which was then reimagined as a key pillar of a "strong nation." Correspondingly, futures trading was recast not only as ethical but also as a patriotic duty (Preda 2009). By 1917, a range of intellectual, political, corporate, and financial leaders had completed their project of reorienting the US political and economic system around universal (and legitimate) investment in financial securities (Ott 2011, 4)—even as deep conflicts over race and class became mystified and more than half of the US population (people of color, women, indigenous people) remained systematically excluded from these systems. The work of the speculative imagination during the preceding decades had been critical in establishing this "national project." A new worldview had settled in, one that reconciled speculation with a new social order in the years leading to the market crash of 1929.[13]

For this project to succeed, speculation itself had to be imagined as a universal force, "intrinsic to human nature and present in all societal realms" (Preda 2009, 176).

After the Great Depression, the state resumed greater political control over the terms of speculation. It did so not by stricter regulation (the securities markets were further deregulated in this period), but by taking up the role of both mammoth creditor (Quinn 2019) and social insurer (and thus correspondingly a mammoth debtor too). The New Deal and the 1935 Social Security Act offered many Americans baseline economic security (including, crucially, deposit insurance)—just as it muted more radical civil-rights movements and continued to exclude millions of Black people from pension schemes and other social policy initiatives.[14] Meanwhile, in the aftermath of World War II, moral antispeculation sentiment lost traction in the public imagination. From the 1960s onward, even traditional gambling would come to be accepted as a mainstream social activity in metropoles throughout the West.

As a result, a good part of the twentieth century will remain "devolatised" (Levy 2012, 313) and largely free of yesteryear's financial panics— "markets and publics" will be now brought under the banner of state-endorsed speculation. This dilution of moral sentiment around speculation and the patriotic infusion of its imagination might appear antithetical to the progressivism of the New Deal era and postwar social security. But, as my so far historical account has shown, these seemingly disparate ideas worked in tandem to furnish the basis of an emerging *homo speculans* that has been taken for granted ever since. For now, the fire of speculative imagination was tamed but not entirely extinguished. After World War II, *homo speculans* was put into a hibernation from which it gradually re-emerged in the new phase of financialization after the Bretton Woods collapse and the state's renewed withdrawal, and then even more vigorously after the 2008 financial crisis.

THEORIZING THE SPECULATIVE IMAGINATION IN POLITICAL ECONOMY

How did students of capitalism understand the historical transformations discussed so far? Capitalism studies have sought to challenge the view of finance capitalism as a sequential transition from a material economy of productive investment and "real value creation" to an abstract and unproductive economy of fictitious values. As we saw in chapter 1, however, critical debates of finance (both historically and at the current juncture) continue to focus overwhelmingly on deconstructing the rational, utility-maximizing *homo economicus* rather than on understanding its successor.[15] Capitalist theorizing has striven without success to reconcile the vexing contradictions of *homo speculans*, whose decisive nineteenth-century ascendancy blurred boundaries between irrational gambling, fictitious trading, rational investing, and even political speculation (the patriotic duty of hedging a nation's uncertain futures). As a result, the speculative imagination has remained mystified in major studies, in spite of its important role.

Economist George Shackle singled out this neglect of the imagination as a major drawback in modern theories of political economy. Shackle argued that imagination offers a way out of "rational choice" dilemmas when faced with uncertain futures: "economic expectations are not primarily the product of reason but of imagination"—a "reasoned imagination" as he called it—and hence "our decisions must be based on how we imagine the future" (Bronk 2009, 72; also see Beckert 2016). His point is especially salient because it demonstrates the need to shift our attention away from deconstructing *homo economicus* and turn it instead to conceptualizing *homo speculans*. This is a critique that I would now like to draw out further. In what follows, I propose a theorization of the speculative imagination that overcomes the historical bifurcation of rationality and irrationality (spawned, in turn, by the conflicted legacies of the Western Enlightenment and Romantic philosophical traditions). Before doing so, however, I would like to consider some first tentative engagements with the speculative imagination in the work of two of the most influential students of the modern economic subject.[16]

▲

Marx's groundbreaking inquiries into nineteenth-century capitalism broadly considered the imagination as a destructive force, undergirding the parasitic function of speculative capital and the alienating power of money ideology. Imagination thus appears in his texts predominantly as a specter or a dark shadow—most vividly in the famous formulation of commodity fetishism, in which finance haunts social life like a phantasm, obscuring and commodifying relations between people. Marx writes of the mysterious commodity qualities that "are at the same time perceptible and imperceptible by the senses" (1887, 1:48)—properties that are therefore at once imagined and real. Finance is a key conduit for traversing between the worlds of imagination and reality, of material and fictitious values. And speculation is paradigmatic of this oneiric function of finance: an imaginary act, entirely detached from the value of the assets it refers to (or the value it could yield), relying instead on how speculators imagine it might appeal, in the future, to others like themselves (Haiven 2011). Volume 1 of *Capital* visualizes poignantly this rapidly growing gap between fictitious and material value forms of capital as a true "horror specter" of blood-sucking vampires.

Marx's use of the vampiric metaphor is especially evocative of the vagaries of nineteenth-century financial traders and their speculative imaginations: their "compulsions, bodily afflictions and spiritual contaminations" (Stäheli 2013, 36). He considers speculation during that period to be an opportunistic activity in essence, albeit one with important material consequences—exacerbating the violence of labor value abstraction (a "destructive fictitiousness"), while enhancing accumulation and expanding capital's reproduction. Yet, on the whole, Marx deals only peripherally (and hesitantly) with the embattled figure at the center of capitalism's specter of horror: the ascendant "money capitalist" of his time.

By contrast, capital's destructive imagination is discussed at much greater length in Marx's analysis of workers' alienation—a condition emerging out of the great uncertainties of nineteenth-century life: ephemerality, insecurity, and the disintegration of community caused by unbound capitalist expansion. Such imagination emboldens the power of ideology, which in turn signals the passage to capitalist modernity, fosters exploitation, and stifles human creativity. As Sayer (1990) notes: "It is this alienation rather than the mere rapidity of change (for which it is the prior condition) which underpins the transitory, fleeting and contingent experience" of workers (56). At the same time, a different type of hushed yet radical imagination underpins the collective struggles of those anxious and precarious laborers: their never fully suppressed power to imagine themselves as the architects of their own history. Marx (1887) speaks vividly of this extremely powerful, generative imagination:

> A spider conducts operations that resemble those of a weaver, and a bee puts to shame many an architect in the construction of her cells. *But what distinguishes the worst architect from the best of bees is this, that the architect raises his structure in imagination before he erects it in reality.* At the end of every labour-process, we get a result that already existed in the imagination of the labourer at its commencement. He not only effects a change of form in the material on which he works, but he also realises a purpose of his own that gives the law to his modus operandi, and to which he must subordinate his will. (1:127, my emphasis)

Human imagination is here crucial because it creates the blueprints for the cells, which workers then go on to erect. Through this extraordinary capacity to "raise the structure" of their products before actually producing them, workers also locate themselves in a broader social matrix, and in doing so they "realise a purpose."[17] But Marx does not link this powerful framing of the imagination with the conditions of alienating uncertainty (from which imagination emerges), nor does he juxtapose it with the speculative specters haunting the modern polity. As Haiven (2011) has noted, capital's role can be seen precisely as encroaching on the generative work of this potentially emancipatory imagination by "offering its material manifestations (money, commodities, institutional hierarchies) as the means through which social relations are imagined and negotiated" (103). A close reading of *Capital* would support this view. Speculative finance exacerbates capital's dominance over the imagination by increasing its power precisely through curtailing workers' capacity to produce social value. To paraphrase Marx, the architects of finance possess a more dominant and pernicious imagination than those enmeshed in the labor process. Hence, the violence of capital's imagination runs much deeper, profoundly influencing the modern political subject, who itself becomes a "fictitious phenomenon" and ultimately "the imaginary member of an illusory sovereignty . . . deprived of his real individual life and endowed with an unreal universality" (Marx 1887, 1: 154). We find in these words a poignant reading of the darkness cast over capitalism's dwellers, marred by an unresolved tension that is innate to the proletarian condition. They are doomed to be enslaved not only by capital itself but by its specter: a speculative imagination binding them to a sovereignty that is purely "illusory."

Max Weber's omniscient rationalizing "iron cage" offers another powerful image of this devastating power of capital to both conscript and stifle the human imagination. Like the "cell" of Marx's labor architects, Weber's metaphor captures lyrically the profoundly alienating forces at the heart of capitalism.[18] His is also fundamentally a negative view of the imagination. Where Marx lays bare the corrosive sociality bred by capital's reifying imagination, Weber is more interested in the force of that imagination to unite markets and publics under the aegis of the iron cage. This view also reflects a crucial departure from the Marxist analysis of speculation in the reproduction of capitalism. Weber's emphasis is placed on speculation's socially constructive (rather than destructive) role in upkeeping reciprocal networks of trading interdependencies, mutual responsibilities, and even solidarity. It is these webs of reciprocal obligation between speculators that led to the complex social fabric of early finance capitalism. As Weber writes in an evocative passage of his magnum opus *Economy and Society*, markets are social because market participants are guided by "the potential action of real or imaginary competitors" (1978, 636).

These formulations contain seeds of the speculative imagination that has preoccupied this chapter. Weber hints at the implications of such a speculative imagination for the emerging subject of finance capitalism in his 1894 pamphlet "Commerce on the Stock and Commodity Exchanges" (see Weber 2000 [1894]), which was written at the height of the legitimacy struggles for speculation in his native Germany. In this essay, he does not altogether condemn speculation as "immoral gambling"; what interests him is that it both incorporates and *exceeds* the instrumental rationality of *homo economicus*. Speculation may be seen, at first sight, as the embodiment of capitalism's "imitative," "atavistic," and "substantive irrationality." For Weber, however, the speculator substantiates a fascinating, "charismatic," and socially embedded creature that channels both tradition and personal authority, both passions and interests (Preda 2009, 42; also see Appadurai 2016). These contradictory entanglements are also explored in Weber's reflections from his visit to the United States in 1904, summarized in his essay "American Protestant Sects" (in Mills 2014). While he refers only briefly to New York City's "fortresses of capital," it is the innerworldly methodicalness of American puritans that fascinates him most. Although he doesn't directly link the spectacular rise of public speculation to the growth of Protestant sects, Weber proposes that Americans' turn to the latter may have been a rational method of socializing the risks of their investment activities.[19]

How are we, then, to understand this emerging subject of early finance capitalism and its great existential struggles in the context of Weber's iron cage? Weber immortalized how the modern capitalist dweller became embroiled in the battle between Calvinist uncertainty and old beliefs of providential certainty (that is, the certainty of grace). Under the mantle of this dramatic experience, a formal "instrumental rationality" came to dominate over substantive, "ethical rationality."[20] Not only did the means of rational action (e.g., wealth accumulation, calculation, coercive proceduralism, and technical control) not coincide with its aims (e.g., salvation), they pushed modern capitalists deeper into the vortex of anxiety, upending them from the magical routines of their religious, traditionalist past. Magic, however, did not entirely go away alongside such old routines—it lingered on. As finance took on a more pivotal role in fin de siècle economies, speculation assumed a more divinatory function to sustain public faith in markets: it became a "great rational prophecy," giving meaning to the irrationalities of speculators' new pursuits.

▲

Both Marx and Weber, then, begin to offer tentative outlines of *homo speculans*, the rising hegemonic subject of early finance capitalism, by bringing its inherent contradictions into sharp focus: for Marx the core tension embodied in the abstracting forces of speculation was between fictitious (unreal) and material (real) values, while for Weber the defining conflict was that between the rationality and irrationality of speculative endeavors. For all their merits, however, their analyses do not engage directly with the unique type of imagination cutting through this ilk of contradiction, the profound force thrusting late industrial societies to the dizzying adventure of speculation—what I have so far called speculative imagination. To understand the limitations of their approaches, we must consider them in the context of their broader philosophical trajectories. Both Marx's dialectical materialism and Weber's idealism were developed under the ominous shadow of Immanuel Kant and the hegemony of German Romanticism on the one hand and the continuing legacy of European Enlightenment rationalism on the other. Though these traditions influenced each thinker in greatly different and complex ways, I would like to draw attention here to one important—albeit unobserved—consequence: the fact that both were left with little desire to foreground theoretically the role of imagination in capitalism.

The idea of imagination (*Einbildungskraft*) in the school of German Romanticism has been intrinsically associated with liberal philosophy's ethos of individual freedom, from which Marx, Weber, and their present-day intellectual heirs have been intent on distancing themselves. At the same time, the conceptual disregard for the imagination has gone hand in hand with a systematic overemphasis on reason. As Bottici (2014) has compellingly argued, the history of Western political thought (from Hobbes to Hegel and from Rawls to Habermas) is riddled with an image of politics in which rationality reigns supreme and imagination is treated instrumentally, left in thrall to reason. This state of affairs has weakened major theoretical critiques from across the spectrum, which have tended to treat capitalism as a particular form of either rationality or irrationality, or yet to focus on "identifying reason's own limits"—often with the deleterious effect of separating theory from politics (Callison 2019; also see Callison and Manfredi 2020).[21] The European Enlightenment legacy of *homo politicus* has in fact been in a close embrace with the persistent heritage of a rational *homo economicus*.

However, as my foregoing history of speculation has revealed, finance capitalism's power struggles were played out within an altogether different arena. They were not merely conflicts between passions and interests, between rationality and irrationality, or between reality and fiction; they were struggles for speculative imagination. It is therefore time to take a further step. Redressing the hierarchical divisions between reason and imagination requires that we move beyond both the structural determinism of economic rationality and the Kantian essentialism of an emancipatory political rationality (which, as we saw in the previous chapter, also begets the current idée fixe of neoliberal reason). We must tackle the role of imagination head-on.

BEYOND POLITICAL AND ECONOMIC RATIONALITIES: CASTORIADIS AND THE REDISCOVERY OF IMAGINATION

No other thinker has scrutinized the imagination in more depth than the philosopher Cornelius Castoriadis. In his wide-ranging project (whose publication coincides with the late twentieth century's period of rekindled financialization, from the early 1970s to the late 1990s), Castoriadis documented exhaustively the historical evolution of the study of imagination in Western philosophy, setting out to address its theoretical neglect across multiple disciplines. In response, he sought to construct a conceptual edifice with imagination at its core, drawing from fields as diverse as mathematics, economics (having spent a twenty-year stint as economic adviser at the Organization for Economic Co-operation and Development), political thought, sociology, and psychoanalysis (having worked as a practicing psychoanalyst for the last thirty years of his life). Castoriadis lamented, above all, the contemporary relegation of the social imagination to the domain of individual psychology, arguing compellingly that this relegation has pernicious consequences for our understanding of modern capitalism. Like Marx, he contended that the specter of capitalist ideology had quelled more radical and emancipatory imaginations. But, in contrast to Marx, he considered such radical imaginations as fundamentally irreducible to the determinist view of capitalism's own self-destruction. Like Weber, he was deeply concerned with the vexing tensions marking modern capitalist pursuits. Yet he suggested inventively that such tensions must be traced in the interplay between different ways of imagining the future, which pull societies toward contradictory paths.[22]

To understand the uniqueness of Castoriadis's theorizing of the imagination, we should first discern two cardinal "misrecognitions" that throw a wrench in the works of dominant philosophical approaches to the imagination.[23] The first is the view that considers the imagination as equivalent to "fiction" and the "fantastical," and thus with the "not real," or that which *is not*. This view has its roots in Western philosophy's "exorbitant ontological privilege granted to the *res* (*extensa* and *cogitans*, each always involving the other)" (Castoriadis 1975, 332). The bulk of Greek-Western philosophical thought hence divides imagination, reality, and reason into opposing camps. This false distinction has a twofold effect. First it delegates the imagination to the ambit of the "instinctive" and the "irrational." Second, it confers a semantic separation of the real from the ideal (the latter can be traced in the Latin root of *imago*, meaning "ideal image"). Imagining is therefore considered an act that aspires to an (inherently) unreachable perfection, a naive striving for utopia—a fantasy.

The second and related misrecognition that we can distinguish is the historical treatment of imagination as a synonym for passive reception. This interpretation has been most prominently adopted by Maurice Merleau-Ponty, who traced imagination's meaning in Greek sources as "appearance" (originating in the verb *phainesthai*, "to make appear"). Under this prism, an image being put forth by the imagination may well be "real," albeit merely as a reflection in the mirror—an *eidolon* (Castoriadis 1975, 3). The function that is emphasized here is that of our ability to perceive (pre-existing) externally given images and to subsequently represent them through "repetition" and "imitation" (as opposed to producing them in the first place). More damningly, an imagination that is conceived as an icon image (*eikon*) can cloud "true vision" and remove us from it, being "essentially an imitation to which is adjoined a false belief bearing on the reality type of its products" (Castoriadis 1997a, 223).

With Castoriadis, each of these misrecognitions is not only refuted but reversed entirely. First, imagination precedes and anticipates "reality," which in turn stems from the human capacity to imagine—reality is nothing but imagination's ongoing outcome. To understand this radical view, we must trace it back to the idea of *phantasia*, the notion of imagination appearing first in Plato and which bears equally on "sensation," "cognition," and "action." Aristotle (1984) substantiated this view: imagination is *phantasia aisthetike*, and the force generating emotions—sensuous *phantasia*—as well as *reason*—deliberative *phantasia* (*Rhetoric* 1370a, 1378b), with which we actively construct the world around us. Therefore, imagination constitutes "a crucial ingredient of our mental life, but it is also something that, insofar as it enables us to deliberate, is a specifically human faculty associated with reason" (Bottici 2014, 19). During the seventeenth and eighteenth centuries, philosophical treatments of the imagination succeeded in severing conceptual links to this idea of *phantasia* and placed it instead within the sphere of aesthetics, where it has remained to this day.

Relatedly, as to the question of why imagination should not be confounded with passive perception and imitation, Castoriadis is steadfast: "Representation is not tracing out the spectacle of the world, it is that in and through which at a given moment a world arises" (1975, 331). Hence, Castoriadis considers images to be generated by a fundamentally creative (rather than imitative or repetitive) act of representation. With creative representation, we have no simple "unmediated access to 'reality,' and further, no interest in 'reality'" (Castoriadis 1997a, 151). The act of "putting" our world "into images" is a twofold process of distorting what "is" (seeing what is absolutely not there in what "is") and of creating forms so alien to "reality" that they cannot even be called distortions but are nonetheless entirely unique "unmotivated creations" (Castoriadis 1975, 247).

Taken together, these core rebukes contribute to a broader important point: human imagination exists on an intersubjective, social level, rather than as an individual faculty. Olson (2016, 41) summarizes neatly this key insight and the ways in which it anticipates Anderson's own concept of imagined communities: "Castoriadis shows how individual ideas, both images and words, can take on the character of shared meaning. By emphasizing the way in which collective imagination constitutes collectivities, he presages Benedict Anderson's work on the imaginary constitution of communities . . . This material dimension is valuable in a more general sense as well: it provides an important antidote to a conception that would turn the imaginary into a kind of phantasm or purely internal, psychological phenomenon" (41). Hence, both capitalist and anticapitalist specters, for Castoriadis, are the products of our own collective imaginations. Let me turn to a passage in Castoriadis's 1975 magnum opus, *The Imaginary Institution of Society*, which demonstrates spiritedly these points by engaging both Marx and Weber and therefore bears quoting at length:

> We recalled above the sketch Marx gave of the role of the imaginary in the capitalist economy, speaking of the "fetishistic character of merchandise." This sketch should be expanded by an analysis of the imaginary in the institutional structure that, increasingly, alongside of and beyond the "market," is assuming the central role in modern society: the bureaucratic organization. The bureaucratic universe is *permeated through and through with the imaginary*. Ordinarily, we pay no attention to it—or only to joke about it—because we see only the excesses in it, an abuse of the routine or "errors," in short, exclusively negative determinations. But there is indeed *a system of "positive" imaginary significations* that articulate the bureaucratic universe, a system that can be reconstructed on the basis of fragments and indications offered by instructions about the organizations of production and of labour, the very model of this organization, the objectives it sets for itself, the typical behaviour of the bureaucracy, etc. (158, my emphases)

Imagination thus undergirds capitalist economy in both market and bureaucratic forms of rationality. It plays both a "negative" and a "positive" role in "articulating" the many fragments of its "bureaucratic universe." In his own critique of capitalism, Castoriadis submits that the "modern pseudo-rationality" of markets "exhibits most strikingly the domination of the imaginary at every level," which tosses modern societies "in the throes of a systematic delirium" (1975, 156). The task of critique, however, should not be to merely suggest an "alternative rationality" that would shake *homo speculans* out of its delirium. Nor, contrarily, should it center on the system's endemic irrationalities as a launchpad for attacking "pure reason."

I have already discussed the problematic assumptions behind critiques of finance, which assume economic rationality as a space of domination over political rationality (while viewing radical forms of the latter as a motor of resistance) and hence conceptualize finance as a vehicle of violence and "demonic anti-politics" (Kotsko 2018, 46; also see Brown 2015).

Castoriadis therefore seeks to overcome the limitations of both idealist and rationalist political economies. His stinging critique of capitalism departs from "materialist-objectivist" and from "idealist-subjectivist" dialectics. For him both are "closed," insofar as they fundamentally presuppose that "all experience is exhaustively reducible to rational determinations" (Castoriadis 1975, 54), reflecting the belief that history is defined by extrasocial forces (such as Marx's laws) rather than society's own laws. An open dialectics must instead be both nonmaterialist *and* nonidealist (56). With a single stroke, Castoriadis repudiates Marx's "Hegelian mystification" of capitalist irrationality and his obfuscation of history's creative imagination: "a revolutionary transcendence of Hegelian dialectics," he purports irreverently, "demands not that it be put back on its feet, but that, as a first step, its head be chopped off" (1975, 56).

Crucially, recognizing this openness represents for Castoriadis the core of a radical (political) project of collective autonomy—a project that goes hand in hand with the idea of self-limitation and, at its root, with the acceptance of death itself as the ultimate frontier of uncertainty's darkness.[24] Working toward collective political autonomy necessitates equally this acute self-awareness of mortality together with the desire for self-alteration. It thus requires that capitalism's anxious subjects act both as diligent insurers and adventurous speculators, recognizing the inevitability of death—life's greatest failure—even as they throw themselves into the whirlpool of the present's chaos. Under the prism of such an open dialectic, social reality can be seen as the ongoing struggle between an institut-*ing* and an institut-*ed* imagination: a creative process (including social anticipations, representation techniques, and interaction rituals) and the imagined, instituted outcomes of that process (the "bank," the "market," or the "nation")—both of which are equally important.[25] Insofar as rationality is generated through imagination in an "instituting" process, once a type of rationality has been "instituted," it becomes a measuring stick for various other images and meanings, rendering them rational, irrational, or even arational.

▲

My intention in this chapter has been to pull the thread of the speculative imagination out of the tangled mess of some persisting conceptual binaries. In doing so, I proposed a theoretical approach that is better suited to the unique dynamism of *homo speculans*, offering us new vistas into the vexing contradictions of finance capitalism. Let me close with a synopsis of these key propositions. Through accepting the radical thesis according to which imagination precedes both reason and affect, we can better understand the historical enmities and alliances among speculating camps in and around financial markets. Finance is not merely a conduit for traversing between the worlds of the real and the fictitious nor between the rational and the irrational. It is a space where these worlds no longer remain insulated from each other. Doomed to permanently inhabit the precipice of the unknown, farmers, workers, populists, and derivatives traders have no choice but to turn to their speculative imaginations—to speculate in order to survive.

The speculative imagination, then, is precisely that essential social force responsible for the open-endedness of capitalism's dialectic: ensuring that even when the future seems fixed, we hold fast to its fundamental unknowability and thus to its openness to change. The concept I have put forward in these pages integrates economy's radical uncertainty as an inherent feature of a self-altering dynamic, rather than a mere outcome of finance-induced alienation. Hence it considers uncertainty an essential resource for the possibility of a more transgressive political subjectivity. Speculative imagination thwarts faith in predetermination, without however replacing it with the certainties of either economic or political rationality. By contrast, it is the inherently imaginative act of taking "collective ownership" over the future's indeterminacy, by giving a—however provisional—image to its chaos, with which we can live.

But to enact a speculative imagination is also to step into a collective quest for resources that would allow *homo speculans* to navigate this path autonomously, and this quest has always been an uphill battle. The emergence of the postwar era's socialized risk paradigms can be seen as an outcome of this ongoing struggle of the speculative imagination to respond to the question of collective autonomy. My foregoing analysis attests to these possibilities of the speculative imagination in political economy. But it has also opened up questions about the forms of sociality and the kinds of politics it has bequeathed to contemporary societies. Having tracked the historical genesis of *homo speculans*, it is now time to delve deeper into its current transformations—to look in more depth at the social bonds it forms and the desires underpinning such bonds; to consider the political collectivities to which it is attached in its new quests for autonomy. Parts 2 and 3 of the book turn to the social and political implications of modern *homo speculans*, as it re-emerges in the modern era.

PART II: SPECTACLE

FINANCE AND SOCIETY

How does the twenty-first century's *homo speculans* differ from its historical forerunner? Today's uncertain struggles for power still occur under the ominous shadow of financial markets, whose grip on everyday life is felt acutely in societies the world over. These struggles have rhymes and echoes of the fin de siècle wars over the moral legitimacy of speculation. The scale and depth of modern technological transformations, however, make our current moment more of a singular event for the speculative imagination when considered from a longer historical perspective.

Therefore, my aim in the second part of this book is to demonstrate how the theoretical framework I have developed explains the integration of *homo speculans* into today's speculative communities. To this end, I will probe the shifting relationship between society and finance by illuminating the ways new digital commodities spread the speculative imagination in society faster than ever before. What I will frame as *speculative technologies* are the core of this process, not merely as mediators of a new relationship between society and finance but also as new expressions of that relationship. Speculative technologies, in short, are the very means by which *homo speculans* becomes embedded in our modern spectacle society. Today's technological opacity tills the soil on which collective speculation grows. Our contemporary speculative endeavors are attempts to foresee the future—not only in the sense of anticipating its uncertain outcomes but also in the sense of navigating our clouded and increasingly obscured reality.

To demonstrate the breadth and depth of these transformations, I discuss a diverse set of prominent speculative technologies: image- and video-sharing apps TikTok and Instagram, astrology apps like Co-Star, mobile dating apps Tinder and Bumble, and Netflix television shows like *Love Is Blind*. While much of my discussion to this point has focused on the conflict between passions and interests, in part 2 my attention shifts to an additional set of struggles experienced with unprecedented intensity in our current techno-world. Specifically, I unravel the tensions between reality and fiction and between that which is (hyper)visible and what remains invisible in modern social life. In doing so, I probe the underlying social and cultural dispositions of *homo speculans*—its new collective bonds, rituals, anxieties, desires, and aspirations. The line of my argument is this: the growing convergence between the world of finance and our everyday digital lives has deepened the sense of confusion for *homo speculans* and has exacerbated its lack of control in forming durable connections. But these contemporary transformations have not entirely hollowed out relations in speculative communities. They have reoriented our pursuits of sociality and intimacy toward more open-ended navigations of the present's uncertainty and, in doing so, they have poked even greater holes in neoliberalism's fading legitimacy.

3: SPECULATIVE TECHNOLOGIES AND THE NEW *HOMO SPECULANS*

On this the occultists live: their mysticism is the enfant
terrible *of the mystical moment in Hegel. They take speculation
to the point of fraudulent bankruptcy. In passing off determinate
being as mind, they put objectified mind to the test of existence,
which must prove negative. No spirit exists.*

THEODOR ADORNO, *THE STARS DOWN TO EARTH*

*Predictive theories can be compared to crystal balls, not in
the sense that they show us the future, but in the sense that we gaze
into them in the hopes of catching a glimpse of the future, and
instead see a vision of ourselves reflected back at us.*

JENS BECKERT, *IMAGINED FUTURES*

Astrology is fake but true.

CO-STAR ASTROLOGY WEBSITE

Speculation has been integral to the history of finance capitalism, yet its impact has not been determined by economic developments alone. A confluence of societal and political factors has produced the highs and lows of the speculative imagination. If the postwar years anointed a devolatilized economy that seemed to suppress speculative impulses, the recent fallout from the 2008 crisis heralded a new period of intense volatility, with staggering levels of uncertainty—and new speculative summits. But ours is also a time of vertiginous confusion. As we turn to smartphones to navigate all aspects of everyday life—from travel and shopping to work and social connection—we find ourselves adrift, suspended over oceans of data that are produced, exchanged, and processed at previously unimaginable speeds. Yet, while information abundance yields enormous fortunes in Silicon Valley and Zhongguancun, it sows befuddlement for most of us. Our routine experiences of the world increasingly unfold through complex technologies, whose inner workings are impenetrable. Data's promise of more or better knowledge remains elusive. Our growing dependence on complex machines and opaque algorithms doesn't make the world more legible or its impending crises more predictable—our ways of seeing are shifting, yet darkness doesn't seem to go away.

Fin de siècle speculative imaginations relished the entanglements of the rational and the irrational, the fictional and the real. As we have seen, nineteenth-century speculators mixed the "magic" of prophecy with an otherwise rational conduct of life—their journeys meandering between the paths of faith and reason. Immortalized by literature classics such as Bram Stoker's *Dracula*, such entanglements reflected a more generalized trend of blending the scientific with the supernatural—a "weird occult doubling of science" (Luckhurst 2011, xxxi)—that became widespread in the Victorian era, with new electrical technologies such as the telegraph and gramophone turning "magic into a daily routine" (Ronell 1989, 35–36). But our current techno-world blurs such boundaries further still. Where Victorian séances often took the form of theatrical performances, our own reality seems increasingly inseparable from fiction. This chapter will examine how today's speculative imagination molds the ways we come to see and represent the world, defining our everyday responses to its chaotic uncertainty and, in doing so, shaping a diffuse and fragile sense of community.

Uncertainty and complexity do not wholly uproot *homo speculans* from the social. Speculation has always performed a social function, animating financial markets' vast networks of codependency and reciprocal obligation. In its most elemental market form, it has determined price formation as a symbolic *representation* of value and as a reflection of a *relationship* between economic actors. As I will argue, today's digital technologies affect both these aspects of speculation. A shared temporality emerges from our virtual routines of image and video sharing, rapid valuation, and self-(re)presentation. At the same time, these routines create speculative modes of relating to one another. They compound our growing disbelief in capitalism's future promises and cement a collective acceptance of "the unknowable."

THE ADVENT OF SPECULATIVE TECHNOLOGIES

Ever since Adam Smith's mystifying evocation of the "invisible hand," finance's "spectral willfulness" (Vogl 2014) has been central to popular visual representations of markets. Marx was not alone when he wrote of capitalism's specters of horror and blood-sucking vampires. In the nineteenth and early twentieth centuries, a rich tapestry of personified and satirical allegories in print media sought to capture something of the markets' lewd irrationalities, bestial impulses, and trickery. Biblical visual tropes evoked the frenzy of market crashes, and animal fables fueled distorted imagery of bloated speculators morphing into monstrous bears, bulls, and malevolent octopuses.[1] However, all visual attempts to make sense of finance's unfolding spectacle ultimately surrendered to its abstraction, "reinforcing the overwhelming power of the market by anthropomorphically depicting it as a kind of sentient being, one quite beyond the comprehension of individual human actors" (P. Knight 2016, 103).

In the aftermath of the 2008 global financial crisis, such spectral representations of finance continued to haunt the popular imagination as public attention focused on the gloomiest corners of the banking system. Robert Harris's 2012 best seller *The Fear Index* evokes neo-Gothic tropes of opaque trading algorithms and AI-supported financial software—a high-tech Frankenstein that feeds on darkness and fear. While the theatrical spectacle of open outcry trading still dominates television news coverage of financial markets, the real action takes place in the darkest corners of dark pools—the technologically powered modern version of upstairs trading: private venues that display no order books or other trading-related data (while transactions themselves remain hidden until they are completed), thus offering total anonymity and invisibility to algorithmic traders. Dark pools are as impenetrable to the public eye as markets can be, epitomizing the abstraction of algorithmically generated finance. Today, more than ever before, the complexities of financial markets are hidden in plain sight, thinly veiled by a world of vast physical infrastructures: phone lines, fiber optics, satellites, cables on the ocean floor, vast warehouses filled with supercomputers, and ultrafast machine-learning trading algorithms.

With the rise of speculative communities, similar complexities are observed—and at the same time occluded—in the communication technologies and digital media animating everyday social life. Image-driven social networking platforms such as Facebook and Instagram and short-form video-sharing apps such as TikTok and YouTube become dominant channels for the diffusion of (moving) images. Their design encourages immersive use and seems to replicate a chaotic order: endless streams of algorithmically produced, visually stimulating stacks of data flow incessantly on smartphone and computer screens. Users' experiences of jarring lip-synching, bot-generated nursery rhyme videos, and repetitive and absurd sketches often resemble the "legibility and logic of a narcoleptic dream."[2] Such platforms increasingly draw on techniques of visualization and obfuscation similar to those of contemporary finance, with similar effects (immersion, acceleration, volatility) on social actors. This tension between visibility (the complexity that we are able to see through the technologies we use) and invisibility (the complexity that remains hidden beneath these technologies) has been central to our contemporary experiences of uncertainty.

How, then, do we collectively respond to the constant stream of images that we seem to find both strikingly familiar and baffling? Adam Smith's invisible hand no longer deals only in money. It carries images, videos, or even menu options and prospective sexual partners to our screens while we nervously tap and swipe on them. Speculative communities form in the eddies and vortices of this unceasing flow of images. To recall a core argument from part 1, whether such images are real or fictional bears little importance. As Anderson (1991) puts it, "communities are to be distinguished, not by their falsity/genuineness, *but by the style in which they are imagined*" (6, my emphasis). By analyzing the ubiquitous role of contemporary technologies, I intend to shed more light onto the collective imaginings that they help fashion. Just as print capitalism catapulted new nationally bound mythologies through the force of narrative tools (from print media and novels to maps, censuses, and museums), contemporary finance capitalism has leaned on speculative technologies to re-narrate modern nation-states.

My use of the term *speculative technologies*, then, intends to account for the dramatic growth of commodified digital, algorithmic, and computational technologies that has taken place throughout the first two decades of the twenty-first century, most notably technologies that feed on images.[3] In what follows, I refer to images in the sense of the term I discussed in chapter 2—that is, as creations (rather than mere pregiven, or imitative, reflections) of society, and thus as a key dimension of the speculative imagination. One important implication of this perspective is that I am interested in a more agentic account of speculative technologies, such that users are not passive consumers (or interpreters) of images but active participants in their production and circulation as a means of connection.

Speculative technologies have enabled a rapid expansion of virtual collectivities during the past decade: platforms like Instagram, YouTube, Facebook, and Reddit emerged out of Silicon Valley and US university campuses before taking major urban centers by storm. Even so, their current demographic spread globally is broader than ever. In the United States, the adoption of image-based social media and mobile dating apps has been increasing across urban, suburban, and rural areas, with impressive growth across all four US regions.[4] The conglomerates behind these technologies are themselves deeply financialized. Their own meteoric rise (and, for some among them, an equally dramatic demise) is shaped by the spectacle of finance, and their individual operations are girded by intense speculation.[5] Technology workers are often paid in stock shares, venture capitalists pay upfront, and a massive user base is cultivated before the companies go public. Appearance (conjuring the image of the "next big thing" in the eyes of the market) is all-important, even if it means running at a colossal loss.

These developments mark a growing convergence of financialization and digitization, which inflects social relations and the formation of the contemporary sense of self.[6] Many investigations of our uncertain times have sought to make sense of this impact. Typically, sociological attention has focused on the growing role of Facebook or Twitter in populist movements that emerged during global liberal democracy's most recent crisis. Such overtly political use of digital technologies is well documented in academic discussions of algorithmic activism and digital populism on both the Right (e.g., Fuchs 2018) and the Left (e.g., Gerbaudo 2018). Less is known, however, about how the quotidian use of new (and less overtly politicized) interfaces, such as video-sharing and location-aware social media apps, influence today's more insidious mode of speculative sociality. My claim is that such popular and commodified media constitute technologies of speculation: they are nourished by speculative imaginations and, at the same time, they spread them like wildfire. Importantly, speculative technologies form part of an interconnected system that binds economic, social, and even intimate spaces together—and, in doing so, they animate finance capitalism in ways that have not yet been fully understood.

Returning to Anderson's original framing of imagined communities, if, as we have seen, today's speculative imagination provides capitalism's new vernacular language, then speculative technologies offer its grammar— forming the skeletal structure of its modern glass house, providing its supporting pillars and rafters. As Anderson (1991) put it, "the colonial state did not merely aspire to create, under its control, a human landscape of *perfect visibility*; the condition of this visibility was that everyone, everything, had (as it were) a serial number. This *style of imagining* did not come out of thin air. It was *the product of the technologies* of navigation, astronomy, horology, surveying, photography and print, to say nothing of the deep driving power of capitalism" (185, my emphases).

In chapter 1, I began to map out the evolution of capitalist technologies under financialization. We saw how digital media, smartphone apps, machine-learning algorithms, and the digital cloud renewed the key functions of simultaneity and standardization, identified by Anderson as central in shaping imagined communities. Today's glass house still offers the means for capital to survey financialized society, circulating data to produce a "totalizing classificatory grid" (Anderson 1991, 184). But, at the same time, its new technologies imbue society with a new "style of imagining," animating speculative communities. And if navigation, astronomy, and photography offered us more or less stable images of a shared future, computational and algorithmic platforms (from social media to popular astrology apps) produce much more distorted and opaque images of such a future.

The act of representation is key to understanding this tension between visibility and invisibility at the heart of our own glass house: the ways we become visible (or invisible) to both ourselves and others, and the images we rely on to endow our speculative communities with meaning.[7] Such images are inherently uncertain—fragments of a fragile and impermanent social reality. Yet, as they course ceaselessly through our smartphone screens, they also shape our visions of the future. Representation itself is a speculative act and therefore crucial in the fulfillment or betrayal of promises made in markets and societies alike—a prerequisite for imagining speculative communities. In that sense, *even chaos and darkness have an image*—be it the line chart patterns of the VIX (the "fear index") representing stock price movements or TikTok's narcoleptic lip-synching videos. Yet the images disseminated by speculative technologies can be at once highly legible and misleading—a "splendid trompe l'oeil" (Anderson 1991, 184) of deceptive optical illusions, binding speculative communities together despite their respective differences and underlying cleavages of power. The glass house's technological obscurity often masks new forms of inequality and exploitation, predicated on people's differential powers of seeing: while some are able to navigate darkness effortlessly without a flashlight, others are paralyzed and forced to stand still.

Successful stakes in algorithmic high-frequency trading cast no light on the price movements that they trigger. They become visible to many through the (often sensationalized) volatility they seed in markets and the vulnerabilities they expose in society writ large by reallocating debt, or through the great environmental impact of high-frequency trading's giant, energy-hungry data centers. How speculative technologies are wielded and to what purpose can make all the difference between profits and misery—just consider how Amazon's and Uber's deliberately ambiguous algorithmic interfaces work to make inhumane working conditions invisible to both their users and laborers (Bridle 2018, 118).[8] It is to this question of power in society's use of speculative technologies that I now turn.

FROM SURVEILLANCE TO "TIKTOK CAPITALISM"

Ever since Durkheim's pivotal theorization of suicide and the "anomic society," sociologists have interrogated the multifaceted impact of capitalist technologies on the formation (as well as the weakening) of social bonds. Durkheimian sociology (the view of society as a social fact where individuals are shaped and conditioned by macro-level, aggregate norms) has had an especially enduring influence: on Hayekian theories of networked markets, on the digital fragmentation of society and the rise of virtual communities (Calhoun 1998), and on the "uncertain connectivities" of a globalized "network society" (Castells 2012).[9] But such major works have tended to focus more on the diffusion of information and data and their role in the development of social ties and less on the creation of collective myths and imaginations made possible through new capitalist technologies.[10] When an emergent algorithmic imagination is considered in its own right, critiques often focus on its surreptitious role "in the organization of exploitation, domination, administration, surveillance, and the emergence of digital Taylorism" (Fuchs 2017, 856). In their influential work, Hardt and Negri (2017), for instance, note that such Taylorian social media algorithms are "increasingly open and social in a way that blurs the boundaries between work and life" in order to generate and capture value "even without the users knowing" (119).

Broader theorizations of the digital have sought to consider algorithmic sociality within bigger theories of contemporary capitalism, offering vital critical insights into the myriad ways social media and data-driven technologies monitor, control, and exacerbate inequalities within their expanding constituencies. Shoshana Zuboff's (2019) work on surveillance capitalism is a particularly noteworthy and far-reaching recent intervention in these debates.[11] Zuboff stresses that the growth of surveillance capitalism poses a serious threat to democracy, considering new technologies as forming a "global architecture of behaviour modification" (vii), spawned by the deregulatory forces of neoliberalism. This process takes place through the buying and selling of behavioral future predictions made on the behest of big tech, unbeknownst to most users.[12] The use of ultra-high-speed algorithmic marketing is the digital industry equivalent of financial high-frequency trading—with social media platforms wielding highly complex machine-learning technologies to track, trace, and sell user data.

Zuboff's (2019) analysis is important because it places uncertainty center stage. Her assumption is that beneath the gigantic, all-encompassing operation of surveillance capitalism lies a systemic desire for minimizing uncertainty—a striving for certainty and absolute predictability. "All that is moist and alive must hand over its facts. There can be no shadow, no darkness. The unknown is intolerable" (241), she writes. Technological behemoths, of course, desire nothing more than turning data into profits, using technology's unique affordances to play the game of algorithmic reward (carrot) and control (stick). Yet, contrary to Zuboff's claim, less uncertainty has not been the secret to Silicon Valley's triumph and astronomic asset valuations in our financialized era. Rather, the industry's greatest strength lies in its successful embedding of uncertainty *within* its complex and opaque platforms—in the ways it reaps profits from the confusion sowed by its algorithms. It is in fact uncertainty itself that becomes a lucrative resource of monetization, much as in the algorithmic wagers of high-frequency traders. To reverse Zuboff's own words, there is *nothing but* "shadow and darkness" in the chaotic, algorithmic universe of digital media inhabited by everyday users—yet it is a darkness they naturally drift toward and come to call home.

Consider Bilibili, a Chinese online video-sharing platform at the sharp end of speculative technologies. Bilibili is designed specifically to generate an aesthetic of intensified confusion while offering users a mode of social navigation and connectivity in the here and now. User-generated streams of live commentary—called "bullet comments" or "rolling comments"—and emojis are superimposed in real time onto accelerated (running in fast-forward mode) video. They aim to create a community around the content shown, while at the same time obscuring the videos they seek to explain. Bullet comments are reminiscent of the bucket-shop ticker tapes around which the first public spectacles of speculation were staged. But they also recall the scrolling news tickers popularized by cable networks in the aftermath of the 9/11 terrorist attacks, when endless streams of news headlines flooded the bottom part of television screens broadcasting the chaos and smoke of burning buildings. News tickers have since become a permanent feature of television news—an all too familiar flashing signifier of a constant state of unease in which media like Bilibili flourish.[13] Or take V-Live, a Korean app that allows K-pop fans around the world to connect with each other through real-time comments streamed while watching live performances by their favorite bands—creating a feeling of emotional proximity among otherwise physically distant fans (King-O'Riain 2020). As Suk-Young Kim (2018) has shown in her illuminating digital ethnography of the platform, the liveness and authenticity projected on V-Live have been key elements of creating this fandom community—affirming ultimately "a sense of being" that offers "affective evidence of life itself" (205).[14]

TikTok is an even more successful Chinese-owned platform that has taken the—extremely lucrative—global video meme market by storm since its launch in 2018. TikTok was developed specifically for the North American and Indian markets, where it rapidly became the single most downloaded app and Facebook-owned Instagram's key competitor (reaching more than 2 billion downloads in 2020).[15] The app is designed around streams of short (under-sixty-second) videos featuring bizarre sketches, nonsensical choreography, and even confessional or political statements set to popular songs. They are sequenced on viewers' screens by the company's famous recommendation algorithm, around which there is a notorious secrecy, with company executives consistently refusing to disclose any information about it. The lack of transparency about the mechanics of algorithmic surfacing (the personalized content generated by the algorithm) on TikTok's #ForYou space has roused intense speculation and even suspicions of conspiracy, but it has protected the company's monetizing model and helped direct even more traffic to the app. The platform itself exists in flux, thriving in the path of the evocative, transient "wall": its endless scroll is even more prominent as a feature than Facebook Timeline or Instagram Stories; there is simply nothing else on the screen to distract users from the constant stream of videos. The overall aesthetic of irreverence is ubiquitous here too and includes more sinister content (often overtly racist and sexist) that is reminiscent of the meme subcultures of anonymous platforms like 4chan, 8chan, Gab, and Reddit. The app is in equal measure preposterous and addictive, representing a reality on the cusp of chaotic incomprehensibility.

It is no accident that critics of such digital platforms lament their distracting role, their manufacturing of a perilous collective ignorance, which suits the profit instincts of proprietary algorithms and further atomizes already fragmented communities.[16] But what exactly are we being distracted from, as our attention veers from everyday life's perplexity to speculative technologies' own virtual chaos? My argument is that the immersive use of these technologies should not be interpreted as a one-way descent into the abyss of collective distraction. It would be a mistake to conflate the muddiness of their disorienting content with vacuity of meaning. Recognizing this, a new generation of technology theorists have challenged the notion of an inexorable, calamitous ignorance in speculative technologies by considering existing—if clandestine—possibilities of reaping benefits from them. In *Stack*, an ambitious work blending software studies and political philosophy, technologist Benjamin Bratton (2015) argues for a critical theory of technology that resists the "apocalyptic panic" of "state surveillance, troll culture, and flash crashes," as well as the "messianic effervescence" of "internet freedom" (xviii).[17] Artist James Bridle (2018) takes a similar view, arguing that the highly complexified gray zones of our computational cloud provide a space in which Silicon Valley–powered surveillance and political conspiracies both flourish. From the perspective of these technology theorists, the darkness of uncontrollable chaos is inescapable, but it also contains more generative possibilities for resistance, counter-surveillance, and more radical ways of seeing.[18]

Such possibilities are not to be found in the grand yet naive techno-optimism of cryptocurrencies, blockchains, and AI automation—rather, in their simplest form, effective resistances may appear in basic software like the TrackMeNot browser extension, which protects data profiling, not by means of concealment or encryption (that is to say, by covering one's tracks) but by deploying the opposite strategy of noise and obfuscation, making "actual web searches, lost in a cloud of false leads . . . essentially hidden in plain view."[19] Obfuscation thus becomes here a defense strategy against surveillance itself (Brunton and Nissenbaum 2016). Or consider the industrial action of UberEats (Uber's food-delivery service) workers, who redeployed the company's secret algorithm (the same algorithm obscuring their own exploitation) and placed strategic orders through the app as a means of assembling coworkers to their picket lines (Bridle 2018).

These insights resonate with an important strand of critical data studies (Seaver 2018; Donovan 2017; Daniels and Gregory 2016), which have also challenged the disproportionate emphasis on the passivity of individual social media users under the shadow of surveillance capitalism. Jean Donovan's (2017) work underlines the complexities of grassroots attempts to weaponize the politics of hypervisibility through the use of image and video data as an activist strategy. Donovan discusses the possibilities and the limitations of this strategy; she shows, for instance, how protesters in the Occupy movement actively engaged in practices of self-surveillance (producing a ubiquitous visual documentation of their rallies) to expose incidents of police violence, but in doing so they also made themselves more vulnerable to police departments that drew on the same data to support their own monitoring of protesters. Nick Seaver's research into "digital traps" (the algorithmic recommender systems that hook users into enduring usage) throws more light onto the problematic dichotomy between coercion and voluntary involvement in today's "encompassing, hard-to-escape (online) cultural worlds" (Seaver 2018, 3). Like Donovan, Seaver demonstrates the inescapability of these new cultural infrastructures but also points to the productive work of users who strive to form relationships within such traps, thereby creating social spaces. The question to ask of traps, he concludes, "may not be how to escape from them, but rather how to recapture them and turn them to new ends in the service of new worlds" (13).

The routine use (consumption and production) of imaged-based data streams such as those I have so far discussed reveals an intricate power dynamic at play in speculative communities. More than just crude or sophisticated instruments of control, digital media driven by recommendation algorithms are sites for the reproduction of the particular tastes, dispositions, and imaginations texturing social life under surveillance capitalism. My contention here is that speculative technologies share a deeper and more profound affinity with finance's cutting-edge infrastructures of derivatives trading. Just as the latter create price volatility and then commodify it into risk, the former financialize and profit from the uncertainty they seed in social media platforms. Giving up data reflects a forfeit of our control over the future—a time when our choices will be shaped by the smart algorithms into which we now unwittingly feed. However, this collective surrender is not merely the price paid in exchange for a painless consumer experience in the present. It is also a collective rite of passage into the speculative community. The ritual use of financialized digital commodities relies on contradictory promises whose exchange fuels anxiety but also renews our speculative imaginations. The promise of received likes on a Facebook post, of views on a posted Instagram story, or even of partner matches that may follow a bout of Tinder swiping are undercut by a compulsive recurrence. They appear at once realizable and elusive, both gratifying in the present and doomed to fail in the future, binding users in an uncertain albeit hypervisual sense of sociality.

Examining this image-oriented, fragile sociality requires us to move beyond the structural perspective of technology companies and consider the dazzling spectacle of speculative communities from the perspective of their lay users.

THE NEW SOCIETY OF THE SPECTACLE

The study of the disorienting and deceptive power of media images in the digital world has a long pedigree in critical theory. From Adorno and the Frankfurt School to Baudrillard, Barthes, and Fredric Jameson, the Marxist theses on alienation and ideology have been deployed to explain the illusionary unity of capitalist societies around signs controlled by material distributions of power. No work, however, has more presciently captured the political economy of images, visibility, and representation under modern capitalism than Guy Debord's (2002 [1968]) hugely influential *Society of the Spectacle*. Debord put forward a radical theoretical proposition:

> In societies where modern conditions of production prevail, all life presents as an immense accumulation of spectacles. Everything that was directly lived has moved away into a representation.... The spectacle is not a collection of images, but a social relation among people, mediated by images. (theses 1–4)

And

> [the] general abstraction of the entirety of production are perfectly rendered in the spectacle, whose mode of being concrete is precisely abstraction. In the spectacle, one part of the world represents itself to the world and is superior to it. The spectacle is nothing more than the common language of this separation. What binds the spectators together is no more than an irreversible relation at the very centre that maintains their isolation. The spectacle reunites the separate, but reunites it as separate. (thesis 29)

The two passages encapsulate two of the most fundamental theoretical suppositions underpinning Debord's argument. One is a transindividualist ontology (shared with Castoriadis's conception of the social imagination), in which people are "never atoms, events, let alone subjects, given once and for all" (Bottici 2017, 97). Put simply, the spectacle itself *is* a type of social relation. Debord underscores the visual dimension of that social relation as a vital force in the shaping of dominant capitalist imaginaries. This emphasis is often misinterpreted as the passivity of a viewer sitting in front of flows of images passing before their eyes. But the spectator is never a mere viewer. The spectacle comes alive in spectators' interactions with others outside the constraints of the media; it is a representation of an imagined community that is reconstituted in the viewers' own everyday lives (Toscano and Kinkle 2015). Debord's analysis focuses on the abstraction and complexity of modern representations and illuminates them by foregrounding the role of mass media in the arbitration of social relations. At the time of writing in the 1960s, television and advertising had forcefully unleashed an overflow of images that saturated social life. Lived experiences became reified and removed into an orbit of representations that was ultimately inaccessible, out of reach. Yet revealingly, the pull of that era's illusionary capitalist promises (e.g., of consumption) remained active (that is, visible), even though they were no longer being fulfilled. Commodification of having was thus superseded by commodification of appearing, and sociality itself became an object of value exchange.

How does the continuing acceleration of such image flows affect the social (dis)connections so astutely observed by Debord over half a century ago? Today more than ever we are incessantly exposed to the gaze of others, simultaneously viewing them ourselves: we are at once agents (creators) and subjects (consumers) of the spectacle. An even more vital change wrought by financialization has been the convergence of the worlds of the hidden and the spectacular (as opposed to the merely visible) as a result of speculative technologies. In today's high-bandwidth, augmented spectacle, it is not only our representations that are held remotely but our personal data too. Stored, distributed, and managed distantly in the digital cloud, everyday data are ceaselessly fed into the banks of online platforms, shaping their algorithms, determining the content that we see, all the while generating huge profits for technological behemoths.

Therefore, on the surface, new digitized social relations are reordered on the model of market relations. The erosion of the socially integrated paradigm of Fordist capitalism has continued during the time of technological acceleration and the visual internet (Chayka 2019): a network that amplifies visual (over verbal) communication in our everyday digital life. Such continuing overabundance of (and overreliance on) images means that we now compete more fervently for what Michel Feher (2018) calls "reputational value" in a market where reputational volatility is the other side of business opportunity. Feher shows how social media become, in effect, technologies of "investee politics," as we compete vigorously in all realms of life to valorize our (human, social, and economic) capital. But the spread of the speculative imagination has been much broader than the quests for creditworthiness that such politics foreground. Current representational forms require us to turn more imaginatively to the study of the spectacles that beguile financialized societies, which represent this infusion of our social relations by the speculative imagination.[20] There is an important distinction afoot here. While the logic of Feher's "investee politics" implies an individual, and mostly rational, quest for maximizing credit, worth, and image reputation, the speculative imagination embodies a more social use of finance-driven vernaculars. Put another way, we are not just competitive collectors of likes and swipes but invested members of anxious communities, yearning for connection at a time of unsettledness and doubt.

Still, such tentative imagined connections are not formed on an equal footing. Updating Debord for this new era of finance, philosopher Chiara Bottici (2014) describes modern spectacles at a time when radical uncertainty saturates both politics and everyday life. Bottici proposes a theory of imaginal politics to describe how global injustice (framed as human-rights violations) becomes a spectacle, reproduced by an abundance of virtual images on our computer screens that raises our incredulity, with the paradoxical effect of rendering them more distant rather than closer to us. This works in concert with the financialization of formerly trustworthy liberal institutions such as news media and universities, as (ill-placed) trust in those former bastions of truth continues to decay. While these new dependencies between reality and image materialize, more equitable forms of sociality that would be able to challenge dominant speculative imaginations are undermined.

At first sight, this issue seems to be heightened by the proliferation of speculative technologies: the dense grayness of our algorithmic cloud makes it even more difficult to occupy an external vantage point that would allow collective representations of this complexity. The cloud, however, can also provide space for alternative, shade-loving imaginations to grow. As artist Hito Steyerl (2009) has powerfully argued (writing a few years before the explosion of platforms like TikTok and Instagram), new digital media have made possible a rapid emergence of what she calls "poor images": imperfect, out-of-focus, low-resolution images that "mock the promises of digital technology" (1) while still circulating within its chaotic premises. Poor images challenge the established visual hierarchies of modern spectacle society (which rewards high-resolution and focused images), and in so doing connect audiences in new visual bonds—"almost in a physical sense by mutual excitement, affective attunement, and anxiety" (7). They encompass "confusion and stupefaction" but also "disruptive movements of thought and affect" (8). They draft users into new roles of active participants in the collective production and circulation of those images.

▲

In nineteenth-century futures markets and bucket shops, bettors' eyes were fixed on prices running through the ticker tapes. Price movement before the eyes of spectator-speculators created a feverish and exciting atmosphere—a fascination that was in part engendered by the challenging task of deciphering information from unfamiliar signs on the ticker tape. This tenuous legibility of hypervisible stock price signs exerted a mystical power over financiers and publics alike (Stäheli 2013). Their attention was captivated by the symbols themselves as they became viewers (and participants) in a spectacle. The kind of abstraction achieved through that early technology of speculation produced a distance between code and traders by obscuring the undergirded values traded behind the mask of price fluctuations. By contrast, abstraction in today's spectacle society works increasingly through *mirroring*: including contemporary speculators' own images in the symbolic universe they help to generate renders the resulting spectacle more familiar. This type of abstraction is qualitatively different, because today, when we look at signs, we often see our own image. Spectator-speculators are thus inscribed even more powerfully in the signs circulated by speculative technologies.

At first glance, then, the work of speculative technologies can be seen as conjuring collectivities that narcissistically reflect ourselves.[21] However, even something as ostensibly solipsistic as the ubiquitous selfie contains a substantial social dimension. Selfies are often used as a means of performing a speculative sociality in both virtual and physical spaces—speculative because, as we have seen, they feed modern people's reputation-seeking anxieties (Rosamond 2020).[22] But selfies also become essential tools for spectators who now increasingly double as performers, who want to be seen. Selfie sociality no longer predominantly consists of overcurated imagery that seeks to mask or embellish reality. In recent years, there has been a notable resurgence of an authentic aesthetic (as opposed to the heavily photoshopped images of influencers in the 2010s)—TikTok's own motto echoes this trend: "real people, real videos." User content *must* look amateur in order to be appealing and successful, for higher visibility amounts to higher income (see, for instance, Bishop 2019). The growing use of short video and "vlogging," which are often broadcast live by users (on Instagram and YouTube and more niche platforms such as V-Live), increases this sense of authenticity even more. Unlike what is often assumed, speculative technologies contribute to a more familiar theatricality (Sennett 1992) in the new spectacle society.

STARS, "STORIES," AND TIME IN SPECULATIVE COMMUNITIES

The antecedents of *homo speculans* responded to the uncertainties of nineteenth-century capitalism by blurring the lines between prediction and divination. To traverse market volatility, the most adventurous speculators turned to the occult, enlisting the services of hypnotists, tarot readers, and, above all, financial astrologers.[23] Their forecasts linked planetary cycles to price cycles and lunar movements to the ebbs and flows of stock values. Occult projections of this kind were not fringe, but mainstream. During the late nineteenth century, eminent stockbrokers such as W. D. Gann, R. N. Elliott, and Charles Dow (of the Dow Jones index) pioneered a practice called "chartist investment analysis," drawing directly on gnostic and astrological fields to hedge future uncertainties.[24] Reciprocally, astrology made appeals to scientific rationality to lend legitimacy to its own forecasts. Some of the most successful financial astrologers demonstrated a solid grasp of astronomy and its underlying mathematics, thus increasing their appeal in the eyes of financiers. In the aftermath of the Great Depression, US exchange markets saw a renaissance of astrological thinking, with J. P. Morgan himself becoming a devout follower of celebrity astrologer Evangeline Adams. The 1935 publication of Luther Jensen's *Astro Cycles and Speculative Markets* was an instant sensation on Wall Street and around the country, with copies selling out quickly. Simultaneously mystical and hardheaded, financial astrology provided a powerful representation of the opaque reality of financial trading.[25]

Like the lay speculation of that time, the ambiguity of such fortune-telling practitioners was attacked as fraudulent for much of the nineteenth century, but it emerged as legally (and for the most part, morally) acceptable in the wake of the twentieth century (Pietruska 2017).[26] Just like legitimacy conflicts around the morality and irrationality of financial speculation hinged on racial and class power relations, the policing and persecution of astrologers and other fortune tellers developed along racial ideologies, gender norms, and class distinctions. Astrologers were berated with the same labels as the bucket-shop gamblers, for example, "vile and unscrupulous hags" and "lying sorcerers" (Pietruska 2017, 210).

Today, astrology is making a spectacular return in speculative communities. In the United States, the astrology app market grew by a whopping

65 percent in 2019 alone, while venture capitalists have been flocking to astrology start-ups.[27] Highly aestheticized and algorithmically powered astrology apps like Sanctuary and The Pattern are becoming popular digital commodities. At the same time, Silicon Valley giants are integrating blockchain astrology into their platforms. Instagram accounts providing esoteric forecasting have seen their followings increasing exponentially, while in 2019, short-term hospitality provider Airbnb partnered with the Twitter astrologers Astro Poets to provide travel horoscopes and recommend "astrologically fitting" destinations. This is not a uniquely Western trend: digital astrology has seen a recent boom in India, for instance, where the 2020 launch of Clickastro caused a sensation, updating traditional Hindu and Vedic astrology (Jyotisha) for the new generation of mobile app users.

Co-Star—"the Uber of digital astrology"—is a leader in this burgeoning market and offers a stark example of speculative technologies. Developed by an alliance of software engineers, amateur astrologers, and literary consultants, the platform mixes the language of algorithmically generated "poetic sarcasm" with a distinctive monochrome visual aesthetic. Its smart daily messages offer an irreverent darkness, instructing its users to "start a cult," "get off the internet," or "check their ego." This unusual function of astrology apps has been hailed as "the new psychotherapy" for Generation Z, or as "psychotherapy plus magic." Unlike psychotherapy, self-help guides, and counseling, however, astrology apps do not provide a space where criticism or judgment are suspended. Rather, they are strewn with sarcasm and covert criticism. At the same time, Co-Star's low-resolution imagery blends nostalgia for the "early internet" age with zine culture and depictions of wild animals, tropical fruits, three-dimensional shapes, and unspecified machinery. Upon downloading the app, such icons are automatically embedded in the user's smartphone, added to their list of emojis, ready to adorn their regular messaging exchanges. As put by one of the first high-profile essays to focus on the resurgence of astrology fueled by Gen Z, apps like Co-Star are "meme machines" that spread "in that blooming, unfurling way that memes do."[28]

The opacity of the algorithmic predictions on the app (and the assorted esoteric iconography) seems to offer apt representations of chaotic everyday life experiences. Such predictions bear out—rather than intervene in—these bewildering experiences, aligning with users' own cynical expectations of the future's gifts. The reemergence of astrology and its spectacular success among today's younger generations has captivated and intrigued mainstream media, which often explain it in terms of its capacity to give us the answers "we already desire," especially in times of crisis.[29] But what if the answer we now seek is uncertainty itself? While the attraction of traditional astrology seemingly lay in the comfort of its determination and prediction, its digital successors make no promises of certainty. Yet their Neptunian fog resonates with the moment's zeitgeist. This new generation of astrology apps offer only an inherently unknowable future. As the Co-Star motto goes, we now need "irrationality to invade our techno-rationalist ways of living." What is more, attraction to the irrationality of these apps does not seem to contradict rational beliefs (Smallwood 2019). While, up until the 2000s, astrology buffs were dwelling in the margins of the obscure, today's astrology followers are more likely to be just as drawn to science—much like Gann and Dow more than a century ago. Google's Artists and Machine Intelligence program calls this marriage of technology, science, and mysticism "algo-séance," one of the most hyped trends in the technology industry for 2020, according to Buzzfeed.[30]

Importantly, astrology apps now harness such representations to connect people, much in the manner of the image-sharing platforms I have already discussed. Co-Star's personal charts are intrinsically social, linked in real time to the charts of users' extended networks of friends (which are fed into the app through Facebook or WhatsApp), and are, for that reason, entirely speculative. This speculative kind of sociality is one of the app's most popular features. It allows users to discover how "compatible" they are with each other, in terms of (among other categories) emotions (Moon), intellect (Mercury), sexual desire (Mars), and idealism (Jupiter). The app deploys the same mischievous irreverence used in its messages to regularly update charts of harmony or discord among one's friends. In India, meanwhile, Clickastro's algorithms apply playfully traditional *dasa sandhi* analysis (for exploring transitions in a user's life from one planetary period to another) and *Kuja dosha* checks (for avoiding unfortunate crossings with the planet Mars) in order to generate reports of compatibility between its users.

The striking popularity of astrology apps reveals a shift in the function of algorithmically powered media: from instruments of forecasting, prediction, and risk control to vehicles of collective uncertainty and incubators of the speculative sociality of our time. While they have little in common with the astrologists of the past, such platforms are part of a rapidly expanding assemblage of speculative technologies, which mediate the ways we imagine and experience contemporary finance capitalism.

▲

To pull the threads of this chapter's discussion together: today's spectacle society, fostered as it is by the speculative imagination, encompasses an unresolved tension between the overabundant, hypervisible images of itself and the disorienting circulation of such image streams by complex speculative technologies. The advance of speculative technologies, which feeds on this contradiction, demonstrates a growing convergence between the worlds of finance and everyday social life. On one level, this convergence evidences the desire of finance to both represent and conceal the complexity of our current social reality in order to create perpetual flows of revenue through the order of the infinite scroll. But what exactly happens as we tap and swipe on such endless image streams? What kind of speculative community is imagined?

In the preceding discussion, I have highlighted two important blind spots in the tropes of technological surveillance: their neglect of the shifting social morphologies undergirding our image-hungry, financialized capitalism and their unhelpful obfuscation of the active roles we play in producing (but also in curating and reposting) the images on which such technologies feed. In the remainder of this chapter, therefore, I would like to consider a final, important aspect of speculative technologies: the distinct, collective temporal experience they generate. I have likened the activity of watching content on Instagram Stories to the reading of newspapers in Anderson's *Imagined Communities*, emphasizing the effects of speed, movement, and impermanence, which, together, lead to a characteristic, speculative simultaneity. Instagram's platform lies somewhere in between TikTok's queasy visual universe and Facebook's more traditional, blended posting structure. Stories are mapped on a social network of followers, whose shared images or videos are organized over users' own posted content, forming a horizontally arranged chronological stream. A right tap on the screen leads you to the same follower's next post, while a right swipe takes you to the next follower's content. The constant flow of posts is intersected by paid content (ads that are generated by Instagram's proprietary personalizing algorithm), which blends in with the familiar stream—sometimes so seamlessly that it can be hard to tell what is real from what is not during a bout of fast tapping.

Unlike reading newspapers (or news tickers, or even the bullet comments on Bilibili), watching stories on Instagram's home feed (but also reading posts on Facebook's news feed or on Twitter's home feed) means that individual users see different content. This more fractured experience of collective time is similar across video-streaming platforms like Netflix or audio-streaming platforms like Spotify, which are themselves becoming more and more embedded in social media apps. In all these media, it is never entirely clear whether others are viewing and sharing the same content—although clusters of users following one another will likely watch a great deal of overlapping streams. The clustering of Instagram communities is further reinforced by practices such as tagging people in a user's post and reposting content that has been uploaded by others (and by doing so also extending the life of a short-lived story). Both practices, as with received likes, induce affective responses as a form of endorsement in a community of users (to be liked, in a sense, is to be included).

Stories also occupy tiny fragments of time (recorded videos and images come in bite-sized spells of fifteen seconds at most) and vanish without a trace after twenty-four hours. Yet, even as content itself becomes impermanent, it is the movements of immersion and repetition that set the tone for engagement with these apps. The increasingly intuitive, embodied, and rapid interaction with circulating data streams consists of vertical swiping gestures that release streams of emojis (conveying a swarm of reactions ranging from passionate approval to vehement rejection). Such streams amplify the addictive familiarity of the disseminated images, whose linear presentation offers in turn a reassuring power to the platform, as it compresses and focuses attention on the present moment—when users view stories, they typically tap or swipe on the screen multiple times in one minute. Lovink (2019) describes the experience as a form of daydreaming: "Swiping fingers assist in moving the mind elsewhere. Checking the smartphone is the present way of daydreaming. Unaware of our brief absence, we enjoy the feeling of being remotely present. We remember what it's like to feel" (38). Meanwhile, a very similar form of ephemerality is also introduced in more text-oriented social networking sites, with Twitter announcing in March 2020 the trial launch of the "fleet": a tweet that lasts only twenty-four hours, promoted by the company as "a way to start conversations about *fleeting thoughts*."[31] Beyond the world of social media, a growing number of commercial apps now also compete in the wider market of short-lived experiences. Take, for instance, Airbnb's partnership with digital astrology—a perfect match for the transient habitus of modern travelers, who move through holiday destinations as slickly as the Sun moves through Pisces and Aries.

As I have argued throughout this chapter, speculative technologies do not merely convert lived experiences into commodified predictive data. They also coproduce and represent the conditions of radical uncertainty that define a speculative mode of social being. In doing so, they integrate *homo speculans* in chaotic yet increasingly interlinked orders. Correspondingly, previous boundaries between realms of life (economic, social, private) catered to by speculative technologies are loosening. Nowhere is this digital tangle more evident than in our virtual navigations of intimacy, love, and sexuality. The organization of individual desires is increasingly charted onto a digital libidinal economy that is at once volatile and immersive. The questions I would now like to ask are, What kinds of intimate relations emerge in this techno-world of radical uncertainty? How do the accelerated temporality and speculative sociality of finance shape the desires of *homo speculans*? Chapter 4 takes up these questions to examine finance capitalism's new speculative intimacies in the world of mobile dating apps.

4: SPECULATIVE INTIMACIES

Make America date again.

DONALD DATERS DATING APP WEBSITE

I don't believe in Tinder, Bumble, all that. . . .
I've come here to meet people organically.

GREG, *LOVE ISLAND* TELEVISION
SHOW CONTESTANT

Economic actions have always influenced how people form intimate rela-tions. In his ruminations on the innerworldly asceticism of modern soci-eties, Max Weber (1992) painted a gloomy picture of the early capitalist subject's intimate world, which was marred by an entrenched "feeling of unprecedented inner loneliness" (104). Such inner loneliness was integral to modern society's "disenchantment." A calculating rationality was en-croaching on the most private corners of capitalist life—even tampering with intimacy itself. We have already seen how the growing mediatization of everyday life ushered in the spectacle society of the twentieth century by binding modern spectator-speculators together in a hypervisible yet con-tradictory experience of sociality. But these developments, as I contend in this chapter, have also made a Debordian spectacle of romantic relations. They have spawned a new, image-based and market-oriented ideal of love that meshes the (profane) consumerism of dating with a (sacred) image of romance. *Homo speculans* is thus jilted in the throes of an even more dazed existence. By the dawn of the twenty-first century, the promise of love un-der neoliberalism was proving to be just as illusory as the promises of em-ployment, upward mobility, and the benefits of entrepreneurial capitalism. The Weberian inner loneliness seemed to return alongside an increasingly distant hope for security sought through tentative pursuits of intimacy.

As our routine navigations of social life become more transient and mobile, our temporal experiences of intimacy shift in similar ways: casual sexual encounters, hookups, flings, friends with benefits, noncommittal and polyamorous relationships (not to mention rapidly falling marriage and climbing divorce rates) are the order of the day. Intimacy itself becomes a fulcrum of the short-lived experience venerated by speculative technologies. And as the receding entrepreneurial logic of *homo economicus* makes way for the more uncertain longings of *homo speculans*, an immersive fixation with images dominates romantic and sexual encounters alike. Nonetheless, capitalist notions of romantic love and sexual desire cannot be fully captured by the frames of disenchantment and individualization—capitalism and intimacy are linked in much more dynamic ways. In her pioneering work, the sociologist Viviana Zelizer (2007) demonstrates that social, intimate, and economic ties all intersect insidiously through individuals' constant relational performances, in and beyond markets. Zelizer challenges the view that money merely corrupts personal relations; ordinary life blends money transactions with the reciprocities of marriage, friendship, and care work, and thus intimate and market relationships cannot be disentangled. Hence, in the following I am less interested in the effect of economic principles (or practices) on these relationships and am more curious about the deeper (and more obscure) impact of finance's distinct speculative imagination on our ephemeral, confused, digitally mediated desires.

My argument is this: contemporary intimate relations, like the social fabric that binds them, are laced with unstable, disorienting (and often disconcerting) images circulated by digital media. Permeated by finance's imagination, *speculative intimacies* are formed through our anxious and doggedly recurrent wagers on intimate bonds, which offer scant hope of withstanding uncertainty. Yet speculative intimacies are not simply the fixed expressions of a new emotional or rational order bestowed on us by an immutable neoliberalism. Like other endeavors of *homo speculans*, they reflect tentative yearnings for connection and for navigating the uncharted waters of an unknowable future in new ways.

▲

Location-aware mobile dating apps are now ubiquitous across capitalist economies in the United States and Europe and are increasingly popular in numerous countries outside the Global North—even in contexts with little pre-existing culture of dating, such as China, Bangladesh, and Egypt.[1] Tinder, the industry's behemoth, was launched in 2012 and has since revolutionized the dating market, making its app a permanent feature in a whole generation's mobile phones. Recent research has shown that Tinder and a host of competing apps like Bumble, Hinge, and Happn have been rapidly substituting for social networks, family, and friends to become the most significant mediators of modern romantic relations. During 2019, it was reported for the first time that the majority of heterosexual couples in the United States had met through such digital apps, surpassing the human intermediary role of institutions that had traditionally facilitated romantic relations until recently (Rosenfeld et al. 2019). The ritual use of online dating has thus become an integral part of everyday intimate life.[2] Yet just as we enter partnerships through these interfaces in greater numbers than ever, their use is being refocused to target the fast-growing constituency of those who remain intentionally unpartnered. Tinder's mission statement as of 2020 reads "We celebrate that being single is a journey. And a great one. Being single isn't the thing you do, unhappily, before you settle down."[3] The company's sleek global marketing campaign, designed by Wieden+Kennedy (the advertising agency behind Nike's "Just do it" tagline), captures this fluid concept of intimacy in the slogan "Single not sorry." People seem to be turning their backs to the pursuit of ideas such as "true love" and a "happy ending," which have long captivated capitalist society's romantic imagination.

It should come as no surprise that public discourse frames Tinder as a pillar of an expanding hookup culture (see, for instance, Wade 2017). Dating apps are typically depicted as the final nail in the coffin of traditional notions of love, binding human relationships even more tightly to the logic of consumption and commodification. They deploy proprietary algorithms to visualize a previously hidden market of sexual and romantic partners.[4] Importantly, they organize such representations (of virtually unlimited choices of available partners) in ways that are familiar from popular social media platforms outside the dating world: Instagram's infinite scroll is replicated in the virtually never-ending stream of partner images on Tinder's infinite swipe. The way such images flow before users' eyes differs little from the constant streams of memetic content seen on TikTok. These features have almost entirely upstaged the apps' more traditional text-heavy or text-driven (desktop) online predecessors OkCupid and Match.com. And, like other spectacles enabled by speculative technologies, spectators' access to visibility is subject to monetization and pricing strategies. Tinder relies on its paid versions for income (called Tinder Plus and Passport), which offer the ability "to like as many people as you could possibly want" (in contrast to the free version, which caps the number of likes and swipes per day). Competitors such as Bumble (launched in 2014 by a Tinder cofounder as a more "women-friendly" dating app) also offer premium features (Bumble Boost), while most other apps offer variants of Bumble's SuperSwipe coins that can be purchased by the most avid users for $2.99 per swipe.

Unsurprisingly, a common criticism of dating apps centers on their routine hypervisualization of intimacy and on the ways they encourage shallow or, in their more sinister form, discriminatory behaviors. Recent qualitative research on the platform (e.g., van Hooff 2020; Thwaites 2020; Krüger and Spilde 2019; Essig 2019) has revealed that dating apps' emphasis on the visual intensifies pressures on users to meet bodily norms of beauty. The effects of the resulting image obsession are especially pernicious for women, queer people, and people of color, whose bodies are often spectacularized and at the same time erased through their trade as commodities. Older forms of violence and power domination, misogyny, macho culture, transphobia, and racism have been rife in some popular dating apps (facilitated by their platforms' conditions of relative anonymity), such as the spread of much-discussed unsolicited "dick pics" and the frequent exclusion and discrimination directed at Black and Asian users.[5]

This issue has been at the center of recent attempts to create new apps that are safer for women and racialized people. Popular platforms like Bumble make specific (though debatable) claims about integrating feminist impulses in their rules of conduct, while apps such as lesbian-friendly Her strive to create safer spaces of interaction for queer people. Yet, as sociologist Laurie Essig (2019) has argued, even when dating apps appear willing to confront systemic vectors of oppression, they often remain faithful to the individualizing ideology of modern capitalist romance: a space of interaction where economic inequalities are concealed and presented as a matter of personal choice. From this perspective, rather than undermining the illusory magic of love, dating apps appear to work in tandem with capitalism's romance ideology, reinforcing "a dreamscape that allows us to get away from our own reality" (Essig 2019, 55). To put it another way, Tinder's infinite swipe is now romantic love's incongruous antechamber. For Essig, societies are thus turned further away from the public sphere and become sheltered in the private sphere—just as intimate life itself becomes more publicly performed than ever. They become distracted from the task of formulating more collective responses to their underlying conditions of emotional insecurity and structural inequality under financialized capitalism.

Nonetheless, a speculative imagination is ever-present during such fantastical traverses: Tinder users often act like curators who filter images of others (Hogan 2010) while also selecting appropriate representations of themselves on behalf of their imagined viewers and potential partners. In that sense, users' ongoing valuations of images in the dating app marketplace form part of a dual process of producing and representing value that is at once subjective and economic, for the "scopic evaluation of others" (Illouz 2019, 141). This should by now be a familiar process. The vast majority of dating app users regularly use the platforms in tandem with image- and video-sharing apps—such as Instagram image albums that are embedded into Tinder profiles, giving additional access to a person's uploaded content. The line between our social and intimate selves becomes fuzzier still.

Recent empirical studies suggest that the rapid, image-based valuations of possible partners can encourage instinctive decisions that "reinvigorate embodied intuition" and "gut feeling" (Krüger and Spilde 2019). The specific temporality of mobile dating apps combines a spontaneity and immediacy that can be conducive to entertainment as well as connection. At the same time, users draw on their imaginations not only to perform binary valuations (right or left swipes) but also to conjure possible viewers—both those they want to meet and those they do not. Their desired self-presentation is continually tweaked even before chatting with a match on the app (unlike Instagram likes, Tinder matches are not publicly displayed) or meeting them in person (Ward 2017, 1655). David and Cambre (2016) capture this microsociological aspect of the all-important swipe gesture through which users "knowingly engage in the proposed figuration of intimacy as levities (volatile, ethereal, and quick), despite its ambiguity" (9). The new visibilities afforded by dating apps (much like the visibilities of their social media counterparts that I examined in chapter 3) are unlikely to restore control over their users' fractured experiences of intimacy. Yet their chasing of immediate gains is not just a futile pursuit of instant gratification (often described as a rush of dopamine)—it is a surrender to a fleeting present. Beneath the mantle of market valuation practices, dating apps foster speculative intimacies. More than just profitable markets, or vehicles for pursuing love and sex, they too form part of the rite of passage into speculative communities.

▲

What are the implications of this immersive surrender to the uncertain space of Tinder's infinite swipe? Critics of neoliberalism, as we have seen, have focused on the breakdown of the Fordist social contract to explain the ascendancy of late capitalism's entrepreneurial rationality and its individualistic risk-taking ethos. In a similar vein, attempts to understand the origins of modern intimate life's nagging uncertainties often center on the collapse of the marriage contract, from which a more individualized pursuit of love emerged. In what follows, I challenge this line of argument. Conventional framings rely disproportionately on what is in essence a critique of neoliberalism and its effects on today's intimate formations, which is too capacious to explain the subtler embrace of speculation engendered by modern dating apps.

Writing in the early internet era, Zygmunt Bauman (2003) argued that the previously reassuring fantasy of a happy marriage was being replaced by an imaginary limitless expansion of sexual possibilities through online dating. Bauman saw nascent digital intimacies as another realm of sociality where the corrosive effect of late-modern consumption was becoming prevalent: (pre-smartphone) online dating was a perfect place where one could shop around mindlessly, without responsibilities or risks and with minimal emotional pain.[6] But with the security of the marriage contract progressively weakened over the course of the twentieth century, the pursuit of love in capitalist society became both more urgent and more uncertain. This, then, was the paradox of modern intimacy, which continued to persist even when an individual pursuit paused and a new relationship began; as Arlie Hochschild (2003) put it, while "culture now invites a couple to aspire to a richly communicative, intimate, playful, sexually fulfilling love," the rising tide of uncertainties in contemporary society conditions people "against trusting such a love too much" (123).

Sociologists have sought to understand this deeply seated instability of contemporary emotional life, not as a matter of individual psychology but as a means for formulating a critique of capitalism itself. Beck and Beck-Gernsheim (2004) depict modern intimacy as the "chaos of love": a society "bereft of any social ties" (2), marching on toward an individualized future, in a "collective trance to abandon marital bliss" (4). Unlike Bauman, Beck and Beck-Gernsheim saw this shift as part of the emergence of risk society, whose transient norms and rituals demand that lovers become risk-takers—to treat love as the blank that they must fill in themselves by drawing on a grotesquely disparate pool of resources, whether pop-song lyrics, advertisements, pornographic scripts, or psychoanalysis. Such a risk-taking animus has effectively turned us into romantic entrepreneurs who use romance as a vehicle "for controlling the future, as well as a form of psychological security" against the profound uncertainties of daily life (Giddens 1993, 42). In a similar vein, Giddens called this process "confluent love," a part of modern societies' inherently contingent project to redefine trust (in a world of waning institutional safety nets) by a reliance on a capacity for self-knowledge. Ultimately, Giddens and the proponents of risk society saw in these modern transformations of intimacy a pathway to autonomy as a "successful realisation of the reflexive project of self" (190)— the possibility of a more democratic emotional rationality that could form the basis for a broader democratization in the community.

Such views of intimacy underpinning the projects of risk society and self-reflexivity have been extensively criticized, most notably on grounds of their gendered, Eurocentric, and exclusionary assumptions. "Self-knowledge" and "choice" inevitably hinge on structural power and mask gender inequalities in areas such as sexual satisfaction, care work, and social reproduction (Thwaites 2020).[7] Moreover, these approaches tend to embrace dominant and universalizing models of intimacy, modernity, and globalization, which privilege a "large-scale process of macro-structural individualisation" (Donner and Santos 2016, 1126) over the alternative modernities (Gaonkar 2001) (and the corresponding alternative intimacies) of local contexts outside the Global North. Donner and Santos (2016) demonstrate this critical point through their ethnographic studies of contemporary intimate relations in China and India. In both countries, they argue, intimacy is being reconfigured by a diverse set of experiences and practices (among them an increasing centrality of individual choice), yet it does not necessarily become unmoored from moral and normative structures such as the "family, larger kin groups, neighborhoods, caste, and other associational identities" (1130). Importantly, they note that in these contexts intimacy represents not only the triumph of affective individualism but also "collective acts of mutual assistance—practices which are simultaneously material, emotional, and meaningful (even if not necessarily verbalised) and which are expected to continue in the long term" (1135).

A further deficiency of the self-reflexivity and risk society approaches to intimacy, which is particularly relevant for our discussion, is the following: for all their cogency in grasping love's unruly nature, these theories prioritize risk over uncertainty in their framings of the modern romantic subject. Specifically, they depict an enhanced sense of risk as the key organizing principle of a volatile intimate life—as a pathway to an emotional rationality through which people continually negotiate intimate relations with the aim of "mutual self-disclosure" (Giddens 1993) and, ultimately, of reaching a new social contract. By contrast, my argument is that speculative intimacies are plural, transient, and increasingly in sync with uncertainty—therefore less geared toward deliberating the risks of love and more attuned to the openness of an immersive present. They are a doorway to the development of a broader speculative subject.

To flesh out this argument, I would like to bring one final scholar into this discussion. Eva Illouz's (1997, 2007, 2013, 2019) vast body of work in the sociology of capitalist intimacy is perhaps the most systematic attempt to illuminate (though ultimately not to overcome, as I will show) these vexed tensions of the modern romantic subject. For Illouz, choice is the dominant trope around which this subject is organized. Capitalist rationalization reconfigures intimate relations, not only through a continuing economization of desire but also through the vehicles of self-help and psychoanalysis to which we turn in droves. Illouz takes here a more critical view than Gidden or Beck and Beck-Gernsheim. She is concerned not only with the fissuring ways in which economic rationality imbues romantic love but also with how it embodies a "structure of feeling" that constantly strives for individual freedom (the freedom to love whom we want), in a turn toward ourselves in order to love better. Illouz (2019) focuses her critique on the "emotional commodities" (228) offered by self-help and the therapeutic industry as defective substitutes for the "ritual structure and normative anchors" (157) of previous sexual interactions. In the absence of such normative rituals with which to generate emotional focus, our attempts at self-reflection are thus doomed to fail, giving way instead to the unmanageable uncertainty of self-management, self-help, and spirituality.[8]

Unlike the proponents of a self-reflexive intimacy, then, Illouz is greatly skeptical of the ideas and possibilities of freedom circulating in the vestiges of risk society. Adopting a rather more pessimistic tone, she suggests that the dissolution of bonds itself becomes the dominant social form (Illouz 2019, 22); the more we linger in the space of uncertainty, the more prone we become to "unloving." Increasingly, we practice what Illouz calls negative choice, that is, the choice to unchoose. To translate it for our world of speculative technologies, we may choose to "unfollow," to "unfriend," to "leave someone on read," or to "ghost"—or to dispose of a Tinder match altogether like any other commodity. Under contemporary capitalism, Illouz contends, love no longer is. But what then fills the void left by unloving, especially as the currency of self-help and therapeutic forms of emotion control seem to be waning among generation Z?

Let me return to the world of mobile dating apps to answer these important questions. There is little doubt that dating apps are lucrative sites of digital consumer markets—sexual fields of short-lived, uncommitted intimacies where body visibility and sexual attractiveness enforce relations of mutual commoditization (Illouz 2013). Tinder's urge to its users to "celebrate being single" offers scant hope for romantic fulfillment.[9] Although promises of a happy ending still abound in major dating platforms (especially those in the heterosexual markets), some of the platforms I have discussed increasingly admit a lack of interest in helping us "find love," calling us instead to embrace the open-endedness of the moment. The emphasis here, as in other speculative technologies, is placed on the here and now, albeit in a manner that does not merely narrate the present as a fleeting instant, or a singular hookup. Instead, the fleetingness of endless partner swipes forms its own ritual; it is pieced together into a more reassuring, coherent experience, intended to be experienced as a journey and given duration.

The dynamic relationship between radical uncertainty and a speculative imagination as a response to it has been a core thread running through this book. As we have seen, speculative imagination draws on promissory instruments as a way of engaging with failed promises and broken contracts. Through their fervent speculative activity, members of speculative communities anticipate unpredictability and submit to life's radical contingencies. In contemporary intimate relations, actual romantic connection is of course itself inherently volatile and largely unpredictable, and in that sense our engagement with it can only be speculative. The redemptive promise of sexual, emotional, and romantic fulfillment (especially when seen as a building block for long-term commitment and family stability) is increasingly at odds with our endorsement of uncertainty itself, our awareness that romantic love is no longer possible—at least not in the way it used to be.

This, then, is quite different from Giddens's self-reflexivity project but also from Illouz's critique of unloving as a practice of managing uncertainty. My argument is that the desires circulating in dating apps are not merely enacted through economic agents' instrumental choices, be they rational or irrational, positive or negative—for both these binaries assume a prevailing economic rationality that sits firmly in the ambit of the *homo economicus*. Accordingly, both framings assume that modern subjects' overall orienting wish is to control contemporary intimacy's uncertainty. Yet the use of modern speculative technologies does not perform mere calculations of risk (of possible disappointment, betrayal of trust, or of unfulfilled love itself)—risk becomes more marginal to our experience of the present. Entrepreneurial neoliberalism (as a dominant model that sanctions risk practices) no longer adequately explains the dynamics of our era's speculative intimacies. Illouz associates this issue with the continuing influence of economization and its rationalizing language on our desires (creating, in her own words, "cold intimacies"), but I want to propose a significant modification to her account. It is our reinforced speculative imagination (rather than a neoliberal rationality) that pervades the accelerated, impatient, and transient nature of contemporary intimacies.

Importantly, this saturation of intimate life by the speculative imagination evokes the type of sociality engendered by the technologies I examined in chapter 3. Mobile dating apps such as Tinder, Bumble, and Hinge, and the overabundance of images they feed on, do not merely satisfy the value-maximizing urges of a romantic entrepreneur, but nor do they represent an absolute lack of commitment. While at first blush they may evoke calculative and evaluative practices like those I have already reviewed, dating apps also insert aspects of the romantic self into the broader constellations of a speculative sociality. Importantly, they do so not by erasing social rituals and replacing them with "psychological self-management" (Illouz 2019, 228) but by auguring new rituals, even if these are harder to pin down. To recall Benedict Anderson's prescient description, such rituals are the "diurnal regularities of the imagining life"—a ceremony that is "incessantly repeated . . . in silent privacy, in the lair of the skull" (1991, 36) of each participant. Algorithmically mediated rituals (like those characterizing the use of dating apps) have the capacity to produce certainty in intimate life because they change the very "terms in which uncertainty is understood" (Appadurai 2016, 86) among participating users. In so doing, they offer a retrospective stability to the inherently volatile conditions of online dating, costaging a repeated certainty alongside uncertainty—and hence recasting this uncertainty through the very agreement to participate in the ritual process. Scrolls and swipes are how we survive the wounds opened by the rite of passage into speculative communities. Yet, at the same time, this extension of temporality achieved through them also contains an element of enjoyment.

A second, related point I would like to propose is this: there exist in these new speculative intimacies some tentative possibilities for connecting scales between intimate, social, and even political planes of everyday experience in speculative communities. Studies of gay intimacy, for instance, have emphasized the more transformative ways in which dating apps can inhabit sexual fields to pursue "connection and community building, which is a very different notion of how to create a better a more secure tomorrow than 'meeting the one'" (Essig 2019, 70). Such connectivities are articulated in mobile apps like Grindr (the world's most popular platform for men seeking men), which explicitly shift focus from the importance of lasting commitment and associated claims of a secure future to a more politicized present experience of sex as an act. Politicized experiences of intimacy may take the form of more radical forms of sociality—like those examined in Dasgupta and Dasgupta's (2018) study of Indian gay men's use of the app PlanetRomeo, which provides "online spaces for articulating a different kind of intimate subjectivity, one that is forged through sharing stories of failure to achieve romantic intimacy or pain and melancholia" (945). Arguably, mainstream and straight dating apps like Tinder are increasingly used like Grindr. The speculative intimacies that they cultivate puncture the false sense of security offered by capitalist romance (the escapism of the "white middle-class wedding fantasy," as put by Essig) and return us (not without shake-ups and trepidations) to the dizziness of the present moment. Taken together, these insights suggest that, contrary to a commonplace view, we have not been "let down" by these technologies. Instead, they have deepened our state of collective suspense. Dating apps' ascending popularity is not a sign of our disenchantment with the world or of the cold reassertion of *homo economicus*. Speculative intimacies can be warmer than Illouz's important work allows.

Nowhere is this clearer than in the new genre of "reality romance" TV that has flooded computer and television screens in recent years.[10] Such productions afford the spectacle of speculative intimacies its greatest visibility. "Happily ever after" narratives have always been part of the consumerist romance industry—and television shows like *The Dating Game* and *Blind Date* have existed since the 1960s. But today's reality romance shows are reflective of the growing fascination and confusion that permeates the mystery of modern intimacy. ITV's *Love Island* (watched by millions of viewers every week) applies a dating app logic to a group of willing participant-performers—in essence, an experiment of the famous Gale-Shapley algorithm (which answers the problem of finding a stable match) stripped down to its basics: half a dozen men and an equal number of women are placed on an island, on a mission to find their match, to pick and be picked by possible partners, for a prize of £50,000. In Netflix's *Love Is Blind*, meanwhile, we have a rather more cynical twist on the old *Blind Date*: after a few dates that take place on either side of a wall, a group of contestants who match with each other have just two weeks to get married or say goodbye forever. The final episode of season one of the series culminates in a sequence of spectacularly failed (absurd, almost) happy endings. One of the grooms hesitates at the altar, in visible discomfort and with trembling lips, when the priest asks him, "Do you take her to be your wife?" He replies, "I do not," and breaks off the "engagement."

If all this sounds chaotic, it's because, unlike their predecessors of more optimistic and wholesome times, these shows do not just put the limelight on the question Who will they choose? Choices, in a sense, matter little. Rather, cameras zoom in on the anxious rituals and misgivings behind that question. In the—often painful to watch—minutiae of interactions between prospective or current couples, what we see most clearly is their doubt and disbelief as they throw themselves into the game (a game that they are nonetheless intent on playing to the end)—a window into a real-time forensic of the nervous motions of their dates and conversations. The gamified format of these shows retains the "in search of love" trope, but at its core it is a testing ground of speculative intimacies, capturing something of modern desire's inherent volatility. Uncertainties abound for the viewer too: Why wait until the wedding day to voice doubt explicitly? Are these even real exchanges or staged performances? My argument is that the messiness of these shows makes sense, because the intimacies they showcase mirror our speculative communities' own uncertain yearnings.

▲

Adorno (2001) famously described astrology as capitalist society's "regression to magic" where "thought is assimilated to late capitalist forms" that are fundamentally "asocial" (173) and where occulting forces not only do not predict the future but craft it in the image of the commodified, reified present. For Adorno, it was precisely this "combination of the realistic and the irrational" that posed a "threat and a remedy in one" (157). The inner workings of dating app algorithms, like those of Instagram or TikTok, remain fundamentally opaque—described by technologists and users alike as a different kind of magic, ostensibly substituting the magic of romantic love. NuiT, launched in 2019, is a new dating app whose matching and connecting algorithm follows astrology and natal chart compatibility—creating, in some ways, a double opacity. Just like star-sign forecasts themselves, NuiT's promises of love to its users are both playful and elusive. The platform can be seen as a natural extension of the social function that is already present in popular astrology apps like Co-Star. But it is also part of a trend that sees traditional dating apps integrating the poetic ambivalence of astrology into their functionality. In 2020, for instance, market leader Bumble introduced extremely popular star-sign filters in their platforms, offering users the option to match with specific star signs, based on their signs' compatibility.

The meshing of digital astrology and popular mobile dating apps is further evidence of our speculative intimacies. Increasingly, dating apps wield their algorithmic intelligence not to find us a future perfect match but to further immerse us in the present's thrill, to reunite us with (rather than separate us from) its uncertainty. In doing so, paradoxically, speculative intimacies make less vertiginous our collective suspension over the oceans of data we deal with. But is dwelling in the speculative, never-ending moment of the swipe all we can hope for? Or could there be a silver lining in the rituals of the short-lived experiences of mobile dating apps? Tinder's infinite swipe is unswervingly repetitive but not entirely without respite. Swipes will, in most cases, eventually bring matches, which will gratify our anxious quests for affirmation yet also make us pause. Our experience of such a pause will be shaped by the speculative imagination rather than by a deliberative (un)choice and, as such, it may also open a doorway into alternative possibilities of inhabiting the unknown. It is therefore the political implications of *homo speculans* that we must now explore in more detail.

PART III: SPECTER

FINANCE AND POLITY

We have seen how the radical uncertainty of the future is endorsed and spread in the everyday life of speculative communities. But what are the current political implications of the revitalized ascendancy of *homo speculans*? How do we account for the political risks of a society taking a whole-hearted plunge into uncertainty? And how are such risks distributed and hedged in today's wavering capitalist democracies? The final part of the book turns to these questions and argues that the speculative mode of everyday life is also reshaping the face of politics in today's financialized capitalism. A specter of speculative politics is haunting liberal democracy as we know it. To dissect this specter, we need to understand the symbolic resources drawn by an incipient political class that is intent on weaponizing our moment's volatility, trailing speculative communities along both regressive and progressive pathways.

The Manichean conflicts in the history of speculation I have so far described across economy and society offer us precursory signals of the current political calamities. Politics during our chaotic time of "post-truth" and "alternative facts" increasingly takes place in a distinctively disorienting and confusing arena, powered by the same technological aesthetic of mystification that is shot through everyday social life. It is precisely against this backdrop that the intersection of modern finance and politics comes into sharp relief. Benedict Anderson (1991) was fascinated by early nationalists' enigmatic desire to self-sacrifice for the idea of an imagined community. Today's ominous surge of a galvanized nationalism is predicated, I will contend, on the rise of speculative communities in financialized societies. The exclusionary nationalist myths of Donald Trump, Boris Johnson, and company are proving popular not (only) because they help restore an injured ethnic identity. At a time when societies have little choice but to submerge in a politics of smoke and mirrors, such myths offer speculative communities much-needed symbolic insurance for hedging an otherwise unbearable uncertainty.

As I will show, however, there is evidence of other responses to this crisis waiting in the wings. *Counter-speculations* are just as elusive as the chaos-inducing practices of populist agitators, wielding similarly volatizing political strategies—albeit with an altogether different aim: to redraw the map of democratic politics. The final part of the book, therefore, attempts to impel the double entendre of speculation—which has preoccupied me from the start—to its furthermost frontier. How can the benefits of inhabiting the land of the unknown be redistributed within speculative communities, such that possibilities for collective autonomy are opened up even to their most vulnerable constituents? To tackle this question, I take inspiration from recent online and offline practices of sabotage and conspiracy (from the Black Lives Matter movement's hashtag hijackings to the "high-vis activism" of France's Gilets Jaunes). I argue that such counter-speculations, while often eluding our comprehension, call attention to the importance of cutting the umbilical cord of inherited modes of political rationality, enabling the speculative imagination to fight financialization more effectively on its own turf.

5: FINANCIALIZED POPULISM AND NEW NATIONALISMS

Populism—I don't think that is a rational approach. . . .
It's a scream of pain.

ALAN GREENSPAN, INTERVIEW WITH THE
FINANCIAL TIMES'S GILLIAN TETT

In estimating the prospects of investment, we must have regard,
therefore, to the nerves and hysteria and even the digestions and
reactions to the weather of those upon whose spontaneous activity it
largely depends. We should not conclude from this that everything
depends on waves of irrational psychology.

JOHN MAYNARD KEYNES, *GENERAL THEORY OF*
EMPLOYMENT, INTEREST, AND MONEY

Hungarian American billionaire investor George Soros was without doubt the arch-speculator of the pre-2008 crisis era. Having made his fortune by betting on currency markets in the early 1990s, he made an alleged $1 billion profit by placing a wager against the Bank of England (in what became known as Black Wednesday), devastating several Asian economies during the tense currency speculation wars of 1998. His reputation as a reckless gambler who exploited political volatility for profit made him a hated figure for progressives everywhere. In the aftermath of the 2008 global financial crisis, Soros found himself in the eye of the storm once again, yet now his fiercest opponents were nationalist-populist figureheads such as Donald Trump, Vladimir Putin, and Hungarian prime minister Viktor Orbán. His infamous market instinct is today confronted by global conspiracies, this time leveled against his own Open Society Foundations (a charity "fighting for freedom of expression, accountable government, and societies that promote justice and equality").[1] Soros's populist foes may pit themselves against his suave global speculation, but they seem to have, in an inverted way, the same disposition: harnessing political uncertainty for previously inaccessible yields. As trade, cultural, and (dis)information wars loom in the popular imagination, spearheading a new speculative fervor in political and economic life, do markets still ally themselves with Soros's open society liberalism? Or has finance drawn closer to Trump's and Johnson's neopopulism?

This book began tracing the historical evolution of speculation by emphasizing how publics and markets have coalesced around the speculative imagination ever since the genesis of modern finance capitalism. Both passions and interests ran high in the Chicago pits of the late nineteenth century, but so did they also at the bucket shops spreading even across the most rural communities of the United States. Speculation and its vicissitudes filtered into economic and social life in the years leading to the Great Depression, which was followed by dramatic public debates about the recalibration of the relationship between government, economy, and society. As I have argued from the start, despite sweeping political reorderings affecting that relationship, markets and publics remained closely connected throughout the twentieth century, and they far from parted ways after the 2008 crisis. In previous chapters, we saw how a revived speculative imagination spread widely in society during financialization's most recent phase, with far-reaching effects on contemporary social and intimate relations. But exactly who are the publics that are now converging with today's machine-learning, algorithmically fueled derivatives markets? And what is the current state of the relationship between *homo speculans* and *homo politicus*?

This chapter will argue that the continuing ascendancy of speculative finance at the dawn of the twenty-first century has molded our time's distinct neopopulist political imaginations. Yet it has done so in different ways than commonly assumed. Finance's wagers on fictive values are matched not only by society's collective submergence in a transient temporality, but also by increasingly fanciful gambles on volatility in the sphere of everyday politics. Speculative and conspiratorial politics such as Trump's trade wars, Brexiteers' expert shaming, and global antivaccination campaigns today dwarf rational decision making and realpolitik. In this hotly debated turn away from neoliberal centrism to a regressive nationalism, one particular claim stands out: the assertion that finance and nationalist populism should be in tension with each other, if not in direct conflict. For one thing, finance is distinctively placeless and tightly linked to global cosmopolitan and neoliberal elites; mainstream US Democratic politics and the right wing of the UK Labour Party epitomize this top-down alliance between neoliberal cosmopolitanism and global finance. As these forces were resoundingly rejected in elections during the 2010s, variants of anti-cosmopolitanism and nationalism (represented by Trump in the United States, or many of the proponents of Brexit in the United Kingdom) emerged as a credible response to the continuing failures of the neoliberal promise. On the face of it, their nativist ideology and interventionist proclamations appeared as an attack on finance's zealously global maxims.

As is now known, where right-wing populists came to power and their ideology became policy, the veneer of rhetorical conflict between ethnonationalism and financial markets quickly dissolved. Few commentators were surprised, for instance, in February 2017 by the announcement of President Trump's first cabinet, which included four prominent Goldman Sachs figures in center-stage positions.[2] Some months later, when the president made a string of racist statements in response to the August 2017 Charlottesville protests, some of the most powerful market leaders (including the chief executives of JPMorgan Chase and Blackstone and the founder of Bridgewater Capital) came out with a strong public statement of support for Trump. The trend was, of course, far from unique to the US and UK economies. Examples of similarly anti-cosmopolitan (albeit squarely financialized) ethno-nationalism have mushroomed around the world: Putin's Russia, Jarosław Kaczynski's Poland, Viktor Orbán's Hungary, Rodrigo Duterte's Philippines, Benjamin Netanyahu's Israel, Narendra Modi's India, and Jair Bolsonaro's Brazil are but a few examples.

The coexistence of finance and populism emerging in these countries represents a new turn in the relationship between finance and polity. Voters appear willing to buy into an unorthodox blend of nativist mythologies, chauvinist sentiment, and speculative finance in populist political agendas. Evocations of both uncertainty and security abound in this discourse. Seemingly incongruent combinations of Pentecostalist revivalism, global trade wars, Hindu nationalism, aggressive interest-rate speculation, Euroscepticism, and so on have been deployed rhetorically alongside an emphasis on "acting swiftly and decisively" and against the "slowness" of liberal democracy. Such discourses are in turn supplemented by a "govern-by-chaos" doctrine, wielded by populist leaders against the technocratic rationality of their neoliberal predecessors.

In the United Kingdom, during the political havoc of Brexit, *chaos* (as a representation of a radically uncertain post-Brexit future) was one of the words most often appearing in media headlines. Yet an unexpected coalition of Brexiteers and City financiers consistently dismissed such assertions as fear mongering and a fantasy. Indeed, despite a cautious skepticism expressed by central bankers (like the Bank of England's Mark Carney), financial markets in the United Kingdom and around the globe seem to generally respond enthusiastically to the news of neopopulist electoral victories. In 2019 Modi's re-election led to a massive boom in the Nifty,

India's stock-market index. In the same year, following Bolsonaro's election, the Bovespa, Brazil's stock-market index, hit a string of record highs. In the United States, the Dow Jones movements have been one of Donald Trump's favorite reference points—used as a real-time measure of his own "political success" throughout his presidency.

However, the unmistakably financialized type of today's nationalist populism appears to be a contradiction in terms. Global capital's speculative character is most often associated with its tendency to erase national and territorial borders and to upend the nativist mythologies fostered within such borders. What is more, some of the constituencies that come to endorse such seemingly heterogeneous programs are among the most adversely affected by years of continuing market deregulation—and, as a consequence, vulnerable to the risk and debt plights suffered in the aftermath of the 2008 crisis. For these reasons, the historical convergence between financialization and neopopulism is frequently addressed as a *paradox*. Attempts to explain the paradox have dominated recent theoretical debates around the rise of populism in social and political thought. Such debates have often been framed within the parameters set by historian Karl Polanyi's hugely influential double-movement theory (e.g., Fraser 2017, 2019; Fraser and Jaeggi 2018; Davies 2018; Streeck 2014).

Diverging from these explanations (which I will discuss in detail in the following section), my claim in this chapter will be that the rise of speculative communities has been at the heart of these political developments, leading to new (and often unexpected) political enmities and alliances. Just as the failures of finance-driven neoliberalism sparked numerous angry revolts against economic and political elites, the forces of financialization reawakened the dormant *homo speculans*. In doing so, they produced new social and political collectivities, even as they destroyed older ones. Thus, although we have been led to believe that a war has broken out between global finance and the new waves of ethno-nationalist populism, this is in fact a false binary.

The new pact between finance and polity has salient political ramifications. To return to the timeline that I sketched out in chapter 1, while the financial crisis of 2008 was a turning point for the exhaustion of the neoliberal promise, the global electoral tremors of 2015–16 marked an apogee of speculative politics. As we have seen, speculative technologies were by then embedded in the fabric of everyday life, suffusing new collective identities and shared mythologies. And while algorithmically generated flows of digital content mediated market trading and social relations alike, the occult memes of Reddit and 4chan leaked out into offline politics, shaping a neopopulist discourse that tampered with trust, liability, and (in)security.

The surge of right-wing populist politics of the 2010s has shown nativist ideologues to be particularly well placed for harnessing speculative technologies. A technologically savvy, chaos-prone brand of populism has been a staple of that decade's global tide of disinformation campaigns. In the United States, Stephen Bannon was the mastermind behind Breitbart, the ultranationalist news network that became imbued with controversy because of its use of misleading stories and alt-right conspiracy theories (such as the infamous Pizzagate) in the lead-up to the 2016 presidential election. In the Philippines, Duterte's rise to power in the same year has long been discussed as a technologically savvy, chaos-mongering project, with armies of paid social media influencers and mercenary trolls deployed to discredit opposing candidates (see for instance, Ong and Cabañes 2018). Meanwhile, in Putin's Russia, notorious spin doctor Vladislav Surkov (a former postmodernist theater-director-turned-Kremlin-propagandist) drew on a mix of advanced computational thinking and the fascist theology of Ivan Ilyin to devise a nationalist politics of speculation aimed at breeding confusion and compounding existing political discord.[3] Surkov's strategy relied on digital platform botnets not to control the flow of information but to amplify the chaotic complexity that already existed within the network; not solely to pollute information space, but to deliberately exacerbate the prevalent state of collective suspense, fostered by the speculative technologies I analyzed in part 2.

Such fact-cynical pursuit of obscurity was captured in a highly contentious UK government job advertisement in 2019 for new recruits in Downing Street (which the *Financial Times* dubbed "the most unusual ever seen"), calling for "true wild cards, artists, people who never went to university and fought their way out of an appalling hell hole."[4] The ad was put out by Dominic Cummings, a rogue senior adviser to Prime Minister Boris Johnson with a keen interest in William Gibson's speculative fiction political novels and an avowed aspiration to run the government like NASA. The story is particularly striking because it seemed to clearly and publicly articulate Surkov's dogma in the nerve center of UK government—making special references to the great value of a chaotic way of conducting politics, doing things that "always look messy," and, importantly, "not caring about trying to control the narrative" (which centrist Labour and Conservative governments had both attempted to do in previous decades).[5]

The muddy-the-waters tactics of neopopulist agitators like Bannon, Surkov, and Cummings looms in the public imagination because it reflects modern societies' own disorienting experiences of searing uncertainty. During a series of election campaigns across the Global North and Global South, calls to embrace the future's radical uncertainty spread as spectacularly as did rhetorical tropes of security and a collective return to mythical pasts. In this tempestuous political space, the operation of speculative imagination appears in full force. At the heart of speculative communities lies the growing conviction of an unknowable future, a condition typically lamented by the variants of insolvent neoliberalism who consider it as a symptom of populist politics. But as I have contended, alongside this political endorsement of unknowability, speculative communities mobilize new forms of insurance in their attempts to hedge the incalculable risks and vexing fears of financialized life. In these new entanglements of gambling and prudence that today become increasingly intricate, a new *homo politicus* has germinated. The question I will address in what follows, then, is, Has finance, contrary to conventional wisdom, revitalized rather than "undone the demos"?[6]

EXPLANATIONS OF THE PARADOX: POLANYI AND CROWD PSYCHOLOGY

Explanations of the paradox of converging global finance and neopopulism often follow the logic of what Karl Polanyi, the noted economic historian, described as "double movement." In his pivotal work *The Great Transformation*, Polanyi (1944) cataloged the history of capitalism from 1830s England to its global crisis in the 1930s, proposing that the movement toward unabated marketization of the political sphere precipitates a countermovement of protectionism and nationalism in response. The double movement both anticipated and sought to explain the rise of fascism and war (which was ongoing at the time of writing *The Great Transformation*). A committed social democrat, Polanyi sought to explain the dominance as well as the renewal of capitalist ideology in two key stages (movements) that are repeated historically: a "disembedding" of the economy from social life (followed, importantly, by the separation of economy from polity) through market deregulation and commodification, and the "(re)embedding" of markets within society, through government intervention, regulation, and decommodification. The disembedding movement occurs as money, labor, and land are treated "as if" they were commodities—what Polanyi terms "fictitious commodities"—thus making societies more vulnerable to the speculative fancies of capital. The re-embedding response is seen as a counter-movement, playing the crucial role of keeping market expansion "in check." This is how society protects itself "against the perils inherent in a self-regulating market system" (Polanyi 1944, 80).

But the double movement is also underpinned by a view of transformative social change in which a participatory demos is instrumental in overturning "reified markets" (Thomasberger 2005). This view, along with Polanyi's explicit concern with the fate of democracy in the aftermath of fascism, helps explain why his work has regained popularity during the nationalist fallout from the 2008 crisis. Counter-movements are considered necessary for providing a sense of security for the future and a politics of redistribution against the ravages of unregulated markets. The government-provided protection and social insurance marshaled by the New Deal (after the Great Depression) are examples of this historical function of the double movement—and so are, by the same token, state interventions such as the controversial bailouts of US and European banks ensuing from the 2008 global financial crisis.

Counter-movements historically have emerged from a diverse set of constituencies that included "workers, peasants, industrialists and land-owning elites," who mobilized to demand national restrictions on markets (Goodwin 2018, 1271). But the kind of counter-movement that Polanyi himself favored was international. Anticipating a new global financial regime, he advocated a framework that would foster market regulation and social provision by democratic welfare states. Polanyi was interested in the *longue durée* of the tensions built within capitalist dynamics rather than in how temporary diversions may become absorbed by it (Peck 2013). His work thus strove to be sensitive to the complex and permanent struggles between traditional and modern forms of capitalism, avoiding a short-sighted view of markets as the (sole) cause of political individuation. One of the most noteworthy implications of the double-movement theory, then, is its view of liberalism as an incubator of its own destruction even when (or precisely when) it appears to be omnipotent.[7]

However, some of the assumptions behind the transformative potential of counter-movements have cast a shadow on the explanatory power of Polanyi's framing, especially in today's context. Nancy Fraser, one of the most prominent contemporary interlocutors of Polanyian theory, has argued convincingly that society can itself be a source of injustice and exclusion rather than a progressive answer to market vagaries. Therefore, counter-movements' celebrated goal of returning the economy to its "proper place" in society is tenuous, for there is nothing inherently "positive" about society that can re-embed markets in a progressive way (Fraser 2017). More worrying to note is that the rise of contemporary right-wing counter-movements represents a hyper-reactionary politics of recognition, which effectively evades the traditional double movement altogether. Neopopulist leaders wield a speculative imagination that mobilizes nationalist myths in bids to appeal to disenfranchised groups (typically, but not exclusively, drawn from the white working and middle classes). This, then, is a course of social re-embedding that is inherently exclusionary and discriminatory.

▲

The logic of the double movement is traceable in contemporary critiques of financialization, which approach its impact on polity through a focus on the tensions (or the overlaps) between the movements of neoliberalism and those of neopopulism. Some of these critiques imply a reaction-formation relation between finance and populism (e.g., Fraser 2017; Streeck 2014; also see Hopkin 2017). They can be considered as an iteration of the anti-financialization argument, which I reviewed in part 1. Let me summarize this view here. The dominance of neoliberal logic (and associated market deregulation) has allegedly driven the rise of an atomized, individualized risk subjectivity. As a result, the new political agent imagined by these critics is at once entrepreneurial and insecure, bound by the spell of risk-taking yet profoundly precarious and anxious. Ultimately, such vulnerable subjectivity becomes an active ingredient in neopopulist disillusionment, leading to fragmented societies of "anxious authoritarians," in the words of Wendy Brown (2017).[8] In turn, the individual grievances of *homo economicus* become fuel for the fire of reactionary and ethnocentric counter-movements (Fuchs 2017; Bonikowski 2017), such as the Tea Party, Dutertismo, or the Hindu Nationalists of Rashtriya Swayamsevak Sangh (RSS). From this perspective, then, the rise of neopopulism is seen as just another consequence of neoliberal rationality's triumph over the domain of politics—another way in which the demos becomes undone.[9]

For others, the conjunction of neoliberalism and nationalist populism is rooted instead in a "conversion" or "evolution" logic. This view draws on Hayek's liberalism and specifically on his conceptualization of economic interests as affects (as opposed to mere rational choices) expressed in the spontaneous organization of markets. In this vein, political economist William Davies (2018) argues that political decisions today are increasingly made on the basis of feeling rather than fact—and therefore the task before us is to understand why expertise and rationality have lost credibility in the era of culture wars. As in the reaction-formation explanations, emphasis is placed on the rise of a neoliberal governmentality: an insidious technology of control, through a political rationality that transfers responsibility to individuals and renders political problems in economic terms. But here *homo economicus* is also shaped by an active rekindling of the affective self, which lays the ground for the rise of a populist subjectivity—what Verónica Gago (2017) describes as "neoliberalism from below." The ascendancy of a Trump-type economic nationalism is thus sustained from the ground up, with publics paradoxically turning to markets to demand neoliberal logic's purification rather than its transformation.

However, by bundling together finance and neoliberalism (in spite of their post-2008 divergence, which I examined in previous chapters), such critiques neglect the deeper shared ground between finance and populism.

An important underlying issue with framing the problem as a paradox is that we are often left with a problematic divide between people and their own (political) desires and choices, as well as between their passions and interests. Certainly, the material effects of a finance-driven neoliberalism (wage stagnation, austerity, a fall in life expectancy, and a crisis of social reproduction) have led to a profound sense of vulnerability, precariousness, and anxiety among the most vulnerable, while blowing wind in the sails of right-wing populist movements. Yet, by insisting that finance's primary effect on the space of politics is fundamentally deconstructive, we risk losing sight of new political vernaculars emerging on the ground level and, importantly, of the connectivities that these vernaculars also forge. In the preceding responses to the question I posed in the beginning of this chapter (Who are the publics converging with today's markets?), we are often left with a polity that is deeply alienated and overcome by its own passions.

As we saw in previous chapters, the paradoxical relationship between the passions and interests of political crowds has a long pedigree in mass psychology. Social psychologists have memorably framed it as a problem of cognitive dissonance (corresponding to what in Marxist parlance could be called false consciousness). Since the days of influential nineteenth-century theorist Gustav Le Bon, both publics and markets have been consistently studied through the lens of crowd psychology. Analyses of Trump's 2016 election as a triumph of the mob have been expectedly popular, with arguments ranging from the regressive to the dismissive.[10] On the one hand, conservative apologists such as Douglas Murray (2019) deride the unjustified anger of the New Left as an explanation for the inflammation of a "mass hysteria," which sets the backdrop for a ("justified") populism such as Trump's. On the other side of this debate, sociologist Dylan Riley (2017, 2018) argues that the indebtedness of societies through increased financialization has atomized precarious wage earners, turning them into what Marx famously described as "a sack of potatoes." More crudely, Riemen (2018) writes of the deplorable "mass man politics" and the "organised stupidity" of Trump supporters. This thesis was plainly shared by Democratic presidential candidate Hillary Clinton, who, in a statement after the 2016 election, referred to Republican constituents as having "a psychological as much as a political yearning to be told what to do, and where to go, and how to live and have their press basically stifled and so be given one version of reality."[11]

Mass psychology, then, may no longer be in the business of defending the moral integrity of *homo economicus*, yet it remains in the service of a liberal political philosophy that imagines people as inherently acquiescent to authoritarianism.[12] Yet, although social collectivities can be repositories of illusions, they also harbor collective imaginations: shared identifications that extend beyond narcissistic attachments to a charismatic leader. After all, even Le Bon's original crowd theory did not consider the role of leaders important (or necessary) for the crowd to function and be integrated.[13] These critiques ultimately consider populism as an individual question, taking individualism (with its irrationalities, manias, and paranoias) as their point of departure.

The second fallacy implied here is a symbolic distinction between the cold, calculating rationality of finance (manifest in the speculative logic of capital) and the emotional capital invested in the type of populist-nationalist politics responding to this rationality (their "attack on reason"). Yet, as we have seen time and again, markets and publics alike rely on a speculative imagination that contains both passions and interests to engage uncertainty. Although markets' amoralism and publics' anger are both undoubtedly real, the opposition between (financial) reason and (populist) feeling can be entirely deceptive. In the culture wars of the Trump and Brexit era, populist passions animate (rather than oppose) the rationality of finance.[14]

A focus on speculative communities brings this juncture into sharp relief. Polanyian debates on populism often center on the (top-down) role of government in the reordering of the relationship between economy and polity, underlining how the state finds itself inexorably embedded in the system of neoliberal and financialized governance.[15] However, the rise of speculative communities implicates publics in this system in new ways, shaping relational political subjectivities through an alliance of strange bedfellows—for instance, between the denizens of Silicon Valley and blue-collar workers in the American rust belt or between France's rural middle classes and the urban poor, under the banner of the Gilets Jaunes.[16] Crucially, the distinction between the spheres of economy and politics implied in the double movement's disembedding logic evades these complex entanglements of financialized populism. As I have argued throughout, the economy and politics are both defined by a set of copresent tensions: anxiety and tenacity, openness and exclusion, and fictitiousness and realism, to name but a few. The double movement neglects the distinctive speculative imagination arising from such seemingly opposing logics and obscures its political importance.

Overall, then, perspectives that focus on the neoliberal rationality of *homo economicus* describe an increasingly fragmented social fabric, a foreclosure of political possibilities, and a wholesale retreat of the *homo politicus*.[17] By contrast, I suggest that over the course of the last decade the demos has enthusiastically embraced finance's speculative imagination and, on some occasions, has deployed it against the markets' (formerly) unchallenged guarantors—though rarely against finance itself. What makes this particular breed of finance-driven neopopulism especially powerful is its ability to hedge uncertainty and political volatility, without access to the material and political resources that previously would have been essential for attaining a sense of security (in the form of employment, income, or other forms of fulfillment). This is made possible thanks to a type of *insurance* that is no longer expected or sought in government but is couched instead in collective myths afforded by a reignited nationalism. In that sense, the renewed coalition of finance and polity is in fact not a paradox at all. In what follows, I show how unexpected affinities between financiers and neo-populists come to light as they enact their respective practices of speculation. It is therefore the insurance (that is, the hedging, ensuring and reassuring) dimension of the new vernacular of speculation that we must now examine to understand this more generative politics suffusing speculative communities.

INSURANCE STRUGGLES IN THE FACE
OF RADICAL UNCERTAINTY

I have discussed how the speculative imagination emerged in the nineteenth century's wars between the first futures markets and bucket shops and resurfaced triumphant in the unresolved tension between risk-taking and risk-hedging arising from the 2008 financial crisis. But exactly how does the insurance side of speculation contribute to the formation of modern speculative communities? What are the forms of political indemnity that become possible when considering the historical function of insurance in political economy?

The origins of insurance lie in speculative gambling, and hence, unsurprisingly, there is a rich history of controversy regarding its moral foundations. Levy (2012) offers a detailed history of the interconnected evolution of the logics of speculation, insurance, and risk, from the days of early finance capitalism in fin de siècle America to the birth of post-1970s neoliberalism. Levy traces the beginning of inscribing insurance (in the form of social security) into the fabric of the American nation after World War II: "a new vision of what it meant to be a free and secure economic actor—premised upon the state providing baseline economic security to its citizens" (314). Importantly, just as in the risk-taking aspect of speculation, insurance, too, trades on promises of an uncertain future: "One party pays cash premiums in return for the promise of the other party to pay a cash sum on the occurrence of a contingent future" (Vogel and Hayes 1998, 151). As Zelizer's (1979) important work has shown, insurance relies fundamentally on the imagination, precisely because we cannot know whether its promise will ever be fulfilled. But although it builds on the instrument of the promise, insurance also anticipates that promise's failure.

Insurance was feared and rejected by Calvinists as morally corrupt because of its interference with Providence. More boldly, Islamic law stressed the important social function of insurance as a collective (rather than simply bilateral) contract, resting on the idea of an imagined collectivity that is willing to share risks as well as responsibilities (see Vogel and Hayes, 1998). Historically, then, the politics of insurance has been paramount in generating and maintaining social relations. Insurance has been a key mechanism for creating, distributing, and, importantly, socializing responsibility. The new types of collective mutuality that were expressed by social insurance in the post-Depression years even threatened the established moral and symbolic purchase of religion and family as pillars of shouldering burdens and thus of managing risk. Life insurance, in particular, turned the uncertainties of life into opportunities for social enrichment, while propelling "collective self-governance and civil society" (Zelizer 1979, 93). Somewhat counterintuitively, insurance has much less to do with individual self-interest than with complex and collective political imaginings, which include the development of social solidarity. Solidarity itself can be seen as the prevention of social insecurity by means of insurance—forming what conservative historian François Ewald (1986) has called *sociétés assurancielles*. The New Deal developments in the United States, which I discussed in chapter 2, enforced this growing role of social insurance, tightly linked to the state's more active postwar role in credit markets.

It is no surprise then that, at our current juncture, insurance continues to play a key role in the economy and politics alike. As a significant technology in the financialization and marketization of uncertainty, it transforms the latter into risk that can be estimated and evaluated, for both the insurers and the insured of speculative communities. In their authoritative work, sociologists Baker and Simon (2002) trace a momentous transition in financialized capitalism, from the postwar insurance model of risk spreading (established by protectionist counter-movements such as the New Deal or Clement Atlee's social security reforms in Britain) to one of risk endorsing, with the explicit intention of reducing individual claims on collective social resources.[18] This shift corresponds to our timeline of modern neoliberal subjectivity underpinning persistent ideas of the rationalizing *homo economicus*. Strengthened individual responsibility and self-insurance undergird this model, borne out in the dramatic reforms of pensions and late-life risks for large segments of society during recent waves of financialization, most notably in sweeping transitions from defined benefit to defined contribution schemes.

At the same time, hedge funds, whose primary function is insurance, became vehicles of profitable risk endorsement for the powerful, while the derivative emerged as the riskiest and most sophisticated form of insurance in securities trading. The credit default swap, the notorious financial instrument implicated in the credit crunch of 2008, was originally an insurance against borrowers defaulting on their loans, before becoming a speculative device on borrowers' inability to repay those loans (Mazzucato 2018). The post-2008 bailouts highlighted the great importance of such insurance for capital but also the corresponding mounting insecurity for society writ large. Meanwhile, the introduction of new techniques of algorithmic prediction further challenges the probabilistic model of risk calculation and distribution, drawing on "big data" and machine learning to produce more "individualized risk forecasts" (Cevolini and Esposito 2020). In so doing, these techniques produce new forms of discrimination and exclusion and pose new threats to the solidaristic model of social insurance, precipitating a further redistribution of responsibility burdens from the state to citizens (McFall 2019).

As speculative communities experience these shifting redistributions of (in)security in all realms of their lives, new populist movements draw on the idea of the nation as insurance policy, in a bid to recollectivize responsibility—while, importantly, bypassing the redistributional role of the state as guarantor of social security. My argument here is that the insurance side of speculation opens up a window into the speculative politics of our moment. Specifically, the notion of insurance shines new light onto the constitution and the usurping of trust relations, the re-evaluation of promises made, and the ensuing reallocations of responsibility within today's fractured polities. The important questions to ask, then, are, What are the underlying assets hedged by nationalist-populists? What are the "premiums" charged by political insurers on their potential followers? And what do the compensations received look like? Whose "claims" are prioritized, and what kinds of exclusion and discrimination are produced? It's now time to examine in more depth some of these forms of speculative politics—and corresponding insurance practices—within contemporary speculative communities.

NATIONALIST FINANCIERS, TEA PARTIERS, AND THE SPECULATIVE POLITICS OF BREXIT

Risk spreading has been the markets' principal insurance mechanism. But modern-day traders on the ground have also continued to rely on age-old forms of sociality and interdependence to perform their routine speculations. I have referred a few times to the image of the twenty-first century's *homo speculans* as an algorithm-crunching chaos doomer residing in the dark corners of shadow trading—a creature that on first sight could not seem more distant from Weber's "charismatic" speculator. It would be a mistake, however, to consider that figure as socially disembedded. Thanks to a growing number of detailed ethnographic studies of such intricate speculative practices within financial markets (e.g., Leins 2018; Preda 2017; LiPuma 2017; Miyazaki 2013; Zaloom 2006), we are now more aware of the social rituals binding modern trader communities together.

Caitlin Zaloom (2006) was one of the first scholars to show that a distinctive, screen-mediated sociality persisted even after the transition from open outcry to electronic and high-frequency trading at the dawn of the twenty-first century. Contemporary traders' speculative communities provide a space for guesswork (that is, of what others value) but also for the continuous work of an "anonymous sociality" (LiPuma 2017) in financial markets. Through screens filled with flashing prices, algorithmic abstraction, and complex visual representations, they acquire a renewed sense of simultaneity (Pryke 2010). Christian Borch's (2012, 2020) recent ethnographic studies bear this out: the shift to screen-based speculation altered but didn't altogether displace practices of mutual anticipation and social integration in algorithmic markets. The algorithmic trading room gives a new visual texture to these complex social routines through a wealth of graphical images, price charts, spread plots, and tree maps, which "become ways of navigating the uncertainty that quantitative modelling is unable to account for" (Beunza 2019, 284).

These important studies show that traders yield their shared obligations and interdependencies as a form of social insurance, which—together with an unrestricted access to the necessary material resources—enables them to place speculative wagers on the volatility of securities prices. It is beyond the scope of my argument to catalog the various forms of social bonds that are engendered through speculative activities (and which the above scholars have dexterously unpacked). However, of particular importance for my discussion of speculative communities is the insight that financiers' sense of collectivity and sociality does not necessarily accord with the cosmopolitan narratives of placeless and globalizing finance. As we have already seen, finance's speculative imagination has been infused with a nationalist sentiment since the early days of Chicago's first futures market, when a highly "patriotic spirit" was marshaled into the transformation of speculative trading (Lambert 2010, 65). Today, financiers around the world remain nationally bound when forming their imagined collectivities, in spite of global markets' cosmopolitan façade. And financialization's most recent tides have far from diffused such nationalist orientations.

In his ethnographic study of US derivatives markets, LiPuma (2017) gestures to a particularly interesting process in the life of finance's speculative communities. For LiPuma, "a sense of nationalism" is one of the "entwined species of rationality that course the financial field," alongside "self-esteem, competitive dynamic," and a "speculative ethos" (14). Nationalism thus blends with traders' diverse anxieties, fears, vulnerabilities, desires, and hopes, all of which are enacted through secular rituals "in which each participant imagines a world/market of imaginary others, similar in mind and interests" (182). Beyond the ambit of US and European markets, the anthropologist Hirokazu Miyazaki (2013) offers an illuminating account of social relations developed in Japan's derivatives market in the face of the great economic uncertainties of the late 1990s. His traders' stories challenge the view of speculation as parasitic on the community and devoid of moral responsibility. By contrast, speculators sought to make "ethical contributions" to the Japanese nation through their routine dealings with risk and arbitrage: "an ethical commitment to embracing the ambiguity and the unknowability of the market" (58).

▲

We can now return to the speculating publics dwelling beyond the contours of financial markets to consider the vernacular imaginations of recent populist movements. In taking up this question, there is a great deal that we can learn from recent empirical work on grassroots movements, such as the influential Tea Party in the United States. Arlie Hochschild's *Strangers in Their Own Land* (2016) offers a noteworthy example of such speculative communities emerging in the wake of the 2008 global financial crisis. Her book presents ethnographic findings from a Tea Party stronghold in the state of Louisiana during the years leading to the 2016 Trump election. Hochschild provides powerful evidence of the severe risk exposures experienced by Louisianans—most devastatingly, environmental risks deriving from the unregulated activity of the oil and petrochemical industries operating in the state. These are real, materially felt risks, affecting hundreds of state inhabitants who experienced (among other forms of insecurity and precarity) ill health and dramatic increases in rates of cancer during the 2010s. A key finding of the study is that the community's engagements with the risks so far described appear to be surprisingly somber, reflecting an acceptance (rather than a questioning) of the growing volatility of their lives as inevitable in the face of broader uncertainties. One of Hochschild's most poignant insights is that, puzzlingly, the higher the exposure to environmental risks among her informants, "the less worried the individual was about it" (2016, 279).

This attitude toward risk and uncertainty is a hallmark of speculative communities. Louisiana's Tea Partiers seemed to reject the neoliberal rationality of risk-taking as a form of investment in their own uncertain futures. Revealingly, their political instincts did not seem to align with the narrative of an atomized and "anxiously entrepreneurial" subjectivity so often found in critiques of financialization. Their disillusionment with the status quo extended beyond the usual suspect of government intervention; while Tea Party members had little sympathy for interventionist counter-movements of risk control and regulation, their responses to the radical uncertainties they experienced dissented from the belief that all problems have a solution (which would have been consonant with the fantasy of neo-liberal reason). Instead, their stoicism reflected an understanding of the inherent impossibility of solution and, more deeply, an acute awareness of inevitable failure. Reading Hochschild's interviews, we acquire a vivid sense of their speculative communities' inability to control the future: signs of a deeper acceptance of the uncertain present's unsettling side but also importantly a disbelief in calculative solutions offered within the liberal/expert paradigm.

Some important implications are afoot here concerning the relationship between finance and populism in the twenty-first century. For large parts of the United States, the 2008 financial crisis lowered hopes and aspirations and led to a growing sense of foreclosure of possibilities. Indeed, Hochschild observes a distinct change in the ways that her informants came to imagine their futures during that time. When grappling with the uncertain consequences of deregulated markets in their everyday lives, they did not merely (or erroneously) assess risks. Rather, they speculated on the (ethical as well as political) values of oil and petrochemical companies responsible for air and water pollution, and also on the values of the local and federal government involved in the (de)regulation of these industries. This generative and relational function of the speculative imagination is crucial here. Rather than growing apart, Louisianans mobilized that speculative imagination as a means to come together in the face of continuing "broken promises." By turning to complex webs of mutuality found in religious congregations, in families, and in other local communities, they were able to reallocate moral responsibilities more collectively. In doing so, the idea that "we're all in this together" helped to cement their sense of belonging to the speculative community, offering a much-needed moral anchoring for hedging their uncertain futures.

Sociologist Robert Wuthnow's (2018) in-depth ethnography of America's rural heartland (conducted during a period overlapping with Hochschild's study) throws further light on this inchoate sense of collectivized uncertainty embodied in grassroots neopopulism—casting it as an integral part of the relational moral self, which is grounded in practices of mutual responsibility. Rather than passively responding to such uncertainty, "left-behind" communities (in Wuthnow's words) employ preemptively "make-shift solutions" (4) to desperate problems, precisely in order to maintain their imagined togetherness. They "workshop" responses to growing economic risks and "don't let themselves get anxious about it" (166), while remaining "realistic about the shortcomings of their communities" (79). Such responses seem to focus the speculative imagination on the present. Contrary to the much-discussed yearning for returning to America's past, left-behind communities' political speculations seemed much more attuned to the here and now (Skocpol and Williamson 2016).

Hence, on closer scrutiny, the vernacular imaginations of these political movements share a great deal with the imaginings of modern traders captured in Miyazaki's and LiPuma's studies. Financiers' anxieties and passions recalibrated their willingness to face uncertainty head-on by circulating practices of myth and providing them with a "surrounding narrative," which morally legitimated "abstractions of society and market." Hochschild (2016) argues that Tea Party members recalibrated their own anticipations of future uncertainty, risk, and loss through what she terms an "emotional self-interest . . . freed from the politically correct rules of feeling" (228). However, emotional self-interest and new "rules of feeling" can only in part explain such grassroots engagements with uncertainty. The ways in which Louisianans developed a sense of togetherness represented the quest for a social insurance that would countervail the community's high-risk exposures. Thus, a more complex picture of these speculative communities begins to emerge. Their shared practices of speculation and insurance challenge the view of the neopopulist *homo politicus* as a monolithic and manipulated subject and render its evolving political alliances less inscrutable. The growing convergence between finance and populism departs measurably from the view of an "anti-political populism" that is generated through "absence of community" and is thus an "outcome" of (or a "response to") financialization and its individualizing forces. The nuanced form of sociality at work within populist movements throws into question this often-homogenizing narrative. The *homo politicus* residing in such speculative communities is a relational speculator rather than a lone, calculative investor.

It is useful to recall here some of the historical struggles of *homo speculans* and, specifically, the dramatic entry of agrarian populism into the US politics of the Gilded Age. Populist Party members generated a complex speculative imagination against the political establishment of the time. Then, just as now, nativism, racism, and antimigrant sentiment were often part and parcel of such imagination (among both antigambling crusaders in the pits and agrarian populists in the farmland). At the same time, for all their great historical differences, fin de siècle populists and Hochschild's

Tea Partiers ultimately sought a pact and not a clash with finance, articulating a desire for harnessing the markets' laissez-faire dynamism to the benefit of their hinterland constituents.[19] Today, however, we witness an even tighter bond between populist politics and the most speculative of financial markets. But since neopopulist communities lack the material resources of LiPuma's and Miyazaki's financiers, their political speculations are less effective in the face of life's debilitating uncertainties. And, in stark contrast to the New Deal era's government policies of "progressive containment," such contemporary uncertainties are now actively cultivated and weaponized by nationalist-populist governments. The populist type of speculative politics is most effective in the global nerve centers of centralized power, rather than in the grassroots.

Let me decipher this crucial aspect in the function of speculative politics that has propelled neopopulists to power. Benefiting electorally from the growing volatility of neoliberal governance does not have to have as its specific aim the latter's future demise. After all, modern derivatives speculators have little interest in whether future asset prices move up or down, as long as they keep moving and remain volatile. Similarly, the potential of speculative politics to disrupt lies not in its ultimate undermining of the status quo but in its capacity to strengthen this status quo even as it destabilizes it in other ways. Clearly, the neopopulism of Trump, Modi, or Bolsonaro has not intended to "defeat" global neoliberalism and replace it with an altogether different agenda. Theirs is a politics that strategically unveils systemic uncertainties where they already exist (or, even more expediently, where it can be shown that such uncertainties had been disguised by liberal forces all along) and inserts them where they didn't previously exist. Climate-change denial is a prominent example of this practice: anticlimate populism has systematically exaggerated real, existing scientific uncertainties in order to contest basic facts around global warming. A chaotic, volatile, and unstable political life (permeated by a spectacle of trade and culture wars) may stifle democratic debate and paralyze the routine functioning of government, or indeed shut it down completely. But in doing so, it bolsters its orchestrators' tentacular power further still.

▲

In the final weeks before the 2016 UK referendum on European Union membership, calls for a "remain" vote urged increasingly for "common sense and practicality" to avoid a "protracted period of economic and political uncertainty" that a "reckless experiment" (such as voting to leave) could trigger.[20] The louder voices of the campaign were certainly those with the clearest neoliberal credentials, from New Labour and centrist figures such as Tony Blair and London's mayor, Sadiq Khan, to the Europhile wing of the Conservative Party. Such voices represented a risk-control logic in their assessment of the future, positioning uncertainty of outcome as a risk factor to ward off by use of distinct measures (be they fiscal or budgetary). In the opposite camp, the most influential players in the "leave" campaign's dizzying spectacle were the country's prominent nationalist-populists, from the UK Independence Party's (and former City financier) Nigel Farage to future prime minister Boris Johnson and cult conservative icon Jacob Rees-Mog. The narrative advanced on the latter side of the debate attempted a reinvention of nationalism's symbolic vocabulary (Molnár 2016) while at the same time defending the openness that was embodied in the possibilities of a "leave" vote—for instance, the global trading opportunities and London's leading position in global financial markets. It was on this latter issue that the "leave" campaign's rhetoric began to converge more clearly with the tropes of speculative finance.[21]

These tropes were repeated throughout the protracted debate over the terms of Brexit that followed the 2016 referendum—with the most vocal Brexiteers placing an even bolder wager on the extreme "no-deal" position. They represented the possible chaotic consequences of exiting the EU without a deal as an opportunity for markets and publics alike (no deal, they argued, was better than a bad deal). Meanwhile, actual risks for London's financial markets from Brexit-related uncertainty (such as those in derivatives trading) were largely hedged in the period after the referendum through a series of agreements between the United States, the United Kingdom, and the EU.[22] However, the type of insurance that was being offered to Brexit constituencies (by these most extreme sides of the neopopulist current) evokes George Soros's own bets on currency volatility, with which I opened this chapter.[23] Such speculative hedging can be seen as a form of predatory insurance—but also as "virtuous speculation" that sanctions the nationalist narrative of "hard Brexit." The power of this distinct speculative imagination wielded by nationalist-populists lies in its capacious integration of insurance and speculation to conjure a new political collectivity, where risks and responsibilities appear to be redistributed.

Yet, for those without access to the markets' premium insurance, such redistribution of risks and responsibilities remained grossly uneven. It is no accident that this particular brand of British populism flourished in the period of "suspended time" between the Brexit vote and the event itself. Above all, the symbolic insurances that were provided were integrated in the chaos of political life that was harnessed by Brexiteers. Such chaos therefore emerged paradoxically as both a reassuring and a more "realistic" response to uncertainty than the "remain" camp's realpolitik. In turn, lingering in this space of uncertainty (as opposed to promising a clear path out of it) paved the way for a Brexit narrative of hope and opti-mism. Brexit itself, then, can be understood as an outcome of the "leave" campaign's volatility-driven politics, galvanized by finance's formidable speculative imagination. At the same time, the ethno-nationalist narra-tives in circulation (such as the control of borders, or the rekindling of an imperialist imagination) allowed for Brexiteers to calibrate their engage-ments with such uncertainty.

In the United States, the Trump narrative operated in a much similar manner. Contrary to "evidence" provided by experts on a range of is-sues, the administration habitually took the position that "things will get sorted"—even when pursuing policies that seem to aim specifically at cre-ating chaos, as during the ongoing political impasse leading to the lon-gest government shutdowns in US history in December 2018 and January 2019. A speculative imagination was mobilized in an attempt to reinstate a more nativist sovereignty through railing against finance's institutional guardians—most notably the Federal Reserve. Consider this passage from Trump's speech at the World Economic Forum in Davos, Switzerland, in January 2020: "To embrace the possibilities of tomorrow we must reject the perennial prophets of doom and their predictions of the apocalypse—they are the heirs of yesterday's foolish fortune tellers." The statement captures vividly right-wing populism's regressive albeit optimistic em-brace of an unpredictable chaos, which runs counter to the "apocalypse" allegedly preached by liberal elites. In that sense, "Make America Great Again" should be interpreted as a politics of "going back to the future"; not just a call for returning to yesteryear's Leviathan, but an optimistic act of divining the future.

MORAL COMMUNITIES, ACTUARIAL CHAUVINISM, AND IMAGINED SOVEREIGNTIES

Let me summarize the discussion so far. Neopopulism's emerging specu-lative communities work like Anderson's imagined communities, though perhaps less obviously. As I have argued throughout this book, specula-tive communities congeal around a continual integration of the future's openness into an uncertain present, thus generating a renewed sense of synchronicity and narrative. In preceding chapters, I have contended that this operation relies on the creation of a spectacle, and that one of the key consequences is the obfuscation of power conflicts simmering beneath. Such obfuscation lends further legitimacy to nationalist narratives. As in all spectacles, horizontality, in the sense of synchronicity and narrative, pulls speculators together across traditional power constellations. It is in this process that we must locate the ascendancy of *homo speculans* as a neopopulist political subject, avoiding the pitfalls of a universalist ontology of cosmopolitanism or of the determinist dismissals of "atavistic" populist crowds.

Trump's political movement hinged on diverse visual and discursive strategies to spread widely a speculative imagination, and by doing so to "narrate the nation": deploying top-down, performative acts of a patriotic leveraging of uncertainty in global risk games such as the US-China trade wars and harnessing subtler speculative rituals performed on the ground by communities of "resourceless speculators" precariously managing the economic hazards of everyday life. Correspondingly, the seemingly paradoxical "evaluations" of populists' own unknowable futures discussed earlier have not merely been the product of an imposed language (such as that of financialization) over deeper social values. They are the means of a more active engagement with collective conditions of uncertainty, driving the integration of modern self and nation—in other words, the constitution of the nation through a shared speculative imagination.[24] To put it another way, the exclusionary myth of autochthony and identity has emboldened the speculative imagination, enabling it to effectively overcome the neoliberal logic of "risk control" by engaging with uncertainty in a more proactive and immersive manner. But the two forces work in tandem—that is, a speculative endorsement of uncertainty also rouses the reassuring nationalist myths of the modern *homo politicus*. This issue has been overlooked by critical observers of (neo)liberalism's legitimacy crises, who correctly identify the doubt and anxiety spawned by the rising popular mistrust of techno-scientific rationality but neglect the complex divinational role of speculation in the public imagination.[25]

Let me now return to the paradox with which the chapter began to illustrate this important point. The politics of neoliberalism might seem at first sight more aligned with the globalized logic of finance, but as the rising tides of right-wing populism endorse finance's deeper speculative orientation, nationalism provides the insurance needed for uncertainty to "embed itself" in speculative communities. Disavowal of the neoliberal promise and anxiety on the individual level are hedged by shared nationalist myths circulating in the community, energizing imagined bonds among its members and allowing them to "short" their governments (thus administering some of George Soros's own medicine). It is precisely in this tension between the closure of nationalist myth and the openness of the speculative imagination that the convergence of financial capital and neopopulism takes place.[26] Seen through this prism, the epoch's culture and trade wars, and its populist leaders' "govern-by-chaos" mantra, are far from contradictory to globalized market principles—rather, they fundamentally embrace finance's intrinsic speculative imagination.[27] President

Trump's sustained offensive against the Federal Reserve's interest-rate policy since 2018 (allegedly in response to his own trade war) included the infamous statement "they are going loco," which turns the disruptive logic of populist "irrational crowds" on its head: chaos-mongering is business as usual, while central bankers' monetary tightness is "wild."[28] In this context, the type of speculative neopopulism ushered in poses the most effective challenge to the logic of There Is No Alternative. This is the terrain of victory over centrist, liberal cosmopolitans, who also draw increasingly to the collective insurance of nationalist myths but remain conspicuously alien to speculation's other constitutive dimension: its full-throated endorsement of radical uncertainty.

Speculative imaginations, however, are not unitary—they are often fragmented and incoherent, forging social bonds and political subjectivities that lead to unwieldly coalitions of disparate actors, from big pharma and derivatives traders to blue-collar workers and small-town churchgoers. Importantly, the speculative communities I have examined in this chapter are moral communities (to use Wuthnow's term) with nation-centered notions of collective responsibility. We can see in these developments a new type of *actuarial chauvinism*—which is distinct from other types of social insurance—whose allocations of responsibility no longer involve substantive redistribution.[29] As the state retreats from both its insurance and its redistributive roles, new collective liabilities fill the void it leaves behind. What unites these communities is their distinctive use of ethnonationalism as insurance against their widely varied experiences of uncertainty. But the "compensations" that are claimed and received through this symbolic insurance differ because people's access to the "underwritten assets" at stake (such as imagined sovereignty and collective autonomy) remains vastly unequal.

▲

So far, I have sought to directly address *homo speculans* as a political subject emerging out of the political developments following the 2008 global financial crisis. I argued that the specific kind of symbolic social insurance involved in neopopulist movements like the Tea Party in the United States and Brexiteers in the United Kingdom contains overlooked invocations of mutuality and interdependency. Yet, as both these cases demonstrate, such appeals are a far cry from postwar forms of social insurance like those established by the New Deal and the Beveridgean welfare state—let alone more radical types of collective action aimed at reclaiming power and squashing entrenched inequalities. The insurance function of speculation seems to operate on affective, performative, and exclusionary registers—a form of social protection made possible by forging a sense of chauvinistic bonding and the exclusion of migrants, Muslims, people of color, and other marginalized groups.[30]

Speculative communities, then, have not erased spaces of division, discrimination, and domination. The speculative politics I have sought to illuminate in this chapter contains an ambivalence, which populist leaders the world over were quick to weaponize during the tumultuous 2010s. But how much longer will those like Trump, Johnson, and company be able to trade successfully on this delicate balance of speculation and insurance? How far will they go in providing no-limit risk protections for the wealthiest, while reserving nationalism's symbolic insurance to the downwardly mobile? And can a speculative imagination be harnessed in more inclusive ways? Can it be weaponized toward more radical progressive projects? My next and final step will be a foray into these pressing political imperatives of speculative communities.

6: COUNTER-SPECULATIONS

*Everlasting uncertainty and agitation distinguish the
bourgeois epoch from all earlier ones. All fixed, fast-frozen
relations, with their train of ancient and venerable prejudices and
opinions, are swept away, all new-formed ones become antiquated
before they can ossify. All that is solid melts into air, all that is holy
is profaned, and man is at last compelled to face with sober senses
his real conditions of life, and his relations with his kind.*

MARX AND ENGELS, *THE COMMUNIST MANIFESTO*

*Speculation is our zeitgeist. . . . Some eagerly buy into
these futures markets, placing their bets; others imagine things
differently. . . . Speculation makes nonsense of the obsessive call
to define agendas, programs, outcomes, or impacts. . . . All in all,
nothing more than speculation and nothing less.*

THE UNCERTAIN COMMONS, *SPECULATE THIS!*

In June 2020, amid the first wave of the novel coronavirus pandemic and
during a global wave of Black Lives Matter (BLM) protests, a string of unusual stories made headlines.[1] On June 5 news media reported that BLM
supporters had launched a coordinated cyber sabotage against the Dallas
Police Department social media accounts after the department had asked
its followers to post video evidence of illegal activity during the weekend's
demonstrations to their iWatchDallas app. By posting a relentless barrage
of fancams (TikTok parlance for video and photo compilations of a K-pop
idol or group), gaming clips, and anime GIFs, the amateur saboteurs overloaded the app, forcing the department to announce that it was tempo-
rarily removing the app "due to technical difficulties." On the same day,
Newsweek ran a story about a separate wave of K-pop fancam spam attacks
on QAnon (the vast network of social media accounts associated with far-
right conspiracy theorists alleging a "deep state" plot against President

Trump). In the days that followed, a number of conservative and neofascist hashtags were also targeted, including #AllLivesMatter, #WhiteLivesMatter, and #ExposeAntifa, all deploying the same method: an onslaught of randomly selected, willfully disorienting off-message images and videos of K-pop bands. The aim of these attacks was to subvert Trump supporters' and white supremacists' efforts to disseminate information and organize meetings through the use of hashtags. The outcome was a resounding success: their messages were almost completely drowned out within hours.

A few days later, on June 10, President Trump announced his decision to host a rally for his 2020 re-election campaign in Tulsa, Oklahoma, in what would be his first major campaign event since the pandemic's outbreak in the country in March 2020 (flouting official public health advice for social distancing). In a matter of days, a call for sabotaging the event went viral on Instagram and TikTok. Hundreds of teenagers swiftly reserved tickets for the event with the express aim of never showing up. On June 20, the day of the event, when the president took the stage, the arena looked spectacularly empty—according to reports, about 6,200 supporters were present in a venue with space for 19,000. Much to the surprise of the Trump campaign, the media, and all those watching, it soon transpired that the majority of tickets had been reserved by TikTok saboteurs.[2] How had that been possible?

The Tulsa fiasco is reminiscent of another much-debated event involving a controversy around the presence of crowds and the blurred line between reality and fiction: Trump's 2016 inauguration. How large was the crowd that gathered on the US Capitol's West Lawn to watch the inauguration speech? Speculation on television networks and social media was rife, and public debate soon turned to photoshopped crowds and other image tampering as well as claims of "alternative facts." The controversy was, in effect, the first episode in the "post-truth" saga that was to mark Trump's time in office. The *Atlantic* characterized it poignantly as an "attempt at weaponized magic."[3] Similar media criticisms were leveled at Tulsa's TikTokers. The culprits behind those attacks were identified as Alt-TikToks—a TikTok subculture comprising young (mostly teenage) users of the popular video-sharing app with a strong community identity. Alt-TikToks are known for even higher levels in the irreverence and obscurity of their uploaded content than those commonly circulated in the app; their posts are seen as "the true chaotic space" of the platform.[4] A popular argument, represented, for instance, by the *Washington Post*'s technology correspondent, cautioned against this group's outlandish practices; it derided this politics as an activism of "online tricksters," claiming that fighting deception with deception is no way "to untangle our world wide web of lies."[5]

Even a president known for denying reality, on this occasion seemed to understand the offensive against him as a hazy act of speculative politics. Yet, unlike the West Lawn's photoshopped crowds, the emptiness of Tulsa's arena was indisputable, plain for all to see. As in the BLM acts I described above, TikTokers did not use technology as a means of creating a fake reality but deployed fakery to create "real chaos." They did not so much manipulate reality as temper it with an already existing "fakeness" to turn deception on its head.[6] Like competent political speculators, they cared little about controlling the direction of their actions' outcomes. Rather, they inserted themselves into the tidal movements of volatility. What is more, their activism did not aim at revealing their targets' evils (a strategy typically favored by the whistleblower activism tradition)—rather, it sought to drown and muddle their opponents' messages. And, unlike the mythical figures of the dark web's code-crackers or the automated armies of bots and algorithm-generated troll farms (deployed by the world's right-wing propagandists), these acts of data sabotage were neither highly complex in their inception nor exceedingly opaque in their execution. They were not so much a case of an elaborate hack as a shot in the dark.

Dexterous coding skills were not required. Instead, these activists possessed a deep awareness of the nuanced politics of visibility and invisibility. Tulsa's sabotage and the BLM hashtag hijackings were in their essence manifestations of a lightly encoded vernacular engulfing its targets like a cloud of smoke. While "lone wolf" hackings fundamentally represent an outsider's unauthorized invasion into proprietary space (typically announcing itself suddenly), the TikTokers' actions worked collectively *within* such a proprietary system by gently (and wholly legally) shepherding the platforms' algorithms toward their own aims. At the same time, Tulsa's saboteurs entered markets by buying rally tickets or, in a simultaneous coordinated offensive, by "holding" Trump campaign merchandise products in online shopping carts and indefinitely suspending checkout payments, both of which fed the campaign bad data and corrupted its election database.

Considered together, these acts had a cumulative effect of disorientation that wasn't immediately perceived as such. While Generation Z's political memes circulated openly on Instagram's and TikTok's proprietary platforms, they seemed even more obscure than the alt-right's subreddits of the 2010s and 4chan's reactionary message boards. K-poppers and Tik-Tokers did not disguise their own identities; they posted from authentic accounts before ultimately covering their tracks by deleting uploaded content within hours of posting it. In doing so, they were practicing the well-rehearsed routines of the short-lived Instagram story and the Twitter "fleet." Their acts, however, form part of a wider phenomenon—a political weaponization of the volatility inhering in today's speculative politics. They are *counter-speculations*: struggles for visibility and obfuscation waged on the turf afforded by speculative technologies.

▲

A blurring of the line between image and reality has been seen as one of the most nefarious consequences of our time's speculative politics: from the growing spread of "misinformation" and populist indictments of "fake news" to the pernicious conspiracies that are increasingly swirled against scientific evidence of all kinds. But what if this very blurring also opens up new paths for interrupting the disastrous cycle of culture wars produced by speculative politics? Contemplating different collective ways of imagining the future, Karl Mannheim (1966) suggested that utopia must be considered distinct from ideology because, while the former "breaks the bonds of the existing social order, the latter aims to preserve it" (Bottici 2014, 161). Is fighting capital with distracting videos and stranded proprietary algorithms offering an alternative to the menacing unreality of culture wars? And are these struggles a spur to a political community endeavoring to be a more autonomous guardian of the unknown?

The counter-speculations I have so far described represent an approach to investing in the here and now, which is nursed in the speculative mode of our financialized times. Trained in a technological environment where contingent ambiguity is a natural ally when confronting uncertainty, K-poppers experimented with the tactical multivalence of the speculative imagination.[7] Yet their attacks were not sudden bolts from the blue. They were made possible not only through the uncertain rituals rehearsed through speculative technologies; they followed in the footsteps of global movements that have thrown themselves in the midst of financialized capitalism's speculative politics—from France's Gilets Jaunes to BLM's own earlier waves of protest. Like the right-wing populism I discussed in chapter 5, counter-speculations endorse uncertainty as a condition of possibility, but unlike Tea Partiers, Brexiteers, and neopopulist groups, they also lay a claim on redressing the unequal distribution of uncertainty's consequences. In the case of BLM, that meant teasing out the intersecting inequalities of race, gender, and class that profoundly condition the ability to gain capital from political speculation. Though hailing from the haze of an uncertain present, such counter-speculations also waged bold claims for defunding a police force channeling racial violence—for instance, through shrewd digital contingents like #defendourmovements and the radical campaigns of Reclaim the Block for divesting police funding in the city of Minneapolis.

Therefore, in this final chapter, I argue that counter-speculations are demonstrative of a desire to subvert power—a "creative duplicity" (Massumi 2018) manifest through participating in (rather than merely rejecting) the workings of today's political spectacles, precisely in order to sabotage them. Where speculative politics tosses the coin of uncertainty to extract exclusive (or exclusionary) yields from a political system that has previously caused it injury, counter-speculations dare to imagine the downfall of that very system for collective gains. We saw how the infinite scroll has been the prevailing mode of sociality mustered through speculative technologies. Counter-speculations seem to emerge from the very space of ephemerality—a temporality that enables radical immersion in a disorienting present with the aim of redrawing the political field in favor of the marginalized and the invisible. In what follows, I consider potential openings in the frames of this negation; possibilities for resistance to the current social order that on first sight may not "look good." My contention is this: counter-speculations offer a much-needed political grammar for progressive engagements with uncertainty in the service of more democratic collectives, at the same time mounting a challenge against the more regressive speculative politics currently on the march.

A DIVIDUAL *HOMO POLITICUS*?

Throughout this book, I have taken a view of finance that seeks to do justice to its multifarious speculative imagination and to the dynamic ways in which it suffuses society from the ground up. Before I consider in more depth the political implications of the counter-speculations framing I have just outlined, I would like to engage a recent body of work with cognate concerns around the generative role of finance beyond a political technique of social control. This work seeks to open up notions of risk and debt in order to account for the bottom-up dynamics of post-2008 financialized politics. A recent study by political economists Bryan and Rafferty (2018), for instance, aims to discern the progressive potential of collective risk-taking as a response to financialization. They examine that potential in practices of "household unionism," "liquidity refusal," and strategies to "block capital's liquidity risk spread" (Bryan and Rafferty 2018, 175). These forms of financial activism are emblematic of a new political subjectivity in which the "citizen-debtor replaces the citizen-worker as the iconic figure of late twentieth-century capitalism" (Krippner 2017, 3). Its many forms include the neighborhood activism of "reinvestment" examined in Krippner's work: tactics deployed by communities of borrowers in marginalized neighborhoods to collectively reclaim credit ownership from financial institutions and to re-assert direct control of resources and assets such as bank deposits; or the debtor activism and mass debt refusal, seen for instance in the ongoing anti-student-loan movement in the United States; or, still, the campaigns for mortgage clemency, the "collective politics of insolvency" discussed in the important work of David Graeber (2014) and Maurizio Lazzarato (2015).

Montgomerie and Tepe-Belfrage (2019) argue that moral norms of debt and indebtedness shape political spaces of action and agency, including small-scale strategies of resistance to debt's authority (and financialization at large) such as "paying it down, diverting expenditures, defaulting, repudiating, cancelling, or paying it off altogether" (310). Importantly, as the 2008 subprime mortgage crisis revealed, such small acts can be extremely disruptive of the regularity on which instruments of securitized debt rely and "lit a firestorm . . . in the underbelly of the global financial system" (316). To date, however, there is scant evidence that conscious, progressive grassroots strategies of debt refusal and risk reallocation can be as consequential as the 2008 domino chain of mortgage foreclosures. Paradoxically, as Melinda Cooper (2020) shows, over the last decade, a surging nationalist Right has been more effective in championing and delivering debt canceling. In Hungary, for instance, Viktor Orbán has unilaterally canceled a quarter of foreign-exchange household debt, acting in apparent disregard for central bank independence.

More insidiously, however, strategies that seek to refute or deny debt can be ineffective because, as has been adeptly argued by Arjun Appadurai (2016) "their architecture poses the moral force of the individual against a process of dividualization that they neither understand nor endorse" (145). Appadurai here takes inspiration from Gilles Deleuze's notion of dividuation, which he uses to describe the dynamic relationship between capital and social control. Instead of a singular identity that is articulated through the process of "individuation," Deleuze saw a separation of the underlying individual and its various attributes analogous to a financial derivative. Dividuation, therefore, is a predatory process by which speculative finance partitions, quantifies, rates, and profiles individual subjects' behaviors and then rebundles them in order to exploit new risks and profit opportunities. Such partitions have become so entrenched that they have rendered irrelevant the idea of the classical "whole" individual. As a consequence, Appadurai argues, any attempt to restore the ideal of the individual as a bedrock of resistance to financial indebtment is doomed to fail, as long as it primarily relies on categories and "stable associations" such as class, race, ethnicities, identities, and parties. The moral battleground of debt politics can feel like quicksand when we fight from within the perimeter of such categories.

Instead, more radical forms of resistance to the pernicious impact of finance should build on a politics of "progressive dividualism" (Appadurai

2016, 145), which responds to finance's own derivative form with a truly socialized dividualism on the ground level. Appadurai explores such strategies by considering the case of India's Mumbai slum dwellers' entry into global risk markets, demonstrating a refusal "to be defined as individuals, in the common modern sense" (that is, to be aligned with a coherent whole in every regard), insisting instead on a collective identity and a solidarity that is built around specific activities of dividuals "grounded in the capacity of such groups to recombine traditional Indian social categories." (121–22). Here, indebtedness is seen as a condition of possibility not because it helps restore old bonds but because it allows future value to be brought into the present in more dynamic ways.

Philosopher Michel Feher (2018), whose work I have already discussed in previous chapters, has explicitly aimed to capture the potential for this more immanent politics of resistance to financialization. Feher's approach, like Appadurai's, goes further than traditional debt activism. He argues that, in order to make such potential materialize, debtors need to cynically embrace the role of investee bestowed on them by creditors, appropriating their own condition so that they can mobilize against it.[8] To do so, they must find the right levers to pull—for instance, using their credit-seeking status as a vehicle for appreciating those assets that are most likely to subvert financialization. Such strategies may include investee activism aiming to exploit corporate social responsibility structures to damage creditor reputation and thus hinder corporate financing (such as the 2016 Standing Rock Reservation's campaign against the Dakota Access Pipeline, which successfully brought extraction pipelines to a standstill). Or they may take the form of contingent workers' cooperative strategies in the gig economy, which invoke a modest ambition of advocating security through autonomy, rather than by pursuing a return to the postwar social-democratic contract. For Feher, while the demands of the Keynesian era's unionized labor were full employment and social security, the task of today's investees must be to imagine the future's new appreciable, creditworthy projects.

These important frameworks, then, sketch a dynamic (and in some ways optimistic) matrix of risk-debt politics, which seeks to overcome the atomizing effect of financialization. Perhaps most valuably, such critical work captures the shifting field of political struggle itself, comprising not mere "cogs in the current regime of capital accumulation" (Feher 2018, 209) but active debtors, creditors, investors, and investees whose collective battles are waged on finance's own turf. What is more, such framing is sensitive to more inclusive visibilities, through an acknowledgment of traditionally invisible subjects' mutual contingencies—chief among which is their mutual indebtedness. Dividual and investee politics endeavors to overthrow the yoke of debt's moral indictment. If the early victors of the fin de siècle wars of speculation fought to reassert the legitimacy of pit trading versus bucket-shop gambling, today's speculators fight in global risk markets to damage their creditors' reputation, their legitimacy, and their access to liquidity. But how does the explanatory capacity of such a *homo politicus* fare when scrutinized from the perspective of speculative communities?

To be clear, I am sympathetic to the inclination to fight fire with fire that undergirds these approaches, as well as to the nuanced mapping of finance's "immanence." But the speculative imagination runs deeper than strategies of risk-debt activism and investee politics. Its power stems not only from a capacity to unite around shared contingencies and harm the reputations of the powerful but from highlighting (and widening) existing gaps, distortions, obscurities, and illegibilities, thereby increasing a volatility that is already operative on some level. The obfuscation strategies deployed by BLM activists and TikTokers with which I opened the chapter did not necessarily aim at causing reputational damage to their targets (the president, his followers, or white-supremacist agitators). Their disillusionment, skepticism, and irony were articulated not against but within an already active spectacle. As I demonstrated in earlier chapters, the postwar social contract of social insurance, and the Fordist model of credit allocation, were shaped by vexed conflicts over both the moral legitimacy and the divinatory power of speculative imagination. These struggles continue to condition the risk and debt politics in today's speculative communities. But now the worlds of reality and fiction appear even more tightly linked by speculation. My next step, therefore, is to probe directly into this entanglement and examine what kinds of counter-speculations are made possible in the "real fake" space of modern speculative politics.

FROM STRATEGIC IGNORANCE TO THE REAL FAKE: SPECULATIVE COMMUNITIES BEYOND LIBERAL COSMOPOLITANISM AND LEFT POPULISM

US Defense Secretary Donald Rumsfeld's infamous 2001 statement about the "unknown unknowns" that had to be reckoned with in the wake of the War on Terror has been watched by millions on YouTube. It has been the subject of documentary films and has sparked numerous debates in media and academia alike. Rumsfeld's statement is broadly seen as having heralded the twenty-first century's new era of security politics: a time when risk is no longer the measuring stick for political decisions, which are driven instead by the incalculable and the unknowable, in turn lending legitimacy to preemptive responses to security threats. These developments have been most influentially captured in sociologist Ulrich Beck's vision of "risk society," which positions uncertainty as the impetus for growing risk control, making twenty-first-century society dependent on security, while encroaching on individual freedom and exacerbating pre-existing inequality (Beck 2008). In part 2 of this book, I tracked the ramifications of the "risk society" thesis for contemporary modes of sociality and intimacy. Considered in the political arena, a key consequence of a security-based approach to risk is an anticipatory (and, most often, reactionary) politics that eschews evidence altogether. Institutions and experts become mistrusted even as demands on their performance increase (Martin 2015, 47).[9]

Beck's thesis has far-reaching sociological implications. In the face of nonknowledge, all social agents must now become risk managers (as opposed to mere risk-takers), competing in a society where risks are increasingly unknowable for all. This widespread risk management of unknowability allegedly eases differentials between experts and publics, although "more knowledge and more science" does not necessarily bring about greater clarity—it may, in fact, compound uncertainty. For Beck (2008), a key consequence of risk society is the creation of a "modern séance": the "staging" of real and manufactured uncertainties around which new cosmopolitan communities coalesce.[10] Hence, the risk of entrapment by late modernity's universal threats also presents an opportunity for activating and connecting actors across borders, through what Beck calls the "enforced enlightenment" of the cosmopolitan moment—a "globalization of compassion" made possible on the one hand through representations of danger in mass media and on the other through opportunities for debate afforded by the internet.[11] The "risk condition" can therefore also become an opportunity for a global democratic politics, mobilized around the mechanism of "self-reflexivity," which I discussed in chapter 4—a process whereby the late-modern individual strives to directly confront what is no longer possible to know, a more "reflexive conduct of life" that reevaluates existing rules in order to develop its own certainties. Beck sees such potential embodied in new social movements pursuing civic, environmental, and transnational agendas.

This argument bears the marks of a well-known thesis in economics on the limited knowledge of all market participants and the superior intelligence of the price system, established most prominently in the works of Hayek and Keynes. Collective ignorance—rather than collective wisdom—drives market equilibrium and social order (Martin 2015). Nonetheless, not everyone is "equally ignorant." Exposing the unequal distributions of nonknowledge is important for understanding uneven experiences of uncertainty in the face of financialization, and thus our speculative responses to it, not to mention our ability to garner capital from speculation. Also, spaces of freedom such as those described by Beck deploy deliberative mechanisms of decision making, resembling Habermas's "communicative democracy," that seek to move from adversarial to consensus politics. Although risk society powerfully captures some of the anxieties of modern capitalism's incipient subject, it plays down the profound conflicts persisting under radical uncertainty. It ignores, in particular, the collective structures of insurance and speculation through which such conflicts are managed and through which new identifications are forged in coagulating polities. As we saw in chapter 5, these collective structures are especially important at the level of nationalism's symbolic capital. Moreover, much of today's progressive politics is firmly rooted in national contexts and is also articulated in ways that seem to contradict the principles of a deliberative cosmopolitanism.

Political theorist Ernesto Laclau has proposed a very different framing of the progressive polities emerging under these uncertain conditions. In his influential *On Populist Reason* (2007), Laclau puts forward a more sympathetic view of the public that is often denigrated by cosmopolitan strands as populism. His approach aims specifically at addressing views that criticize progressive populism for inevitably anticipating authoritarianism and nation-centered xenophobia. Laclau argues instead that polities are able to articulate progressive demands, which can be unified under any emerging "empty signifier"—a role often filled by a leader—in order to avoid centrifugal tendencies as their communities grow larger. Such empty signifiers can encompass multiple, diverse, yet equivalently marginalized "publics" under the aegis of a single counter-hegemonic movement. Parting ways with the traditional Marxist Left, therefore, this view of progressive populism accommodates identity claims and heterogeneous demands, seeking to combat reified and regressive notions of "the public." Laclau's project of rehabilitating populism is a tour de force traversing the intellectual history of crowd theory, collective behavior, and psychoanalysis to counter the systematic dismissal of populism in critical theory and to defend the crowd's own "populist reason." This significant contribution demonstrates how such systematic dismissal, in Laclau's own words, "has been part of the discursive construction of a certain normality . . . from which [populism's] dangerous logics had to be excluded" (2007, 19) in order to separate the normal (rational individual) from the pathological (irrational crowd).

Yet the image of *homo politicus* that emerges in this critique conjures new specters of political rationality. Although Laclau takes an important step toward a more relational understanding of that figure (specifically by foregrounding "vagueness" as an important constitutive element of populist reason), such counter-politics ultimately remains a closed language. Echoing the legacy of Hobbesian theory, Laclau contends that political communities are discursive formations—and, by that token, they must be traced and examined at the level of signification. To put it simply, political identities are constituted predominantly through words. Verónica Gago (2017) has offered, in my view, the most comprehensive account of this issue in Laclau's rendition, evaluating it through an illuminating empirical study of migrant worker movements in Buenos Aires. The thrust of her argument is this: the idea of populist reason as a means for dismantling "theories of enlightened government elites" is based on the "unicist rationality" of popular life, which in turn relies overmuch on the logic of "perverting language" (Gago 2017, 225-26). Put another way, the linguistic framing of the Laclauian critique focuses rather narrowly on the discursive nature of political claims.

More broadly, both these influential lines of thinking are, from quite different starting points, ultimately wedded to a belief in the liberating promise of (a type of) rationality. For Beck (2008), such promise exists in the self-reflexive navigation of risk society's maze of real and manufactured uncertainties; for Laclau (2007), in the "equivalential power" of the "people's" empty signifiers. Both approaches seem to implicitly subscribe to the Polanyian double movement, positing uncertainty-ridden capitalism as the movement and a counter-movement of emerging responses—a Left populism for Laclau and a cosmopolitan "micropolitics" of local alliances with global ambition for Beck.[12]

Although I do not wish to quarrel with the spirit of such defenses of a more democratic polity, I propose that a further move is needed—beyond what is allowed by these counter-movements and their concomitant political rationalities. The questions I would like to pose, specifically, are, How can speculative endorsements of the moment's uncertainty exceed the closed principles of a cosmopolitan "rationalist enlightenment," or the discursive universalism of "populist reason"? How can resistance to financialization find more equitable articulations under conditions that are outside its control?

▲

Reflecting on his famous 2001 statement in Errol Morris's 2013 documentary *The Known Unknown*, Donald Rumsfeld professed that the proliferation of unknown unknowns had in fact been a "failure of the imagination."[13] His phrase was evocative of the answer given to another question (frequently cited in uncertainty studies) that Queen Elizabeth asked the Bank of England in 2009: "How could you not see the financial crisis coming?"—to which the bank's chief economist answered (in a much quoted open letter) that the crisis was a "failure of the collective imagination of many bright people."[14] At the dawn of the twenty-first century, then, the failure to imagine in the face of unpredictable uncertainty had become a commonplace among the Global North's political and economic power centers. But why did such mighty imaginations fail in the first place, and why were those responsible for the failing so quick to admit it?

One way of answering this question is by interrogating the strategic positions that were taken by such institutions toward unknown unknowns. The growing field of the "sociology of ignorance" (McGoey 2012, 2019; Davies and McGoey 2012; Gross and McGoey 2015) offers a view of ignorance as "a productive asset" that—like volatility—can be leveraged by institutions "to command resources, deny liability in the aftermath of crises, and to assert expertise in the face of unpredictable outcomes" (McGoey 2012, 553). Hence, especially at times of profound uncertainty and confusion, references to unknown unknowns should be seen as "not accidental, but rather a political accomplishment" (553); in short, as "strategic ignorance" weaponized by legal and political institutions as tactics of political control.[15] Modern societies' perennial confusions and anxieties about the future are unequally distributed—not only because knowledge itself is unevenly accessed but because the capacity to mobilize ignorance is widely unequal. Strategic ignorance is thus a powerful tool of "class domination and corporate power," as opposed to an "individual act" of ignoring (McGoey 2019, 118). Crucially, McGoey and colleagues trace in the history of Western Enlightenment a pathway toward such structural and exclusionary ignorance—specifically,

> the belief that knowledge inevitably increases one's political power or leverage: these are inheritances of an Enlightenment era marked by the assumption that prejudice can and should be tamed by making knowledge more universally accessible. But what about *when people do not wish to know?* What about when, through the principle of *not seeing*, certain groups are rendered more vulnerable, more at risk of exploitation or punishment by legal systems that purport to function free of prejudice? What is the role of ignorance in societies that hail the importance of knowledge even as we court ignorance in a myriad of ways, at once obvious and less apparent, pernicious and commendable in turn? (Gross and McGoey 2015, 3; my emphases)[16]

Indeed, as Achille Mbembe (2003, 2017) has powerfully shown, critical theories of capitalism often privilege normative theories of democracy developed around the concepts of rational knowledge as the foundation of a "second modernity" and a "topos of sovereignty."[17] Mounting a spirited critique of Rawls's and Habermas's liberal philosophies (which, to put it crudely, view knowledge as the path to liberty), Mbembe (2003) contends that the "distinction between reason and unreason (passion, fantasy)" has enabled "late-modern criticism to articulate a certain idea of the political, the community, the subject" within which "reason is the truth of the subject and politics is the exercise of reason in the public sphere" (13–14). The idea of strategic ignorance proposed by McGoey can make inroads into opening up such problematic and exclusionary political rationalities of Western modernity. This is not a question of discerning a conflict between (a certain type of) knowledge versus (a certain type of) ignorance, but rather asking how strategic ignorance can be mobilized from the ground up as a more equitable political strategy. Answering the latter question is neither the cynical rejection of evidence nor the positing of a new type of rationality (populist, cosmopolitan, or otherwise).

At the same time, these ideas also lean away from popular explanations that equate ignorance with irrationality or the overpowering strength of our emotions in the face of uncertainty. This is typically reflected in the commonplace view of "publics" as "malleable" in a world where emotion becomes the only reliable compass for navigating "lies" (such as those underpinning the logic of culture wars, but also those echoing the critiques of populism I discussed in chapter 5). It is a trope I have sought to debunk through my framing of the speculative imagination, whose open dialectics invite a shake-up of Eurocentric universalism. One of the issues with the dominance of Kantian idealism in Western modernity's critiques of reason (over the imagination) has been precisely its exclusion of certain categories of people—most prominently, people of color (see Charles Mills 1997, 2017). Indeed, one of the most detrimental domains where routinized ignorance can be found is what Charles Mills has called "white ignorance," the "belief systems and mythologies that white colonizers, as part of the European imperialist project, actively constructed as factual reality" (1997, 5).

Taken together then, these insights call for a shift of attention, from struggles that seek to defend a notion of enlightened (and procedural) rationality to a resistance that pierces the deceptive reality it is called to accept and counteracts it instead with its own myths, narratives, and fictions. A key argument I have put forward so far is that speculative communities no longer live (and perceive) their clouded reality through modes of "anticipation" or "control" alone but by endorsing its uncertainty as an inherent feature of today's spectacle societies—what we could call a notion of "real fake." The real fake is where the politics of progressive counter-speculation germinates—directing the speculative imagination toward modes of strategic unknowing that are just as alert to the falsities of liberal democracy and neopopulism as they are open to our own vulnerabilities and those of others. Such strategic ignorance, then, can articulate a more radical framing of equality in speculative communities. This view calls for an important modification of what has been a joint premise in some strands of "Left populist" and postcolonial theory, which have sought to foreground heterogeneity over an ideal political subject that is European, masculine, and white. Indeed, counter-speculations reject this subject, but in doing so they move beyond the principle of heterogeneity, hinging on the dynamics of uncertainty and (in)visibility to mobilize subaltern perspectives through the speculative imagination's open dialectics. They don't push for the "coexistence" of multiple identities but rather for the productive unknowability of identity itself.

When all is in flux, endorsements of the "real fake" often take the well-known form of conspiracy, which emerges with greater power. As we have seen, conspiracy sits well with toxic and exclusionary political agendas whose denial of reality fuels a disavowal of difference rather than a community of "equal unknowers." It has thus been common to consider conspiracy a "fantasy narrative," an expression of crowd irrationality that is typically juxtaposed with the "reality" and "truth" of scientific reason. In finance, the markets' irrational crowds have long been considered linchpins of conspiracy—vectors along which false information (about stock prices) spreads fast and rumors (about insolvency) fly around. Legitimate speculation in formal exchanges has represented, in that sense, the very ability of speculators to cut through such conspiracies and place "lucid" wagers by positioning themselves ahead of the "conspiring herds."

My contention, however, is that even the most "maximalist" and "pathological" practices of speculation embody a political dynamic that should not be dismissed altogether. If, as we have seen, speculation is predicated on the sociality of trading interdependencies and reciprocal obligations, conspiracy has a similar capacity to satisfy societies' yearnings for connection. And as with all types of speculation, it encompasses both an insurance (in the form of orienting myths that offer a sense of narrative to otherwise baffling and destabilizing events) and a wager (that seeks to yield returns from such destabilizing events). For these reasons, Bridle (2018) provocatively suggests that conspiracy can be "the extreme resort of the powerless" (205), or in the terms of this book, a longing to "be seen" and rise above the haze of uncertainty enveloping financialized life.

To demonstrate the deeper implications of the discussion so far, I now consider two very different examples of counter-speculation from recent years, which nevertheless represent distinct ways of inhabiting the political space I have mapped.

COUNTER-SPECULATING WITH FRANCE'S GILETS JAUNES AND GREECE'S OXI MOVEMENT

One of the most intriguing slogans of the Gilets Jaunes over the months of chaos in France's urban centers during the winter of 2019 was "*Coucou, Macron!*" (loosely translated in English as "We see you, Macron!").[18] The phrase is interesting because it challenges the monopoly on perception that the all-seeing eyes of capital have created through the algorithmic data centers of banks and technology companies. Here, activists simultaneously recognize and adopt the power of an omniscient supercomputer crunching algorithms under chaotic circumstances. President Emmanuel Macron was the one who had to keep guessing where his enemies were. In Paris, Lyon, Toulouse, Bordeaux, and other major French cities, protesters from the rural hinterlands in their high-visibility yellow safety vests (*gilets jaunes*) burst into streets and squares to protest the government's newly announced green tax on fuel. They included road blockages and occupations, as well as "flash mobs"—a practice of sudden organized assemblies aimed at catching people by surprise originating in the early 2000s, later politicized by the Occupy movement, and honed by the recent climate-change activism of the Extinction Rebellion movement.

At the same time, protesters used imaginative practices of counter-surveillance to target some of France's largest corporations, most notably luxury-products behemoth LVMH (owner of brands Louis Vuitton, Givenchy, Möet, and Dom Pérignon, among others). Their speculative offensive included a barrage of mocking video posts on Facebook and YouTube (viewed by millions) attacking Macron and prominent business figures like LVMH's chairman and chief executive, Bernard Arnault.[19] Meanwhile, demonstrations managed a blow to these brands' physical sales, as many of their flagship stores were located at epicenters of the weekly rallies, such as the Champs-Élysées in Paris. Yet protesters' occupations of traffic circles in the cities' nondescript peripheries were just as widespread. Their strategies relied on both hypervisibility and invisibility, expressed through an amorphous presence online and offline. The weekly descent of yellow-vest-wearing farmers and rural commuters at the Champs-Élysées was a sight no less strange than that of the K-pop fans' takeover of the iWatchDallas app and the Trump 2020 merchandise website. Hence, the Gilets Jaunes protests eschewed identification; they were distinctively unstraightforward, difficult to anticipate or to pin down. The lack of a general consensus about their demographic makeup, their diverse ideological origins, and their heterogeneous demands befuddled France's liberal commentariat. The movement was steeped in confusion and conspiracy.[20] As historian Enzo Traverso put it, the weekly Saturday protests were "a strange and unclassifiable object, either naïvely idealized as the announcement of revolution or obtusely stigmatized as dangerous and potentially 'proto-fascist.'"[21] State news broadcaster France 24 called the ongoing demonstrations "an unconventional insurgency that caught Parisian elites sleeping, rattling the government, baffling commentators."

The high-visibility yellow vests worn by protesters were a particularly distinctive protest technology. Legally required for motorists in cases of road accidents and emergencies, they became a totemic object representing the movement's transience, urgency, and distress. Vests hence complemented the role played traditionally by masks: the veiling of protesters' faces to protect them from security forces and safeguard their anonymity. When worn outside the life of protests, the yellow vest also signifies a "special legitimacy" to disrupt normality (for instance through traffic obstruction or roadwork), marking someone who is both building and disrupting. Their fluorescence drew attention to protesters' shared struggle to be seen, "to assume physical form in the sphere of appearance" to use Judith Butler's (2020, 6) formulation, but also to appear to each other in the political spaces of that struggle (Arendt 1998). Such weaponizing of the power of seeing and the politics of (in)visibility is reminiscent of tactics used by the May '68-ers—participants in the famous Paris uprisings that formed the backdrop of Guy Debord's (2002 [1968]) *Society of the Spectacle*. On closer inspection, however, the Gilets Jaunes' hypervisual campaigns are emblematic of our own era's counter-speculations.

Their use of images has affinities with the cynicism of meme culture, which they brought offline to streets and traffic circles, where real violence also took place. As Paul Torino and Adrian Wohlleben put it in an essay reflection of their own involvement in the protests, the movement was not so much "us[ing] memes to make symbolic demands" as it was "a form of movement as meme."[22] The Gilets Jaunes were a "coalition of invisibles" who had not previously come together under the same banner—the rural working class, the peri-urban middle class, high-school students, the unemployed, urban environmentalists—who blended demands for recognition and redistribution. The most emblematic of such demands centered on the traditionally right-wing territory of antitax grievances. On the face of it, protesting an anticarbon fuel tax would be the natural territory of climate-change deniers and anti-environmental conspiracists. Yet here protesters leveraged a counter-speculation that was purposely aimed at revealing the power inequities behind the government's policy. They denounced a "pseudo-environmentalism" with no intention to "punish the actual polluters" while doing "much to make daily life just that bit harder for many more" (Stetler 2020).

In doing so, the movement also mobilized a speculative politics against the government's own entrepreneurial imaginary of France as a start-up nation of citizen-investors.[23] Crucially, its claims did not center on demands for a dialogue in tune with a procedural Habermassian democracy. Protesters repeatedly declined invitations to speak to television news through representatives and made few attempts to dispel negative rumors about the movement. Dialogue was President Macron's way of appeasing the public opinion: the government staged a series of *grand débats* (grand debates) in early 2019 as part of a "nationwide public consultation" in response to the Gilets Jaunes protests. Both the content and the style (hierarchical, formulaic) of the debates were ostentatiously out of tune with the movement and its demands. In a display of self-fulfilling prophecy, Prime Minister Édouard Philippe concluded at the end of the process that a "more deliberative democracy is needed."[24]

▲

In the years preceding the eruption of the Gilets Jaunes movement, countries in Europe's southern periphery had been marred by a deep sovereign debt crisis. On July 5, 2015, that crisis came to a head when citizens in Greece cast their votes in a politically charged yes (*nai*) or no (*oxi*) referendum that would define the country's future. On June 28 Prime Minister Alexis Tsipras (having achieved a historic first-time victory as head of Syriza's left-wing government only a few months earlier) had declared a snap referendum in a dramatic televised address, to take place within just a week. The public was asked to accept or reject the terms of a loan agreement proposed to Greece by the "troika" of institutions responsible for managing the country's debt (the European Commission, the European Central Bank, and the International Monetary Fund). The *oxi* outcome—with a staggering 62 percent of the votes cast against the proposed deal—sent shockwaves through the European Union and took global observers by great surprise.[25] On the face of it, the vote could be seen as a political act of collective debt refusal: voters had not only rejected a desperately needed loan but had also challenged the dominant neoliberal narrative of austerity propagated by the country's creditors. On a deeper level, however, I suggest that the vote can be interpreted as a mass act of counter-speculation—a wager that endorsed rather than averted a volatile future.

At the time, I had spent an extended period in Athens observing these events unfold, and I was in the capital during the seven dramatic days from the announcement of the referendum to the voting day. Time in the city felt strangely compressed, suspended. Capital controls were imposed and banks had to shut their doors on June 28 (for the first time since World War II) to prevent bank runs, sparking a sense of palpable, existential insecurity that seemed impossible to ignore and just as impossible to resolve. It was clear, then, that the voters' decision would not be taken from conditions of relative political and economic stability (as could be said was the case in the United Kingdom's Brexit vote) but from a position of a deeply uncertain present. Against this backdrop, "endorsing chaos" was not so much an act of self-sacrifice as a survival strategy. During that week, even the matter of whether the vote would actually take place was uncertain, with Greece's highest court ruling it constitutional (following an appeal) only two days before the referendum. Confusion seemed to be embedded in the ballot question itself. Speculation was rampant about the phrasing of the question, with the government being accused of using overly complicated and misleading language, making it difficult for voters to interpret.[26]

Ultimately, voting under these circumstances was an act taken straight out of the Uncertain Commons' (2013) playbook, which I quoted in this chapter's epigraph: "mak[ing] nonsense of the obsessive call to define agendas, programs, outcomes, or impacts" (15). But what made the *oxi* vote counter-speculative as opposed to merely speculative was the agenda in which the moment's profound uncertainty was channeled. Such an agenda seemed to run counter to the programs that were formally articulated on either side of the political debate around the vote. On the one hand it showed skepticism toward a Left populism that was advocating an "immediate rupture" with the creditors (associated with the position of returning to a national currency as expressed by the platform of the Left faction within Syriza) but, on the other, it rejected the market-friendlier—albeit deeply xenophobic—nationalism represented by the main opposition party's *nai* supporters.[27] By venting such disillusionment, the skepticism of *oxi* was cultivated not as displacement toward external threats (such as migrants and people of color) but against what were seen as oppressing power structures threatening people's livelihoods. My argument, then, is this: the speculative imagination of *oxi* voters did not so much represent the positing of a clear new meaning—a path "out of the crisis"—as it did a generative awareness of the crisis. Against demands (from both sides of the political map) for articulating a viable or "realistic" alternative, the vote expressed a communal way of dwelling with the unknown. It was made possible during this period of collective suspense in daily mass rallies, bustling cafés, and, most poignantly, in the long but orderly lines forming outside shut banks. The image of the future conjured by citizens during these days may not have offered "an alternative," but it strove to imagine a "collective ownership" of indeterminacy, to recall Castoriadis's rendition—a future that was unclear, but that was at least theirs.

NEW SOLIDARITIES AND THE
RADICAL POLITICS OF EPHEMERALITY

The diverse instances of counter-speculation I have so far outlined offer us significant insights about the possibilities emerging from waging speculation's double entendre. TikTokers' attacks, Gilets Jaunes' protests, and the Greek *oxi* vote exemplify distinct forms of a transient political tempo-rality.[28] Whether a seven-day immersion in the life of politics under bank shutdowns, a weekly drive from the rural hinterlands into the city center, or a barrage of abstruse videos disappearing soon after posted, counter-speculations consciously inhabited spaces of action that were inherently ephemeral and profoundly uncertain. They showcased collective acts that were grounded in a recognition of crisis not as an impasse but as an oppor-tunity. "Nothing is true and everything is possible," declares Peter Pomer-antsev (2017)—but what *are* such imagined possibilities? Paradoxically, the distinctive cloudiness of the present reality has a transparent obscu-rity allowing us to peer into struggles of imagination that were previously hidden: instances when the "speculated upon" rise to wage their own bets on the future. Crucially, such instances unveil possibilities of re-imagining that future. As new speculative communities emerge out of the invincible There Is No Alternative doctrine (so deeply cemented in the political ho-rizon of financialized neoliberalism), the challenge ahead of us is learning to occupy this new unmapped territory of "everything is possible." Can we both expose the nefarious forces of exclusionary and dogmatic ignorance and find ways to retain our trust in a shared reality or, better yet, acknowl-edge that such a shared reality contains myths of our own making?

Let me return to the issue of endorsing the "real fake" that I have sketched in the foregoing pages. It is often argued that today's publics turn their backs on facts and shun scientific consensus; that they are routinely misled, too distracted by raging misinformation to prevent their falling prey to the epoch's conflicts of ideology and the base identification of cul-ture wars. Following this view, twenty-first-century democracy's major challenge emerges as a project of restoring faith in scientific truth over the lies of "uncertainty doomers." Not only is this a fallacious view, it also underestimates today's fiery speculative conflicts—its lenses are ill-fitted for the incongruous (nondeliberative) forms taken by such conflicts. Trust itself looks different when predicated on our speculating together rather than on understanding each other. Ultimately, it, too, requires a specula-tive imagination, in the sense of being able to imagine ourselves occupying the positions of others, but not necessarily to understand or to empathize. This is not a Rawlsian veil of ignorance, in the sense of a rational device that allows equal citizens to make fairer choices. Rather, it looks more like a trust fall game, in which participants share each other's relinquishment of control.[29] Forging horizontal forms of trust will thus never generate greater certainty, for as philosopher Martha Nussbaum (2001) has pointed out, the most radical forms of trust are inherently uncertain too; they re-quire a leap of faith that doesn't seek to align different forms of resistance into one unified whole.

My point, then, has not been to refute that a financialized reality exists, nor to argue that its puzzling volatility is imaginary, but to suggest that such reality comes to pass *through* the speculative imagination. Counter-speculations, in their essence, acknowledge this very process. It follows that distrusting the institutional guardians of the real fake (which may include both experts and populists) does not necessarily amount to disbelief, irrationality, or fantasy but can be an apt identification of the spectacle we find ourselves immersed in. Importantly, by positioning themselves at the point of friction between reality and fiction, speculative communities have greater chances of achieving the goal—vital for any social movement—of bringing the ideal a little closer to realization. Bottici (2014, 122) calls such practice, after Rousseau, a "homeopathic method," an inclination to fight today's whopping political spectacles by injecting small quantities of the very same evil. Bridle (2018) suggests a similar radical strategy when he urges us to accept that the binary of truth versus lies no longer represents our reality and we should therefore "make peace with the otherwise-irreconcilable, conflicting worldviews that prevent us from taking meaningful action in the present" (213). Being counter-speculative, as exemplified in the case of corporate callouts waged by the BLM and the Gilets Jaunes, or by the TikTok saboteurs' hashtag hijackings, means retaining a flexibility to mobilize speculation according to the problem at hand. In other words, the dispensing of a *pharmakon* adjusted to the need of each patient.

▲

Blaise Pascal (2008) remarked four centuries ago that "we never keep ourselves to the present moment," that people are so "vain" that they only dream about times "which no longer exist and allow the present to escape without thinking about it" (20–21). On the surface, the idea seems to resonate with modern critiques of an immature, flippant, and self-indulgent generation that is perpetually distracted by the lures of digital choice. Nevertheless, it doesn't capture the vertiginous condition—the "perpetual now"—of our contemporary moment. As I have argued from the outset, modern societies' "daydreaming" is oriented toward the here and now rather than the future, thus greatly influencing how we act as political agents. The type of imagination that has been re-animating *homo speculans* is characterized by an openness to indeterminacy, which is not synonymous with an openness to "all possibilities" but with a way of acting in the present. We can call this open-endedness *kairos* (the Greek word used to demarcate time that is opportune for taking action, as opposed to chronological time, or to distinguish "weather" from "climate"), in Castoriadis's words, "a moment of decision, critical occasion, conjuncture" (1984, 7). Sociologist Hartmut Rosa (2019) views such active engagement with the accelerated present moment from the "acoustic" perspective of what he calls "resonance." People relate to the unpredictable nature of the present's staggering acceleration through its echoes and reverberations. This is nevertheless quite different from existing in "harmony" with that accelerated present. My reading of Rosa's insight about resonance is that it offers an apposite image of our dwellings in speculative communities, in which we form social relations not through our attempts to avoid uncertainty's waves by "slowing down," but by inserting ourselves into the present's storm at the pace set by such waves.

Let me step back one final time and consider the political forms of counter-speculation I have discussed in this chapter. Today, those residing in the disadvantaged corners of speculative communities share an even more profound sense of urgency from experiencing the immediate consequences of issues ranging from systemic structural racism to anthropogenic climate change: precarious gig economy workers faced with exorbitant living costs and desolate housing conditions, incarcerated people of color in US prisons, refugees in Europe's shameful and overcrowded refugee camps, small-scale farmers in coastal farmlands exposed to rising sea levels and flooding. These are constituencies that are simply unable to "be distracted" by the current vortex of uncertainty, and hence their immersion in the condensed temporality of the present can be even greater. For many, living with such consequences is inescapable and, often, paralyzingly anxious.

So far, such anxiety has loomed in the background of my discussions of today's precarious and disoriented political subject, manifest across all aspects of the everyday life of *homo speculans*, from labor and housing precarity to a crisis of social reproduction. Indeed, as Mark Fisher (2009) tirelessly argued, there can be no understanding of contemporary anxiety's proliferation without a critical investigation of its social and political causes. Capitalist anxiety diminishes societies' horizons of possibility, often stoking a calamitous skepticism toward democracy and cementing the ascendancy of authoritarian populism. But can the condition of anxiety also become a source for a still inchoate yet more radical collective resistance? My joint work with Max Haiven (Haiven and Komporozos-Athanasiou 2019) has challenged universal narratives of passive acquiescence in the face of such foreclosed possibilities. In our recent studies of the so-called anxiety epidemic in UK and North American university campuses, for instance, we found hints of more generative politics that may appear unfamiliar (taking the form of retreat, ambivalence, disengagement, and practices of uncoordinated refusal) but contain a counter-speculative potential. Students today are just as capable of knowingly undermining their universities' technocratic management systems (for instance, by tactically using "extenuating-circumstances" forms to disrupt the bureaucratic administration of "student support services"), as they are of more overt political organizing such as protests and sit-ins. Simply put, speculative communities can be sites of anxious solidarities, formed around unseen and often "unseeable" struggles that cannot be answered under the guise of individual psychology. They often unfold in the darker corners of speculative technologies—in Instagram posts and Facebook comment threads, where students' anxiety reverberates but at the same time also blends with irony, playfulness, and routine expressions of mutual aid, care, and fellowship.[30]

I have emphasized that our fuzzy navigations of speculative technologies create bonds within ephemeral digital spaces through rituals that are not necessarily a "symptom" of anxiety but can be a way of countering it as a pathologized individual condition. Such rituals thus diverge from the self-destructive nihilism epitomized by the condition increasingly described as "doom scrolling" condemning people to vicious circles of narcissism and negativity. In their most radical forms, "doom scrolls" can deliberately channel such negativity against the perpetrators who have inflicted precarity in the first place—moving from self-sabotage to collective acts of political sabotage, aimed at revealing anxiety's systemic causes.

I have also argued, moreover, that such ritual navigations of uncertainty contain enjoyment too. Although an abundance of psychoanalytic readings of such "anxious enjoyment" is undoubtedly in store, I would like to consider here a sociological interpretation through the concept of counter-speculations. From TikTok's slapstick humor and Instagram's animated memes to Tinder's "it's a match!" moments and Co-Star's mischievous riddles, the uncertain routines of our everyday life offer more than just consolation or distraction from (or denial of) our fears of the unknown. The avoidance of discomfort has been a hallmark of consumer culture, configured by a short-term convenience economy, but such digital routines do not bode well for carefree acquiescence. The experience is captured beautifully by Silvia Federici (2020, 127), who, in ruminating on a very similar feeling of "joy" in the present moment, describes an "active passion" that doesn't convey "satisfaction with things as they are." To quote a passage from her recent book *Beyond the Periphery of the Skin*: "It is feeling our powers, seeing our capacities growing in ourselves and in the people around us. . . . It means . . . that we understand the situation we are in and are moving along in accordance to what is required of us *in that moment*. So, we feel that we have the power to change and that we are changing, together with other people. *It's not acquiescence to what exists*" (127).[31] I find Federici's view especially evocative of what unites the disparate examples of counter-speculation I have discussed in this chapter: political practices that contain no finite lessons for where to move toward yet nevertheless represent important ways of dwelling collectively (and consciously) with the unknown.

▲

In chapter 2, I proposed that all work toward collective autonomy demands of capitalism's anxious subjects to act both as diligent insurers and adventurous speculators, to recognize the inevitability of failed promises and live with life's many broken contracts. What makes our time's counter-speculations distinct from the broader speculative politics currently on the march is their unwillingness to simply replace one external broken promise with another. As Ann Mische (2014) has astutely argued, imagining the future has always vexed sociologists because imaginings ultimately exist "in our heads." In her own work, Mische has looked for "proxies" to trace more radical re-imaginings in contemporary social movements, different "externalizations in text, talk, and material objects, which make them accessible to empirical study" (438). They can be found in what she calls "hyperprojective" settings: communicative spaces such as Rio de Janeiro's 2012 People's Summit, where participants brought their "fragmentary, semi-submerged narratives to the level of reflective consciousness" (448) with the aim of projecting more radical and sustainable futures.

The spaces of counter-speculation I have sought to chart in this chapter display few such "externalizations." Most importantly, their defining features are not discursive articulations in the traditional sense of public debate. Rather, I traced them in a more heterogeneous mix of political gestures that blended voting and prefigurative activism with the effervescence of swipes, scrolls, and posts. Nor did such gestures' potential necessarily emerge in acts of slowing down to cultivate a discursive space like that of traditional liberalism. Radical movements—such as BLM's ongoing campaigns against anti-Black racism and state-sanctioned violence—often work in the margins of mainstream political space before a full-scale eruption.

My analysis, however, also calls attention to the margins of temporality from which such eruptions emanate. Even when they take recognizable political forms, counter-speculations are sensitive to the uncertainties and frictions entrenched in all manner of political protest, votes, or referenda, preserving an element of conflict that is often lost in deliberative forums. Importantly, just as with the speculative socialities and intimacies I examined in part 2 of this book, counter-speculations are never mere binary choices—a single left or right swipe—but rather a way of investing in doubt's openness. Louise Amoore's (2020) important work has revealed that, in our algorithmic techno-world such uncertain openness can be found in the "excess" of the code's 1-0 binary output by paying closer attention to "the moment of writing" that leads to any such output. It is there, in the code's if-then conditionality, where moments of nonclosure reside, "where the making of a threshold of marginality is a necessary condition of the meaning of the dominant output" (Amoore 2020, 105).[32] This, as I hope to have demonstrated, is just as true for speculative communities' virtual swipes as it is for our navigations of the binaries with which we are presented in today's politics.

In our radically uncertain and financialized times, Walter Benjamin's (1969) assertion rings perhaps truer than ever before: we are surrounded by the debris of the past and the obscurity of the future. Counter-speculations work as a homeopathic strategy, a cure for finance's deleterious speculation on our lives, the placement of small everyday stakes on more equitable futures. We administer small doses of speculation to give speculators a taste of their own medicine and thus speak directly to the clouded future in front of us—even if we can only see it from the corners of our vision.

CONCLUSIONS

*To think is not to get out of the cave; it is not to
replace the uncertainty of shadows by the clear-cut outlines of
things themselves, the flame's flickering glow by the light of the true
sun. To think is to enter the labyrinth; more exactly, it is to make be
and appear a labyrinth when we might have stayed "lying among
the flowers, facing the sky." It is to lose oneself amidst galleries
which exist only because we never tire of digging them; to turn
round and round at the end of a cul-de-sac whose entrance has
been shut off behind us—until, inexplicably, this spinning round
opens up in the surrounding walls cracks which offer passage.*

CORNELIUS CASTORIADIS,
CROSSROADS IN THE LABYRINTH

*I am in a labyrinth. A labyrinth, not a maze: I hadn't really
thought about the difference before, but it has become clear.
A labyrinth's winding paths lead, finally, to the meaningful center.
A maze, in contrast, is full of cul-de-sacs, dead ends, false signals;
a maze is the trickster God's domain.*

TEJU COLE, *EVERY DAY IS FOR THE THIEF*

This book has argued that as a haze of uncertainty engulfs global economies, the speculative spirit of financial markets is no longer confined to
the obscure dealings of hedge funds, equity firms, and derivatives traders.
Speculation has become the very practice around which modern societies
coalesce, the vernacular through which we express our collective disbelief
in the waning legitimacy of neoliberalism. By bringing these social practices to the fore of my analysis, I have sought to open up the black box of
financialization and show how finance percolates through our everyday
lives in uneven and contradictory ways. A core argument of the book has
been that, contrary to popular narratives, finance's dominance arises not

only from the subordination of our collective values to market rational-ity. If finance reigns supreme today, it is thanks to the generative power of its unique speculative imagination: its unswerving capacity to draw profit from the unknown and in so doing to forge unexpected connections in so-ciety at large.

The book has traced a key historical shift—from neoliberal capitalism's totemic *homo economicus* to a more socially embedded *homo speculans*—to demonstrate this pivotal, if elusive, role of the speculative imagination. Speculative communities, I contend, are not the sum of individual gam-blers and opportunists. Beneath individual struggles for survival in the face of growing insecurity, collective imaginations shape our shared wagers on the future.

Such imaginations are critical if we are to understand contemporary shifts in the course of politics and the constitution of the public sphere. Rather than arising from rational calculations, today's vexed political con-flicts emerge out of an impatience with the promises of contemporary capi-talism. Grounded on speculations of other futures, movements from Left to Right break the mold of historically "rational" forms of politics (such as the politics of parties and bureaucracies) and rely heavily on the promises of speculation as a way of creating communities and building support. This is not the Habermassian public sphere of consensus politics, nor is it a bar-ren space of irrationality and delusion. Against these commonplace views, I have sought to dispel flippant dismissals of crowds and publics as dupes of neoliberalism's ideological capture. I have suggested that this incipient political domain is in fact grounded in institutions like finance—despite our intuitive understanding of those institutions as antagonistic to grass-roots political movements.

Finance, then, seems to tear up the familiar script of political and social life. Yet, as the insights I have marshaled throughout the book reveal, even if modern social relations are more loosely scripted than before, they are not altogether eroded. In *Imagined Communities*, Benedict Anderson (1991) envisaged collectivities that were conjured "in the turn of the page"—in the ceremonial reading of a narrative novel or a morning newspaper. Today, finance venerates the instantaneous, calling forth a more transitory social reality marked by immersive rituals of scrolling and swiping. Speculative communities are formed in these rituals, which are social inasmuch as they connect us into a set of shared symbols and values. But what is distinc-tive about them is that, unlike Anderson's imagined communities, they are built on more ambiguous and ambivalent forms of belonging. The stream of distorted and opaque images reflects our own convoluted experiences: a dizzying spectacle that feels oddly intimate. In this way, image-hungry technologies like Instagram and Tinder become the mystical devices of our shared entanglement with pervasive uncertainty—our way of orienting ourselves within a fragmented world. Imagined in this state of flux, speculative communities are fluid social constellations that do not always cluster along traditional lines of class. Their boundaries are defined more tentatively by the twin practices of speculation and insurance, which set in motion an open-ended dialectic between real and imagined futures. This dialectic undergirds the contradictory collective wagers of today's politics—whether the swelling currents of evangelical populism and the rising "fake news" conspiracies or the abstruse gossip of online meme culture and the sabotage practices of fandom communities.

In the wake of capitalism's current crisis, the novel coronavirus pandemic, peculiar alliances have been fashioned through the uncanny speculative politics I examined in chapters 5 and 6. For instance, the anti-lockdown demonstrations that rocked the world's cities during the pandemic's second wave saw neonationalists and QAnon conspiracists marching alongside rainbow-flag-carrying identitarians, yoga enthusiasts, and even "pro-Enlightenment" libertarians. My intention has been to show that these groups are molded neither through a shared belief in a consistent promise (such as the nostalgic return to an idealized past) nor through an appeal to an image of a "new order." A bizarre tapestry of images of the future—blending together outlandish conspiracy and Enlightenment rationality—orients these actions. It offers respite in a world where promises of a better future are all but silenced.

Still, gender, race, and class inequalities continue to structure those ostensibly disparate collectives. Predictive algorithms and surveillance technologies compound the hypervisibility of racialized groups, making them more vulnerable to forms of police and extremist violence (anti-lockdown protesters in the United States and Europe have been overwhelmingly white, while people of color have suffered disproportionally from the pandemic's devastating impact). Sexual and gender minorities remain broadly excluded from idealized images of community circulating on smartphone screens and in populist discourse alike. But, as I have contended, structural injustice now also cleaves speculative communities in subtler ways, affecting their ability to reap the benefits of more emancipatory political wagers. Most markedly, it does so through invalidating lay modes of "strategic ignorance" that challenge hierarchical power and by conditioning their differential access to resources (capital, time, and technologies) needed for successfully hedging uncertainty.

Yet more radical possibilities emerge from the cracks of capitalism's failed promises. As I argued in chapter 6, such possibilities inhere in the politics of counter-speculation, mobilized when those most subjected to speculative violence (women and racialized and queer people) form their own subversive ways of inhabiting uncertainty collectively. What distinguishes such politics is that it doesn't merely exploit an existing crisis but seeks to cultivate more consciously the specific conditions of confusion and volatility in which a new generation of capitalist subjects has come of age. Certainly, as Miranda Joseph (2002) has argued so well, we must remain alert here to the risks of fetishizing community through universal framings that adhere either to celebratory discourses of a unitary identity or to empty celebrations of heterogeneity. New subaltern solidarities such as those between anxious students, K-poppers, and the Black Lives Matter movement or the unwieldy alliances between climate-change activists and the rural anti-fuel-tax movement, make no claims to the "commons" of a fabled past (from which traditionally marginalized social groups were excluded). In that sense, counter-speculative movements are not just symptomatic of our moment of flux but also constitutive of it.

The question that arises, then, is whether such movements merely write another page in capitalism's manual or are actually turning the page to a new chapter altogether. How do we avoid reproducing the system these movements seek to undermine and sabotage? How can the circularity of the new rituals, as it were, be opened up (Bottici 2007)? Any effectual critique of finance cannot avoid facing this normative question. For my own part, I have attempted to move beyond a pessimism that bears the marks of Boltanski and Chiapello's (2018) hugely influential critique in *The New Spirit of Capitalism*: a view that centers on late capitalism's parasitic power to feed on counter-imaginaries and to thus integrate them into the existing social order ad infinitum. I have offered a different reading of what is typically framed as a crisis of capitalism, contending that our current state of suspense challenges the often-cited Gramscian "interregnum thesis" that the old is dead and the new cannot be born. There is no deceased *homo politicus* to be revived, but a world of immanent possibilities in the politics of *homo speculans*. I have thus aimed to unveil a mode of critique that is *already here*, in present practices of resistance that do not shy away from the darkness by wishing uncertainty away. Such critique nibbles at the edges of a confusing world that cannot be straightened out, and—why not?—widens the distortions and illegibilities of this—our own—world.

Let me dwell on this final point, by way of conclusion. In recent years there has been a striking insistence, across the mainstream ideological spectrum, on "exposing" the lies infesting political life the world over. Just as "fake news" became a shorthand for stoking the flames of global right-wing populism, a noble defense of "truth" emerged as liberal politics' foremost project. The latter laments conspiracy, misinformation, and lies for their corrosive effect on democracy's fraying fabric and individuals' capacity for reasoning. For some, this effect extends even into social and intimate lives beset by "phony friendships" and virtual sex. Under this logic, we are asked to think of the current political conflict as an "epistemological crisis."[1] Joe Biden's pyrrhic victory in the 2020 US presidential election (which saw Trump increase his support base in much of rural and suburban America) was presented overwhelmingly as a "win for truth" in the war against "lies" and conspiracy. Such a victory seems to offer a return to normal, even if—given the pandemic—this will be a new normal.

However, the political tumult of recent years serves as a warning against these framings. Much as Trump's electoral defeat is a welcome development, it is not in itself sufficient to taper the grassroots appeal of the speculative politics that catapulted Trumpism to power in 2016.[2] As I have argued throughout this book, dominant political rationalities are themselves underwritten by falsehoods and are steeped in fiction—from the Washington Consensus and the Deficit Myth to the American Dream and There Is No Alternative.[3] States of unreality do not originate within conspiracy; it is in finance itself, capitalism's crown jewel, where they express themselves with the most force. Reality and fiction are imbricated within speculative communities; fighting to untangle them can become a futile distraction from the perennial struggle for more democratic and autonomous ways of living. Instead, we must engage the recondite fictions of our time with the same resolve as if we were entering a labyrinth. Faced with repeated crossroads, we cannot know in advance whether they will lead us to an exit, but that does not mean we wander in vain. The labyrinth's pathways may be puzzling, but they are the outcome of our own digging; their twists and turns are not the whims of "a trickster," to use Teju Cole's words. By digging the proverbial labyrinth, speculative communities give form to chaos and create a world that allows them to endure collectively the vicissitudes of financialized everyday life.

Finance has shaped our very ability to create narratives, paving the way for new communal inhabitations of the unknown. How will this terrain shift in the years to come? Which routes of counter-speculation might give rise to more radical redistributions of responsibility and greater collective autonomy? Will speculative communities coagulate around the symbolic insurance offered by regressive nationalism as they did during the tumultuous 2010s? Or will they experiment with new forms of social and symbolic capital such as those gained in practices of sabotage and counter-conspiracy? What leaps of faith will counter-speculation require, and which leaps into the future will they initiate? I have argued throughout that we navigate our spectacle society by dwelling in speculative communities. They enable us to "move" toward the undetermined—that is, "somewhere" not yet defined. But move we do. As we step forward into the unknown, our speculative imagination no longer settles for visions of certitude in response to the uncertainty perching at the core of our everyday lives. Speculative communities are here to stay. How equitably their powers are wielded and to what ends will define our collective responses to the crises yet to come.

ACKNOWLEDGMENTS

This book would not have been possible without the many colleagues and friends who supported it from its inception in distinct ways. My ongoing collaboration and friendship with Chiara Bottici and Max Haiven provided continuing intellectual inspiration, and their brilliant work has been a stepping-stone for my own forays into the speculative imagination. They both read extensive parts of the manuscript and pushed me to move beyond my comfort zones without losing sight of the "bigger questions." I am particularly indebted to Jens Beckert for believing in the project from the start, and for his deep engagement with the book's arguments over the years I worked on the manuscript. I am thankful to Juan Pablo Pardo-Guerra, one of the readers for the University of Chicago Press, for offering insightful comments that helped me anchor my analysis more firmly on important debates in the social studies of finance.

I am deeply grateful to all the wonderful scholars and writers who were kind enough to read and comment on chapters of the book when I asked them to (sometimes on very short notice!). Melinda Cooper has been an invaluable interlocutor throughout and made crucial suggestions for my framing of key contributions, especially in chapter 5. Kristian Bondo pointed me to important works on the history of speculation, which greatly benefited my analysis in chapters 1 and 2. Ahmed Dailami cast a keen eye on various chapters, sharing with me his in-depth historical expertise. Ed Kiely's attentive reading of the manuscript and his thoughtful input were vital in tying together some of the loose ends of my argument. I am also grateful to Julia Ott for her insightful comments on chapter 2, which were especially helpful in historicizing my discussion of speculation in the United States.

Tom Geue was the godfather of my *homo speculans* and my most precious editorial genie, always there when his help was needed. His expeditions into the ghostly anonymity of Latin literature loomed in the background of my own ruminations on the queasiness of capitalism's unknowns.

Michał Murawski was one of the first people to read the embryonic ideas in my book proposal, offering me vital advice for moving forward. My framing of the "real fake" of speculative communities was crystallized partly thanks to his remarks on the book's final chapters. Marc Aziz Michael was an important early reader of the manuscript, encouraging me to explore more systematically the double entendre of speculation and insurance, as well as to engage the work of Polanyi in greater depth. I finally owe a special thanks to Alina Kolar, my most kindred soul, for lending some of her own art-critic imagination to key parts of chapter 3.

I couldn't have wished for better co-panelists and interlocutors on the various occasions when I presented the book's arguments—I want to thank in particular Arjun Appadurai, Jean-Phillipe Bouilloud, Benjamin Bratton, James Bridle, Judith Butler, Nancy Fraser, Rahel Jaeggi, Julia Ott, and Jamieson Webster for all the stimulating conversations, suggestions, and critiques. For responses and thoughts, I am grateful to audiences at the New School for Social Research, Sciences-Po Paris, Panteion University of Social and Political Science, Copenhagen Business School, ESCP Paris, Université Paris Diderot, City University of London, Birkbeck School of Law, and the University College London Institute of Advanced Studies, as well as the annual conferences of the American Sociological Association, the Society for the Advancement of Socio-Economics, and the meetings of the Finance and Society Network. I treasure the engaging discussions of the book's arguments with art students and artists at talks I gave between 2017 and 2019 at the Slade School of Fine Art, the European Art Biennial "Manifesta," and the Ural Industrial Biennale of Yekaterinburg in Russia.

I am also grateful to those who opened their homes for me to write during the summers of 2019 and 2020. Key parts of the manuscript were written in the outskirts of Alicante on the Costa Bianca, in Saltaro at the Stockholm Archipelago, and on the Greek island of Aegina. My deepest thanks go to Carlos Cueva, Tora Färnström, and Alexia Liakounakou for their generous hospitality. The sun's light in each of these beautiful places shone through the mist that sometimes clouded my writing. During the 2020 lockdowns, and while University College London was closed, Sandy Oliver generously offered me office space in her London flat when I most needed it. A very special moment in the course of writing this book was when, in February 2019, Zoé Castoriadis kindly opened the doors to her Paris flat allowing me to peer through Cornelius Castoriadis's own annotated copies of Weber's *Economy and Society*.

Last, I want to thank my editors at the University of Chicago Press. Priya Nelson believed in the project from the start and championed it at its earliest stages when it was still a loosely formed idea, taking time to work closely with me on improving the text's style in interim drafts. Elizabeth

Branch Dyson stewarded the book dexterously through its final phase ensuring a smooth publication process, and Mollie McFee offered brilliant editorial support throughout. Any errors are of course my own.

Unpayable debt is due to my parents, Giorgos Komporozos and Eleni Athanasiou, without whom my own tentative wagers would have been impossible to place.

NOTES

INTRODUCTION

1. As Bottici (2007) demonstrates, narratives and myths are inherently linked, especially in the sphere of politics: "Political myths are narratives that coagulate and reproduce significance. They consist of the work on a common narrative by which the members of a social group or society represent and posit their experience and deeds. As such, they are an important part of what, following Castoriadis, can be called the social imaginary" (201).

2. See for instance, the *Atlantic*'s March 2020 special edition on "disinformation wars," which describes the 2020 presidential election as "a referendum on reality itself." https://www.theatlantic.com/magazine/archive/2020/03/the-2020-disinformation-war/605530/.

3. Since the 1970s, dozens of important works in economic sociology have examined these entanglements; latterly in the bourgeoning field of social studies of finance. A cursory and far from exhaustive list includes cultural theorists Randy Martin and Max Haiven; anthropologists Arjun Appadurai, Laura Bear, Karen Ho, Edward LiPuma, Caitlin Zaloom; sociologists Jens Beckert, Christian Borch, Greta Krippner, Juan Pablo Pardo-Guerra, Alex Preda, Sarah Quinn, and Viviana Zelizer; and philosophers Michel Feher, Joseph Vogl, and Franco Berardi.

4. Recently, there have been important critical studies of finance that challenge the fallacious separation of real and material economy and make illuminating inroads into the tenuous yet important sociality of finance, most influential among which the work of de Goede (2005) and Appadurai (2016). Such work has tended to consider finance primarily as a discursive domain, focusing on its "textual nature" and the power of its language (following Judith Butler's [2019] core insights of performativity), mapping the discursive constitution of finance's "material practices," prices, costs, and capital. Correspondingly, both limitations and conditions of possibility in finance (however contingent) are often located within discursive domains.

5. Harvard political philosopher Michael Sandel (2013), for instance, has recently proposed precisely such an argument.

6. For an in-depth review of financialization as an economic, social, and political phenomenon with multiple facets and corresponding interpretations, see van der Zwan (2014).

7. The violence of this bloody history was immortalized by Hobbes's (2017 [1651]) depiction of money as "the blood stream" of the nation-state's body politic.

8. As variously traced by different observers' accounts, the history of speculation goes all the way back to ancient Mesopotamia or, closer to its modern financial form (in the sense of stock trading) to medieval Europe. The 1637 tulip mania in the Netherlands is typically cited as the first occasion of a speculative bubble (de Marchi and Harrison 1994; also see de Goede 2005).

9. This period corresponds to Giovanni Arrighi's (2009) cataloguing of the shift from the British to the US regime of capitalist hegemony.

10. Correspondingly, much of my discussion takes the United States and the United Kingdom as its main geographical focus. However, the emergence of speculative communities speaks to a broader set of recent social and political developments around the world—most salient among them the pact between speculative finance and nationalist neopopulism in major economies of both the Global North and the Global South and the global proliferation of speculative technologies in everyday life (as demonstrated by the meteoric rise of digital apps like TikTok, Instagram, and Tinder throughout non-Western contexts).

11. See, for instance, Pomerantsev (2017).

CHAPTER ONE

1. Weber (2000 [1894], 333) describes the small speculator as a "superfluous parasite."

2. See Juhel and Dufour (2010) for a detailed discussion of Proudhon's theoretical engagement with speculation.

3. Although latterly, from a distance of over a decade since the 2008 meltdown, some fictionalized accounts of speculation appear more attentive to its complexities and nuances. Sam Mendes's hugely successful *Lehman Trilogy* play (produced in 2018 by the United Kingdom's National Theatre) offers one such somber study of the speculative imagination driving the journey of Lehman Brothers from its apogee through to its collapse. In the words of the *Financial Times* review, "Rather than greedy criminals, bankers ultimately emerge here as highly-strung obsessives in thrall to mercurial, systemic forces beyond their control." https://www.ft.com/content /ee06bc5a-521111e9-8f44-fe4a86c48b33.

4. Zeckhauser (2014, 8–9) calls for more systematic economic research into uncertainty, rather than risk: "Economists now understand that risk is a terrific subject for gamblers, for students in high school math, and for insurance companies having data that enable them to predict the probabilities of micro-outcomes with reasonable reliability. But for investors, business folks, government officials, physicians, international diplomats, those in romantic pursuit, and parents of young children, indeed for almost anybody else, risk is an intriguing subject that bears little relation to the real decisions they face. Unknown outcomes confront these players every day, and the probabilities are virtually never known nor knowable. Uncertainty, not risk, is the difficulty regularly before us. That is, we can identify the states of the world, but not their probabilities."

5. For a detailed discussion of this court case, which was particularly significant in the history of regulating speculative activities see Fabian (1999).

6. Appadurai (2016) proposes that this operation of derivatives is unique because it does not merely reflect but also produces the contingencies characterizing modern contracts, relations, and promises traded—and ultimately value itself. It does so through providing "a continuous and reliable source of collective effervescence through which the valuation of underlying assets can be enhanced and leveraged" (99).

7. Or they will look for leverageable volatility elsewhere—the famously volatile cryptocurrency markets, for instance, which saw a surge of speculative investment during their bubble moment in 2018, just as high-frequency trading appeared to plateau. Deutsche Bank demonstrated a direct correlation between VIX (the volatility index) and cryptocurrency prices (as volatility in traditional assets drops, the price of bitcoin and other mainstream cryptocurrencies rises). See: https://www.insider.com/bitcoin-price-wall-street-volatility-index-correlation-deutsche-bank-2018-1.

8. "Warren Buffet on Derivatives," edited excerpts from the Berkshire Hathaway annual report for 2002, can be found here: http://www.fintools.com/docs/Warren%20Buffet%20on%20Derivatives.pdf.

9. He expressed this alarm in an interview with Gillian Tett in the *Financial Times*, August 18, 2018, https://app.ft.com/content/0e20f113-f559-4f8e-85b3-6773e96c75b0. Greenspan's fame outside the banking world has been achieved partly thanks to his famous Delphic interventions, which often had the explicit intention to confuse rather than to illuminate—a practice that, as we will see over the course of this book, has become endemic in modern speculative communities.

10. I unpack *hedging* as a key constitutive dimension of speculation in part 3, where I discuss how myths, mutual dependencies, and ideals of security become sources of symbolic and political insurance within speculative communities.

11. The image is perhaps most memorably evoked in Robert Harris's (2012) novel *The Fear Index*, to which I return in chapter 3. Caitlin Zaloom (2006, 177) draws the outlines of this "new variant of economic man" of the early digital trading era, who represents a "newer affective order, more distant from direct competition, more reflective, and quieter."

12. For a detailed discussion of the incongruences of these approaches, see Kotsko (2018).

13. Brown's view, as I show in subsequent chapters, has been critiqued from a variety of perspectives. Amin Samman (2019), for instance, argues that the eclipse of the *homo politicus* by *homo economicus* in Brown's Foucauldian analysis of neoliberalism misses the important noneconomic structuring of "timescapes": "the narrative logic of historical reason" that "works away at the margins or in the background of other discourses, providing a sense of antecedent, trajectory, and possibility that would otherwise be missing from a purely economic or financial perspective" (9).

14. I am grateful to Arjun Appadurai for this point, which he made during our workshop discussion at the New School of Social Research in February 2019.

15. In subsequent chapters, I deepen the analysis of this contradiction in Weber's discussions of speculation.

16. Konings (2015, 254) puts it thus: "a faith that does not idly hope for magic but assumes personal responsibility for ensuring the transformation of fictions into facts. Such austerity itself takes the form of speculation: it involves a willingness to gear the creation of new symbolic forms to the validation of past promises."

17. A consensus that seemed altogether scrapped in the wake of the multitrillion emergency credit released by major economies to address the global pandemic crisis in 2020.

18. Stimilli (2017) writes about asceticism as a paradoxical form called into play in contemporary capitalist forms of power. As she argues, the premise that accumulation and profit are no longer retraceable to renunciation (that is, to the ability to delay the gratification of needs and desires for the sake of the accumulation of wealth) is contrary

to Weber's analysis, which is in line with the sacrificial paradigm. Instead, Stimilli claims that accumulation and profit are in fact traceable to the compulsive drive to enjoy and consume and hence that there is no ascetic practice lurking in the background.

19. The interlock between particular educational and administrative pilgrimages provided the territorial base for new imagined communities in which natives could come to see themselves as nationals (Calhoun 1991, 140).

20. Here Anderson is quoting Walter Benjamin (1969, 263).

21. Anderson did not examine the content and style of the first widely read printed novels in detail but focused instead on their mediating role (through narrative form) in vernacularizing social connectivity. Speculative technologies, too, do not belong exclusively to the domain of the digital. Today, the world of narrative fiction and the contemporary novel may not be as central in the mediation of such connectivity, but a distinctly speculative genre of narrative fiction captures powerfully the radical uncertainty of our contemporary moment. Ben Lerner, whose writing is considered emblematic of this style, returns obsessively to the image of "double representation" in all three of his novels, while this is also a central question in the extremely popular biographical fiction of Karl Ove Knausgård.

22. I reprise these discussions in part 2, where I unpack in detail the role of speculative technologies in the constitution of social and intimate relations through digital commodities.

23. Anderson (1991, 23–24n5).

24. Anderson (1991, 47) gives the following definition of Creole people in the Americas: "1. Creole (Criollo)—person of (at least theoretically) pure European descent but born in the Americas (and, by later extension, anywhere outside Europe)."

25. Part 3 of this book examines in detail the implications of *Imagined Communities* for studying today's populist movements, taking the Tea Party and the Brexiteers as exemplar case studies.

26. The constitution of the "narrative readership" of speculative communities is an issue I discuss at length in the following chapters. While key technologies of connectivity mentioned here emerged on liberal university campuses, recent studies show a demographic spread of users that has expanded exponentially beyond the white millennials of urban and metropolitan areas, spanning a wide range of geographical areas and age groups.

27. Importantly, Anderson (1991) does not use the concept of imagined communities merely to speak of the originary "nationness" of the Creole and Indonesian insurrectionaries but also to discuss the rise of nationalism in the core European states during the second half of the nineteenth century, as well as the last wave of the post–World War II period. The concept of imagined communities is thus historically relevant.

28. The passage from *Imagined Communities* outlining these three elements reads "What, in a positive sense, made the new communities imaginable was a half-fortuitous, but explosive, interaction between a system of production and productive relations (capitalism), a technology of communications (print), and the fatality of human linguistic diversity" (Anderson 1991, 41–42).

CHAPTER TWO

1. Poem written in 1926 by Florence Sherman, secretary at the Chicago Mercantile Exchange. Cited in E. Harris (1970).

2. See, for instance, Agamben (1993).

3. I use the term *genealogy* in the Nietzschean sense: not as an attempt to reconstruct the history of the concept but to form a critique of key debates about the speculative imagination and their presuppositions (also see Bottici 2007, 10).

4. Although people's minds would more naturally go to New York City's Wall Street as the main stage of global financial history, Chicago's unique futures and derivatives markets have long attracted sociological interest, with several important studies published in the last two decades. See, for instance, Hochfelder (2006), Zaloom (2006), and MacKenzie and Millo (2003).

5. Fabian (1999), cited in Sapien (2009, 412), traces the origins of the term "bucket shops" in 1820's England, "where the urban poor gathered to drink dregs of beer which had been collected in buckets from larger saloons." As the Chicago Board of Trade's official historian Charles Taylor noted in 1917, initially at least, bucket shops "were not viewed with particular alarm" but regarded as "a sort of democratized Board of Trade, where the common people could speculate."

6. Hochfelder (2006, 345) captures vividly the great pace of bucket-shop growth during that time: "In 1887 CBT president Abner Wright resorted to drastic measures to prevent bucket shops from obtaining the board's quotations because he estimated that such shops accounted for 80 percent of the speculative business derived from broadcast quotations. In 1889 the New York Times estimated that the patrons of the nation's bucket shops wagered the equivalent of a million shares a day. By way of comparison, the average daily volume on the New York Stock Exchange in June 1888 was roughly 140,000 shares."

7. De Goede (2005) and Fabian (1999) offer the most detailed accounts of this historical conflict about the moral legitimacy of speculation and gambling that I am aware of. De Goede's approach provides important insights into the discursive means by which the former dominated over the latter. However, it does not consider the underlying imaginations driving the opposing moral arguments, nor the role of political speculation among the emerging constituencies of farmers and agrarian Populists during that time. Fabian also sketches a rich history of slave labor, racial violence, and class politics as key aspects of the legitimacy conflicts leading to the ascendancy of speculative capitalism. For both scholars, these dramatic conflicts herald the dominance, legitimation, and dissemination of the twentieth century's "economic rationality." For a more detailed critique of Fabian's undue emphasis on the assumed pervasiveness of "'economic rationality" in her study, see Masur (1991).

8. This formulation offered legitimacy not only to formal speculative markets in the United States but also in Europe.

9. Cornelius Torp, "Speculation and Gambling in Germany and Britain around 1900," seminar given at the German Historical Institute, London, March 11, 2020.

10. It is beyond the scope of my account to provide a detailed review of crowd theories and their pivotal role in the study of markets, but interested readers can consult the comprehensive accounts of scholars such as Borch (2012, 2020), Preda (2009) and Stäheli (2013).

11. There are numerous—and often contradictory—historical accounts of the nineteenth-century US Populist movement, which foreground different interpretations of the "nature of Populism." James Turner, whom I cite here, provides a comprehensive review of those accounts, including major historical works such as John D. Hicks's *The Populist Revolt* (1931) and Richard Hofstadter's *The Age of Reform* (1956).

Postel's (2007) own influential study finds significant controversy among historians in the account of the Populist record on race matters in particular—with a clear division across the South and the North memberships of the Party. Gerteis and Goolsby (2005) note that while Populists "were known for their demands for the inclusion of black voters into their political coalition" and "figures such as Georgia's Tom Watson risked (and lost) a great deal in order to build a biracial coalition," at the same time, the movement "was distinctly xenophobic in many respects, and despite the largely sincere attempt to build a political coalition of black and white members, most Southern white Populists remained avowed racists" (205). Beyond these important issues, it is undeniable that the populist movement significantly influenced debates about the relationship between publics and markets during the speculation wars I focus on here.

12. Similar developments are observed in the European centers of financial speculation at the time, including London, Berlin, Paris, Le Havre, and Bremen.

13. Preda (2009) demonstrates how the pervasiveness of speculation in the social realm works to challenge but also to cement "order." He analyses a wealth of sources from that era, from political and financial speeches to Zola's *L'Argent* (1891) to unpack links between speculation and social mobility, foresight and progress, and peace-but also wild adventure. Speculation, he argues, was seen as a "civilising factor and untamed natural force at the same time" (179).

14. Quinn's (2019) masterful historical account of post–New Deal US credit markets demonstrates that governments systematically used credit as a policy tool with which to uphold racial hierarchies, most notably by defining inequality issues (from higher education to healthcare) as financial problems.

15. When looking beyond their own disciplinary boundaries, sociologists often castigate economists for their perseverating on the rationality principle (a nest of assumptions around rational choice theory, utility maximization, and market equilibrium). For a review—and cogent rebuttal—of these sociological critiques, see Beckert (2016).

16. Here I am interested in the ways finance appears to affect the capitalist imagination through the emerging dominance of the figure of the speculator. For a thorough historical analysis of speculation alone in the works of Smith, Hegel, Marx, and Weber, see Preda (2009).

17. In the original text, this social-collective framing of the imagination is indicated by the use of the word *Vorstellung* rather than *Einbildungskraft*, which is used by Kant and thus carries an (undesired by Marx) association with the individualist and idealist philosophical traditions.

18. Weber's view of capitalist rationality is less rigid than the iron cage metaphor implies. It is worth noting that the German term used by Weber (1992) was *stahlhartes Gehäuse*, rendered "iron cage" by Talcott Parsons in the first and most influential English translation. *Stahlhartes Gehäuse*, more accurately translated as "house made of steel," allows greater flexibility in the construction of capitalist bureaucracy, casting a prevalent rationality that is more codependent with its ensnared agents.

19. Cornwell (2007) notes that "sects offered an alternative to relying on a personal network made up mainly of kinship and friendship ties as a foundation for credit and investment" (276).

20. Weber considers rationality most notably in relation to technical control through calculative thinking, although there are texts where he "admits that the irrational element applies to every experience" (Sica 1988, 172). Thus, he is resistant to calling a

certain type of human action rational and another irrational: "The good question was not to ask: is this action rational . . . but rather to explore what is the rationality of this action" (Szelenyi 2016, 5). Weber ultimately appears aware of the possible return of reenchanting prophets and "a new magic" in the memorable final passage of *The Protestant Ethic*.

21. Kotsko (2018) shows powerfully how the aim of "saving the political," and keeping it open against the closing ranks of neoliberal rationality, has been undermined by the very deployment of this binary. His analysis leads us to question the practice of bifurcating the political and the economic (understood as "anti-political"), which constitutes the kernel of Polanyian critiques of neoliberalism. I examine this issue closely in chapter 5, but for now, I want to insist on the importance of reinstating the concept of *imagination* (as opposed to rationality) within political economy itself.

22. For a detailed discussion of Castoriadis's engagement with the works of Marx and Weber, see Arnason (2015).

23. For more in-depth reviews of Castoriadis's ontological framework of the imagination and its links to other important philosophical works, see Bottici (2014).

24. Castoriadis, as a practicing psychoanalyst, is interested in the process of self-understanding of the uncertain social subject—and this interest greatly influences the ways he seeks to overcome the limitations of traditional political economies. In his own words, a "reflective and deliberative subjectivity . . . is critically and lucidly open to the new; it does not repress the works of the imagination (one's own or that of others) but is capable of receiving them critically, of accepting them or rejecting them" (Castoriadis 1997b, 112).

25. Paul Ricoeur, in a series of lectures given at the University of Chicago in 1975 (the year Castoriadis's *Imaginary Institution of Society* was published), took a resonant view of Castoriadis's open dialectics. By emphasizing the ceaseless struggles between ideology and utopia in society, he proposed that a rich dialectic is always at play between conservative (represented by ideology) and radical (represented by utopia) forms of social imagination. See Ricoeur (1985).

CHAPTER THREE

1. For a detailed history of popular and artistic representations of finance, see Crosthwaite et al. (2014), and P. Knight (2016).

2. The *New Yorker*: https://www.newyorker.com/magazine/2019/09/30/how-tiktok-holds-our-attention. Also see Bridle's (2017) essay on the disturbing universe of algorithmically generated YouTube videos targeted at young children: https://medium.com/@jamesbridle/something-is-wrong-on-the-internet-c39c471271d2.

3. For a detailed review of the historical shift to the social media image that succeeded the networked image of the 2000s to become the new dominant cultural visual form of the 2010s, see Hochman (2014).

4. Detailed data of dating app use spread across regions in 2016 can be found here: https://medium.com/@sm_app_intel/conquer-love-with-these-crucial-dating-app-statistics-2870ec5493cd. For data on the overall growth trends of social media app adoption from urban to suburban and rural communities, see https://www.pewresearch.org/internet/2013/02/14/social-networking-site-users/ and https://www.pewresearch.org/internet/fact-sheet/social-media/.

5. The case of precipitous demise is evidenced, for instance, in the case of Snapchat.

6. Vogl (2014, 5) calls this a "euphoric alliance between information technology and finance capital," between Wall Street and Silicon Valley—an alliance that also has been documented by Frank Pasquale's (2015) influential *Black Box Society*.

7. The glass house metaphor captures this tension powerfully, in multiple ways. It functions as a greenhouse (offering comforting warmth) and as a magnifying glass (also coinciding thus with the meaning of *speculum*—the root word of speculation), combining the effects of transparency and reflection.

8. Bridle (2018) also describes the obscure ways in which Uber visualizes the movement of cars on users' phone screens, inserting "ghost cars" into the platform's map and deliberately distorting real car positions on the map to make it appear more responsive than it actually is.

9. See Birner and Ege (1999) for an exploration of Durkheim's influence on Hayek in particular. Contemporary dominant algorithmic imaginaries (e.g., Bucher 2018) have also been associated with Hayekian ideas of order and long-standing mythologies such as Adam Smith's invisible hand (Ziewitz 2016).

10. The predictive capacity afforded by such technologies is itself a form of speculation.

11. As critical reviewers of surveillance capitalism have remarked, while much debate centers on surveillance, too little is discussed about capitalism itself. For a critique expanding on this latter issue, see Morozov (2019).

12. Zuboff (2019) shows how such computational technologies are drawn in Silicon Valley as the driving force of a new field of competition and commodification: the market for the best predictions, which are the most powerful speculations. But even computational algorithms for modeling and predicting the future often fail because of the inherent unpredictability of human behavior. Arguably, the single greatest success of computational technologies has been their harnessing of the multilayered complexity that has enveloped all human activities.

13. See *Time* magazine: http://content.time.com/time/specials/packages/article /0,28804,2032304_2032745_2032850,00.html.

14. The fans' strength of attachment and identification with K-pop idols recalls the mode of "para-social interaction" between television performers and spectators that is discussed in Horton and Wohl's influential 1956 essay (see, for instance, Elfving-Hwang 2018). However, the kind of togetherness described here by Kim shows how intimate bonds also develop among fans themselves through what she calls the "liveliness" afforded by the digital social rituals of their (imagined) fandom community.

15. At the time of writing, the United States had announced plans to ban TikTok altogether as part of an escalated ongoing dispute with China, and India moved to ban the platform on June 29, 2020. See https://www.bbc.com/news/technology-53225720.

16. Wendy Brown (quoted in Callison and Manfredi 2020, 57), for instance, describes the pernicious role of new digital technologies: "technological platforms for 'communication' that enshrine ignorance and enable public invective."

17. Here is a longer description of what the stack consists of: "Today's political geographic conflicts are often defined as exceptions to that normal model, and many are driven, enabled, or enforced in significant measure by planetary computation: byzantine international and subnational bodies, a proliferation of enclaves and exclaves, non-contiguous states, diasporic nationalisms, global brand affiliations, wide-scale

demographic mobilization and containment, free trade corridors and special economic zones, massive file-sharing networks both legal and illegal, material and manufacturing logistical vectors, polar and subpolar resource appropriations, panoptic satellite platforms, alternative currencies, atavistic and irredentist religious imaginaries, cloud data and social-graph identity platforms, big data biopolitics of population medicine, equities markets held in place by an algorithmic arms race of supercomputational trading, deep cold wars over data aggregation across state and party lines, and so on" (Bratton 2015, 6).

18. Such political possibilities are the focus of my discussion of counter-speculations in chapter 6.

19. From the browser extension's website: http://trackmenot.io.

20. Of course, some of the most deleterious aspects of financialized spectacles can still be found in the sphere of material economy itself, for instance in real estate's harnessing of user-generated computational data (through tags, check-ins, and posts) to speculate on value, to drive urban restructuring, and to purge communities of their poorer inhabitants. See, for instance, https://failedarchitecture.com/the-extractive-growth-of-artificially-intelligent-real-estate/.

21. As Faucher (2018) notes, "Social media may appear to be heavily dominated by narcissistic behavior from a proliferation of selfies, the diligent archiving of the details of everyday life, the dogged pursuit of online social capital, and conspicuous acts of digital display—a digital form of narcissistic behavior watched over by the corporately owned networks of loving grace" (88). Other critics argue that a similarly narcissistic imperative drives the design of modern dating apps—see, for instance, https://www.theguardian.com/commentisfree/2018/may/03/tech-love-rightwing-game-facebook-dating-app.

22. Murawski (2020, 2021) explores the increasingly prominent use of what he called "the public selfie" in the context of new urban park developments in Russia and the United States. He argues that the public selfie is reflective of "the ongoing rise of a global paradigm of publicness and selfhood," and he discusses the example of High Line redevelopment in New York City as paradigmatic of a public space in which (acceptable forms of) spontaneity, performance, collective self-valorization, and scripted "wildness" are valued as exemplary characteristics of a new "dramaturgical flâneurship."

23. Astrological interest seemed to peak especially in the immediate aftermath of market crises and crashes.

24. As Crosthwaite et al. (2019) put it, "the 'real value' of chartist investment advice—and especially that of its two most renowned exponents—lies precisely in its close kinship with astrology and other branches of occult lore, if we understand that value as inhering not ultimately in a capacity to make profits trading stocks, but in entry into an intricate and enveloping system of privileged knowledge that provides an alluring alternative vision of the forces shaping the stock market and the world at large" (678). Economic forecasting as a practice of enlisting science to temper the future's uncertainty began in earnest during fin de siècle America and intensified in the wake of World War I, when statistical tools were used systematically to solve this ancient problem. For an excellent review of this history, see Friedman (2013).

25. For a detailed overview of financial astrology works of the time, see Cochrane (2017).

26. Pietruska (2017) notes that "state courts ruling on antidivination prosecutions by the 1910s disallowed predictions that made claims to certainty but permitted those that acknowledged their own indeterminacy, thereby constructing a new legal framework for fortune-telling that accepted uncertainty embedded in claims of occult foreknowledge" (201).

27. For detailed data on the astrology app market growth, see https://sensortower .com/blog/astrology-apps-2019-revenue-downloads. On the rising venture capitalist investment in astrology apps, see https://www.nytimes.com/2019/04/15/style/astrology -apps-venture-capital.html.

28. Julie Beck, "The New Age of Astrology," *Atlantic*, January 16, 2018, https://www .theatlantic.com/health/archive/2018/01/the-new-age-of-astrology/550034/.

29. See, for instance, https://www.nytimes.com/2020/05/09/style/coronavirus -astrology-predictions.html.

30. See https://www.wired.co.uk/article/astrology-apps-technology.

31. Statement taken from Twitter's official blog: https://blog.twitter.com/en_us /topics/product/2020/testing-new-conversation-settings.html.

CHAPTER FOUR

1. For some recent data on the uptake of dating apps in these countries, see https://www.economist.com/international/2020/05/09/casual-sex-is-out-com panionship-is-in.

2. Dating app users in the United States were projected to exceed 25 million in 2019, while the total size of online dating services was in excess of $3 billion in 2018. See https://www.businessinsider.com/dating-app-usage-growth-slowing-tinder-match -bumble-analysts-say-2019-6.

3. Tinder is part of the multibillion-dollar Match Group, which also owns apps like Hinge—the dating app whose global downloads more than tripled in 2019 after Democratic presidential candidate Pete Buttigieg's revelation that he met his future husband on it. However, unlike Tinder, Hinge has been established as a more elite app, operating only in specific urban zones, being more popular with white university graduates. For some relevant data, see https://www.vox.com/2015/3/19/8257357/hinge-explained.

4. The algorithms behind these movements are just as treasured a secret as those underpinning TikTok's recommended content. Introduced in the second stage of growth in the market by apps such as OkCupid, AI-based dating algorithms essentially took over control from users, learning from their preferences (as revealed during their swiping activities). Ironically, during their first years of growth, these computational tools were speculated to be versions of Gale-Shapley (also known as the stable marriage algorithm), which was supposed to yield stable matchings by identifying patterns of likes and swipes. But, as their emphasis shifts toward the present moment and the short-lived experience (rather than a future outcome), dating apps are now cautious to not replicate gaming principles on their platforms—famously, in 2019 Tinder dropped their use of the controversial "Elo Score," which ranked attractiveness of users when generating partner options.

5. Even the space of speculative intimacies has encompassed elements of nativism that resemble the use of ephemeral image boards and anonymous online forums such as 4chan. At the same time, dating apps like Righter and Donald Daters have been developed to cater exclusively to Tea Partiers, conservatives, and Trump supporters.

6. For Bauman, online dating was "liquid love" par excellence—that is, a relational manifestation of the social condition he termed "liquid modernity." I do not wish to present in detail Bauman's broader account of liquid modernity (the transformation from a modern to a liquid modern world), but it is important to note the association with the financialization thesis (a move from solid rational-bureaucratic values to an irrational, formless, and ambivalent social order) that are plain to see in his work. (On this, also see Best 2019.)

7. For a comprehensive critique of Giddens's theory of intimacy, see Jamieson (1998, 1999).

8. Illouz pointedly suggests these developments can be explained by "the epistemic imperialism of psychology in the emotional realm" (2019, 226).

9. Or consider Hinge's "most compatible" feature: outputs of the platform's recommendation algorithm that purports to match users that are more likely to be attracted to each other—but, importantly, these recommendations are inherently elusive, as they themselves disappear without a trace after twenty-four hours, exactly like an Instagram story or a fleet.

10. A slew of such dating shows include ITV's *Love Island* and Channel 4's *First Dates* in the United Kingdom and US-produced *Dating Around* and *Love Is Blind* on the online streaming service Netflix. The unmistakably speculative nature of these productions is captured by the contradiction of the term *reality romance*—traditionally, reality is what "ruins romance"—we therefore already get a hint that we are not only in for happy endings but for ruins too.

CHAPTER FIVE

1. Open Society Foundations website, "Who We Are: George Soros, Founder/ Chair," https://www.opensocietyfoundations.org/george-soros.

2. Although, many consider another incident as preamble to this spectacular alliance: when Rick Santelli, CNBC's market reporter, delivered his infamous 2009 Tea Party rant—a theatrical outburst of populist anger against Barack Obama's multibillion-dollar economic stimulus on live television. Surrounded by cheering traders inside the Chicago Mercantile Exchange's pit, Santelli protested "subsidiz[ing] the losers' mortgages" instead of rewarding "the people that could carry the water instead of drink the water. . . . This is America . . . the silent majority" (pointing to the traders behind him) and completed his tirade with the proclamation "We're thinking of having a Chicago Tea Party." Also see https://www.politicalresearch.org/2011/08/01 /tea-party-new-populism.

3. Surkov's techniques of postmodern propaganda are described most vividly in Peter Pomerantsev's (2017) best-selling memoir *Nothing Is True Everything Is Possible: Adventures in Modern Russia*. Pomerantsev has also written extensively about the inner workings of other recent disinformation campaigns, including those in the Philippines, Serbia, and Ukraine.

4. This description bears astonishing resemblance to the maverick quants of Robert Harris's (2012) novel *The Fear Index*, which we encountered in previous chapters.

5. The full call can be found on Dominic Cummings's personal blog at https://dom iniccummings.com/2020/01/02/two-hands-are-a-lot-were-hiring-data-scientists-proj ect-managers-policy-experts-assorted-weirdos/.

6. Here, and in subsequent discussions, I allude to the evocative title of Wendy Brown's 2015 book *Undoing the Demos*.

7. Goodwin (2018) distinguishes two principal approaches to this question of temporal dynamics in contemporary applications of the double movement: "The first sees the double movement revolve around economic liberalism, while the second views it as a fundamental contradiction in market capitalism. Scholars in the first group focus on the neoliberal stage of capitalism, seeing this as the start of a new cycle of the double movement. Authors in the second camp point towards underlying continuities in capitalist development, interpreting the double movement as a longer-term, continuous historical process. Exponents of the former reading suggest the double movement can be eased or overcome through reform, while advocates of the latter claim more radical solutions are required" (1269).

8. Critics such as Jodi Dean (2016) challenge Brown's argument on the grounds that it risks rehearsing apocalyptic accounts about a collapse of democracy, which are similar to some of the neopopulist narratives of the rise of neoliberalism.

9. This view is captured succinctly by Gonzalez-Vicente and Carroll (2017), who argue that "the emergent forms of populism and nationalism evident are predictable responses to the consolidation of the world market and the formation of an elite consensus around market-oriented policy as being beyond politics" (993).

10. In the immediate aftermath of the Trump election, there was a surge of published volumes positioned at the sharp end of this moralistic critique of populism. For a popular example of this type of critique, see Mounk (2018).

11. See https://www.theguardian.com/world/2018/nov/22/hillary-clinton-europe -must-curb-immigration-stop-populists-trump-brexit.

12. I discussed the role of mass psychology in the legitimacy conflicts about the fin de siècle figure of *homo economicus* in chapter 2.

13. Indeed, even in the cautionary tales of Greenspan and economists Akerlof and Shiller, which we encountered in chapter 1, populism may well emerge as a collective expression of the publics' own "'irrational exuberance."

14. As Appadurai (2011) puts it, the "heroes of the financial imaginary are precisely not about the taming of the 'passions' by the 'interests' . . . but rather are about the animation of the interests by the passions" (524).

15. Konings's (2018) criticism, for example, focuses on the state's inherent deep endorsement of speculative finance (e.g., through its role as guarantor of major banks) in a way that serves to sustain neoliberalism. As he emphasizes, "the Polanyian countermovement" fails to materialize, as neoliberalism manages to "suspend its contradictions and to defer its demise" (127). Konings points here to the inherent overlap of passions and interests in the constitution of neoliberalism. The policy implications of this view are that financial markets and their governance do not have to be reembedded, for they should not be considered disembedded in the first place.

16. Melinda Cooper (2017) offers one of the most prescient analyses of neoliberalism's "strange hybridity," which includes forms of resistance shaped around the strengthening of traditional forms of connection such as the family.

17. There are, of course, arguments that see a progressive potential germinating in the present crisis of neoliberalism, but they invariably tend to address it through "improvements" of the double movement. The political vacuum left by the "withdrawal of neoliberal consensus" (Streeck 2014) has opened up a space for political experimentation—an interregnum that Nancy Fraser (2019) describes as a curious disjuncture. As Fraser (2017) argues: "While today's crisis appears to follow a Polanyian structural

logic, grounded in the dynamics of fictitious commodification, it does not manifest a Polanyian political logic, figured by the double movement" (31). Fraser (2017) proposes that a third movement be added in order to overcome the current stalemate: "emancipation." For an alternative approach that departs from the Polanyian current altogether, see Riley (2017, 2018). Riley offers an analysis of Trump's populism that considers it not a fascist threat to democratic institutions but a potential stimulus for injecting "a shot of adrenaline to a moribund system."

18. For Levy (2012), even social security "was dependent upon the instruments of corporate risk management" (314). It was thus "an extension of the insurance principle" and hence "predicated upon notions of male individual entitlement and right rather than the shared obligations of a truly national risk community, solidified by an egalitarian ethos of citizenship" (314).

19. There is evidence of even more speculative responses to political and economic uncertainties in rural constituencies of other country contexts (where a similar genre of financialized, right-wing populism has recently been on the march). Anthropologist Carol Upadhya (2020), for instance, describes how farmers in the southern Indian state of Andhra Pradesh threw themselves enthusiastically into land speculation to navigate uncertainty and to "renegotiate their futures" (19). Revealingly, Upadhya notes that those farmers' new "speculative economic habitus" (20) was not a case of neoliberal co-optation but reshaped instead by local citizens, in a project where "regional capital and political actors . . . inserted themselves into the development and planning process, drawing on a regional cultural economy of speculative accumulation and caste affiliation, in turn infusing land with new values as they reconfigure their own lives and futures" (20).

20. See Tony Blair, "Brexit's Stunning Coup," *New York Times*, https://www.nytimes .com/2016/06/26/opinion/tony-blair-brexits-stunning-coup.html.

21. It is worth noting that markets did not align with the argument made by politicians of the "remain" campaign, nor did they show similar levels of panic at the prospect of Brexit.

22. See https://www.theguardian.com/business/2019/feb/25/uk-us-brexit-deriva tives-trading-deal-eu.

23. Former Conservative chancellor Philip Hammond tweeted in October 2019, "Johnson is backed by speculators who have bet billions on a hard Brexit—and there is only one option that works for them: a crash-out no-deal that sends the currency tumbling and inflation soaring." To which the response of the sitting business minister was that such accusations were "a conspiracy." See https://www.bbc.com/news /business-49898289.

24. As we saw in part 2, speculative technologies do not merely subtract lived experiences into commodified predictive data; they are nodes for circulating the radical uncertainty that defines a speculative mode of being. Ethno-nationalist populist movements have channeled their digital activism right at the heart of the spaces afforded by such technologies; the connectivities and cleavages evident in the steady growth of these platforms' constituencies now extend far beyond the fringe, achieving magnitudes of mobilization that traditional social movements have previously lacked. Sociologist Paolo Gerbaudo (2018) has emphasized this affinity between digital technologies (their dependence on and use of contradiction, opacity, and confusion) and neopopulist publics.

25. This is not an entirely new phenomenon. As I argued in chapter 2, US agrarian populists molded their distinct speculative imaginations through attempts to navigate the post–Civil War period's radical uncertainties, which cast serious doubt on probabilistic models of forecasting.

26. Although, we should not discard the nuances in the dialectics between openness and closedness, which are contained not only between but also *within* the concepts of finance and nationalism. Randy Martin (2015) hints at this immanent dialectic of finance when he observes that the root of the French word *finance* (*fin*) encompasses both bringing a transaction to a close and also, importantly, pursuing the opportunity opened up by that ending. Openness and closedness also coexist in the imaginary production of the nation, as Anderson (1991) puts it, "Seen as both a historical fatality and as a community imagined through language, the nation presents itself as simultaneously open and closed" (146). Finally, Amoore (2020) uses the metaphor of aperture to describe the simultaneous possibilities for openness and closure contained in decisions made in the darkness of our computational world's algorithmic clouds.

27. Again, we can find examples of this convergence in a variety of contexts, as in the cases of Eastern European (seemingly statist-welfarist) populists like Hungary's Orbán and Poland's Kaczynski, who have become much more deeply embedded into global speculative financial mechanisms than have their openly neoliberal predecessors. Consider, for instance, Poland's public refusal to accept Syrian refugees in 2017 (justified by the ultra-right discourse of the "Islamization of Europe"), while at the same time pursuing a conscious policy of opening domestic labor markets to economic migrants from South Asia through large corporate brokers. See https://visegradpost.com /en/2018/08/24/lacking-manpower-poland-relies-on-asian-immigration-besides -ukrainians-and-belorussians/ and https://www.economist.com/europe/2020/02/22 /poland-is-cocking-up-migration-in-a-very-european-way.

28. In September 2019 Trump launched another Twitter attack in response to the Federal Reserve's meager interest rate drop by 0.25 points: "Jay Powell and the Federal Reserve Fail Again. No 'guts,' no sense, no vision! A terrible communicator!" In 2020, amid the coronavirus pandemic, the Federal Reserve's rapid technocratic response (injecting billions of dollars' worth of liquidity into the US economy) contrasted even more sharply with Trump's flippancy, but by that point of the crisis the conflict between experts, central bankers, and populists had entered a new chapter.

29. I am indebted to Melinda Cooper for suggesting the term *actuarial chauvinism* to me.

30. In the United States, even the Obama administration's Affordable Care Act, for instance, went simply too far for Tea Party Republicans and Trump supporters.

CHAPTER SIX

1. For a sample of indicative news reports, see https://www.vox.com/2020/6/8/21 279262/k-pop-fans-black-lives-matter-fancams-youtubers-protest-support and https:// www.nytimes.com/2020/06/21/style/tiktok-trump-rally-tulsa.html.

2. President Trump's 2020 campaign manager tweeted shortly after the rally, "Radical protestors, fueled by a week of apocalyptic media coverage, interfered with @real-DonaldTrump supporters at the rally. They even blocked access to the metal detectors, preventing people from entering. Thanks to the 1,000s who made it anyway!"

3. See https://www.theatlantic.com/politics/archive/2019/01/the-absurdity-of-do
nald-trumps-lies/579622/. The political debate about the question of facts and fake
news intensified in the lead-up to the 2020 US presidential election. In May 2020 the
Trump campaign launched TheTruthOverFacts.com: an anti-Biden website named after the Democratic candidate's slip-up when he mistakenly said "We choose science
over fiction, *we choose truth over facts*" (emphasis added) in an appearance at the Iowa
State Fair during August 2019. See https://www.msnbc.com/rachel-maddow-show
/why-trump-campaign-prioritizing-truth-over-facts-n121028. Meanwhile, the BBC's
Our World program characterized the 2020 US election as the "TikTok Election." https://
www.bbc.co.uk/iplayer/episode/m000nyst/our-world-americas-tiktok-election.

4. In its original inception, subcultures' fancam spam was deployed to innocuous
mockery of the millennial and boomer generations or to target competing social media threads for popularity. See https://www.buzzfeed.com/stefficao/alt-tiktok. Other,
more sinister, emerging subcultures include Borrowing TikTok, a growing community
of rebellious shoplifters sharing videos of best "borrowing" practices, mixed with overt
anticapitalist messages and deliberate political targeting of corrupt corporations.

5. See the full article here: https://www.washingtonpost.com/opinions/2020/06
/23/darker-side-tiktoks-trump-rally-trolling/.

6. When pressed, Facebook (Instagram's parent company) explained that that there
was no reason to regulate these specific posts because they did not count as "harmfully
deceptive" or as "co-ordinated inauthentic behavior," according to the platform's official policy, which can be found here: https://www.facebook.com/communitystandards
/inauthentic_behavior.

7. As Kim (2018) has shown in her study of K-pop activism, fans' recent political acts
of sabotage build on well-versed ("convoluted and devious") practices of group action
in the K-pop community, including online hazing of idols and sabotaging rival groups'
concerts. See also https://www.nbcnews.com/think/opinion/k-pop-stans-anti-trump
-black-lives-matter-activism-reveals-ncna1232327.

8. A key example of such strategic appropriation tactics can be found among trade
unions and in their historical use of wages for wielding their position as dependent laborers to legitimate their fight against capital.

9. For this reason, Martin (2015) describes our current state as one of manufactured
uncertainty.

10. In one of his last published essays, Ulrich Beck (2011) engages at length Benedict Anderson and applies the idea of imagined communities to his own transnational
concept of "risk cosmopolitanism."

11. Beck develops these core theses in a process of continuous refining of his original risk society (Beck 1986) framework during the 2000s and 2010s (around key events
such as the war on terror, the growth of environmental movements, and the 2008 financial crisis) until his death in 2015.

12. Endemic to the Polanyian schema, as I have earlier proposed, is a view of reinstating the social as an essential move for combating capitalism's uncertainties. A
perennial issue with this move is the belief in restoring a form of tradition that is able
to reembed a fugitive economic rationality in more socially cohesive ways. Angela
Mitropoulos offers a particularly scathing critique of this view: "For Polanyians, 'tra-
ditionalism' is rendered as the only proper anticapitalist strategy because Polanyians
systematically re-describe 'capitalism' as the erosion of 'tradition' (that is, 'traditional'
concepts of property law and right). By that view, those who do not serve the restoration

of 'tradition'—or the reproduction of 'the social' in the face of uncertainty—are implicitly cast as traitors to the cause" (Mitropoulos's blog entry at https://s0metim3s .com/2019/03/27/streeck-sociology/).

13. Rumsfeld gave the following response to a relevant question in Morris's film: "In my confirmation hearing . . . the best question I was asked was, What do you worry about when you go to bed at night? And my answer was, in effect, intelligence. The danger that we can be surprised because of a failure of imagining what might happen in the world."

14. July 26, 2009—excerpts from the letter were published by the *Guardian* and can be accessed here: https://www.theguardian.com/uk/2009/jul/26/monarchy-credit -crunch.

15. On a more general level, philosopher Renata Salecl (2020) recently argued that a proliferating willful ignorance has become a means of survival, taking the form of a (pervasive and pernicious) collective denial of reality.

16. In her more recent work McGoey (2019) offers further examples of such deliberate and exclusionary darkness in which political and legal institutions sequester marginalized groups to quash their resistance. One of her examples is the decision of England's Court of Appeal to overturn an earlier ruling made by the High Court about the legality for Britain's Home Office not to have provided information about two thousand children living in the Calais camp and about the reasons for rejecting their application to join family members in the United Kingdom: "The less they are informed, the British government appears to have speculated, the weaker the children's legal case" (2).

17. Epitomized by calls such as Steven Pinker's (2018) neorationalist manifesto *Enlightenment Now*.

18. Jeremy Harding wrote in the *London Review of Books* about the political strategies of the Gilet Jaunes in March 2019: https://www.lrb.co.uk/v41/n06/jeremy-hard ing/among-the-gilets-jaunes.

19. Much in a similar manner, BLM activists fiercely condemned solidarity statements about police reform made by companies such as Amazon, whose facial recognition software was used by many of the country's police departments (using an algorithm that caused controversy over disproportionately misidentified crime perpetrators in communities of color). Amazon's corporate instinct to publicly support BLM and adopting the movement's logo on its Instagram and Twitter accounts led to a wave of activist attacks on these very media, voicing a rejection of the company's pernicious duplicity. See details of the controversy here: https://www.theguardian.com /technology/2020/jun/09/amazon-black-lives-matter-police-ring-jeff-bezos.

20. Accusations of conspiracy within the movement were widespread in popular media. The tabloid *Daily Telegraph*, for instance, ran the story "Six Out of Ten 'Yellow Vests' in France Believe Diana, Princess of Wales, Was Murdered, Finds Survey," https://www.telegraph.co.uk/news/2019/02/11/six-ten-yellow-vests-france-believe -diana-princess-wales-murdered/.

21. The longer passage from Traverso's essay expatiates on this point: "Observers have been surprised and puzzled by the unusual forms, symbols, and practices of the Gilets Jaunes. Everybody recognizes the protest's radicalism, determination, and remarkable duration, but their movement remains in many respects a strange and unclassifiable object, either naïvely idealized as the announcement of revolution or obtusely stigmatized as dangerous and potentially 'proto-fascist.' The Gilets Jaunes

are supported by both the Left and the Right but claim their independence; they do not accept any political representation or recuperation." See Verso blog, https://www.versobooks.com/blogs/4242-understanding-the-gilets-jaunes.

22. The full essay can be found here: https://www.metamute.org/editorial/articles/memes-force---lessons-yellow-vests.

23. In 2017 President Macron vowed to make France a "start-up nation" at the opening of the technology incubator Station F in Paris. See https://www.nytimes.com/2018/05/23/business/emmanuel-macron-france-technology.html.

24. See https://www.france24.com/en/20190408-france-debate-philippe-justice-equity-yellow-vest-protests-macron-tax.

25. The majority of pollsters in the week leading up to the vote had been predicting a very tight outcome, or a victory for the *nai* camp.

26. The full text of the ballot question was "Should the deal draft that was forward by the European Commission, the European Central Bank and the International Monetary Fund in the Eurogroup of June 25, 2015, and consists of two parts, that together form a unified proposal, be accepted? The first document is titled 'Reforms for the Completion of the Current Program and Beyond' and the second 'Preliminary Debt Sustainability Analysis.'"

27. Several opinion polls after the vote suggested that the majority of those voting *oxi* did not favor "Grexit" (the severing of all ties with the EU). Images of openness versus exclusion were mobilized in a manner that was a reverse of the United Kingdom's Brexit referendum, which took place in the following year. Antonis Samaras, the defeated right-wing leader of the opposition, defended a pro-Europe vote by stating in his closing rally before the referendum: "Our world focuses on security—we aim to secure our borders against illegal immigrants. In contrast, Syriza is asking for open borders. They will drive us to anarchy, together with their communist allies in Europe. They will destroy Europe!" Quoted in Boukala and Dimitrakopoulou (2017).

28. In this chapter, I have examined the three political examples in reverse chronological order to demonstrate the historical depth of some of today's most readily recognizable counter-speculation movements.

29. For a critique of Rawls and his "veil of ignorance" notion from the perspective of the political imagination, see Bottici (2014).

30. Such practices are the topic of the podcast series *The Order of Unmanageable Risks*, which I coproduced with Max Haiven in 2020. More details and episodes can be found at the project's website, https://www.anxious.community.

31. There are echoes of Georges Bataille's (1991) view of joy in this passage: a visceral experience responding to sudden ruptures of stable social order, which alert us to the openness of the unknown.

32. The "if-then" formula is also how financial derivatives write contingency into their function.

CONCLUSIONS

1. The phrase was used by former President Barack Obama in an interview with the *Atlantic*. Vice President-Elect Kamala Harris's victory statement made a similar claim on the importance of a prevailing truth that was represented by the Biden victory: https://edition.cnn.com/politics/live-news/trump-biden-election-results-11-07-20/h_59d6a19d74b8848691263f000e83cf24.

2. There is even less cause for optimism in other emblematic right-wing-populist strongholds. In the face of the pandemic, key figures such as Israel's Benjamin Netanyahu were managing to cling to power, while leaders like Brazil's Jair Bolsonaro and India's Narendra Modi were widening their popular support. See https://www.reuters .com/article/us-brazil-politics-idUSKCN25A1JX and https://www.nytimes.com/2020 /05/16/world/asia/coronavirus-modi-india.html.

3. For a systematic review of the persisting deficit myths plaguing global budgetary policy (typically associated with the false idea that federal government should budget like a household) see Kelton (2020).

REFERENCES

Adorno, Theodor W. 2001. *The Stars Down to Earth and Other Essays on the Irrational in Culture*. London: Psychology Press.

Agamben, Giorgio. 1993. *The Coming Community*. Minneapolis: University of Minnesota Press.

Akerlof, George A., and Robert J. Shiller. 2010. *Animal Spirits: How Human Psychology Drives the Economy, and Why It Matters for Global Capitalism*. Princeton, NJ: Princeton University Press.

Alexander, Jeffrey C. 1990. *Durkheimian Sociology: Cultural Studies*. Cambridge: Cambridge University Press.

Amoore, Louise. 2020. *Cloud Ethics*. Durham, NC: Duke University Press.

Anderson, Benedict. 1991. *Imagined Communities: Reflections on the Origin and Spread of Nationalism*. Rev. ed. London: Verso.

Appadurai, Arjun. 1990. "Disjuncture and Difference in the Global Cultural Economy." *Theory, Culture and Society* 7, nos. 2–3: 295–310.

Appadurai, Arjun. 2011. "The Ghost in the Financial Machine." *Public Culture* 23 (3) (65): 517–39.

Appadurai, Arjun. 2016. *Banking on Words: The Failure of Language in the Age of Derivative Finance*. Chicago: University of Chicago Press.

Arendt, Hannah. 1998. *The Human Condition*. Chicago: University of Chicago Press.

Aristotle. 1984. *Complete Works of Aristotle*. Vol. 1. Rev. ed. Oxford trans. Princeton, NJ: Princeton University Press.

Arnason, Johann P. 2015. "The Imaginary Dimensions of Modernity: Beyond Marx and Weber." *Social Imaginaries* 1 (1): 135–49.

Arrighi, Giovanni. 2009. *The Long Twentieth Century: Money, Power and the Origins of Our Time*. New ed. London: Verso.

Ascher, Ivan. 2016. *Portfolio Society: On the Capitalist Mode of Prediction*. New York: Zone.

Ayache, Elie. 2010. *The Blank Swan: The End of Probability*. Repr. Chichester, UK: John Wiley and Sons.

Baker, Tom, and Jonathan Simon. 2002. *Embracing Risk: The Changing Culture of Insurance and Responsibility*. Chicago: University of Chicago Press.

Banner, Stuart. 2017. *Speculation: A History of the Fine Line between Gambling and Investing*. Oxford: Oxford University Press.

Bataille, Georges. 1991. *The Accursed Share.* Vol. 1. Translated by Robert Hurley. Repr. New York: Zone.

Bauman, Zygmunt. 2003. *Liquid Love: On the Frailty of Human Bonds.* Cambridge, UK: Polity.

Bear, Laura. 2020. "Speculation: A Political Economy of Technologies of Imagination." *Economy and Society* 49 (1): 1–15. https://doi.org/10.1080/03085147.2020.1715604.

Beck, Ulrich. 1986. *Risikogesellschaft: Auf dem Weg in eine andere Moderne.* Frankfurt: Suhrkamp.

Beck, Ulrich. 2008. *World at Risk.* Cambridge, UK: Polity.

Beck, Ulrich. 2011. "Cosmopolitanism as Imagined Communities of Global Risk." *American Behavioral Scientist* 55 (10): 1346–61.

Beck, Ulrich, and Elisabeth Beck-Gernsheim. 2004. *The Normal Chaos of Love.* Cambridge, UK: Polity.

Beckert, Jens. 2016. *Imagined Futures: Fictional Expectations and Capitalist Dynamics.* Cambridge, MA: Harvard University Press.

Beckert, Jens. 2020. "The Exhausted Futures of Neoliberalism: From Promissory Legitimacy to Social Anomy." *Journal of Cultural Economy* 13 (3): 318–30.

Beckert, Jens, and Richard Bronk, eds. 2018. *Uncertain Futures: Imaginaries, Narratives, and Calculation in the Economy.* Oxford: Oxford University Press.

Benjamin, Ruha. 2019. *Race after Technology: Abolitionist Tools for the New Jim Code.* Medford, MA: Polity.

Benjamin, Walter. 1969. *Illuminations: Essays and Reflections.* Edited by Hannah Arendt. Translated by Harry Zohn. New York: Schocken.

Berardi, Franco. 2017. *Futurability: The Age of Impotence and the Horizon of Possibility.* London: Verso.

Best, Shaun. 2019. "Liquid Love: Zygmunt Bauman's Thesis on Sex Revisited." *Sexualities* 22, nos. 7–8: 1094–1109. https://doi.org/10.1177/1363460718795082.

Beunza, Daniel. 2019. *Taking the Floor.* Princeton, NJ: Princeton University Press.

Bhattacharyya, Debjani. 2019. "Provincializing the History of Speculation from Colonial South Asia." *History Compass* 17 (1): e12517. https://doi.org/10.1111/hic3.12517.

Birla, Ritu. 2009. *Stages of Capital: Law, Culture, and Market Governance in Late Colonial India.* Durham, NC: Duke University Press.

Birner, Jack, and Ragip Ege. 1999. "Two Views on Social Stability: An Unsettled Question." *American Journal of Economics and Sociology* 58 (4): 749–80. https://doi.org/10.1111/j.1536-7150.1999.tb03393.x.

Bishop, Sophie. 2019. "Managing Visibility on YouTube through Algorithmic Gossip." *New Media and Society* 21, nos. 11–12: 2589–2606. https://doi.org/10.1177/1461444819854731.

Blokker, Paul. 2012. "A Political Sociology of European Anti-politics and Dissent." *Cambio* 2 (4): 17–31.

Boltanski, Luc. 2009. *De la critique: Précis de sociologie de l'émancipation.* Paris: Gallimard.

Boltanski, Luc. 2011. *On Critique: A Sociology of Emancipation.* Cambridge, UK: Polity.

Boltanski, Luc, and Eve Chiapello. 2018. *The New Spirit of Capitalism.* Translated by Gregory Elliott. Repr. London: Verso.

Bonikowski, Bart. 2017. "Ethno-Nationalist Populism and the Mobilization of Collective Resentment." *British Journal of Sociology* 68: S181–S213.

Borch, Christian. 2012. *The Politics of Crowds: An Alternative History of Sociology.* New York: Cambridge University Press.

Borch, Christian. 2020. *Social Avalanche: Crowds, Cities and Financial Markets*. New York: Cambridge University Press.

Bottici, Chiara. 2007. *A Philosophy of Political Myth*. New York: Cambridge University Press.

Bottici, Chiara. 2014. *Imaginal Politics: Images beyond Imagination and the Imaginary*. New York: Columbia University Press.

Bottici, Chiara. 2017. "Bodies in Plural: Towards an Anarcha-Feminist Manifesto." *Thesis Eleven* 142 (1): 91–111. https://doi.org/10.1177/0725513617727793.

Boukala, Salomi, and Dimitra Dimitrakopoulou. 2017. "The Politics of Fear vs. the Politics of Hope: Analysing the 2015 Greek Election and Referendum Campaigns." *Critical Discourse Studies* 14 (1): 39–55.

Bourne, Clea, Paul Robert Gilbert, Max Haiven, and Johnna Montgomerie. 2018. "Colonial Debts, Imperial Insolvencies, Extractive Nostalgias." *Discover Society* 60.

Bratton, Benjamin H. 2015. *The Stack: On Software and Sovereignty*. Cambridge, MA: MIT Press.

Bridle, James. 2018. *New Dark Age: Technology and the End of the Future*. London: Verso.

Bronk, Richard. 2009. *The Romantic Economist: Imagination in Economics*. Cambridge: Cambridge University Press.

Brown, Wendy. 2015. *Undoing the Demos: Neoliberalism's Stealth Revolution*. New York: Zone.

Brown, Wendy. 2017. "Apocalyptic Populism." *New Humanist*, December 4. https://newhumanist.org.uk/5256/apocalyptic-populism.

Brunton, Finn, and Helen Nissenbaum. 2016. *Obfuscation: A User's Guide for Privacy and Protest*. Repr. Cambridge, MA: MIT Press.

Bryan, Dick, and Michael Rafferty. 2006. *Capitalism with Derivatives: A Political Economy of Financial Derivatives, Capital and Class*. New York: Palgrave Macmillan.

Bryan, Dick, and Mike Rafferty. 2018. *Risking Together: How Finance Is Dominating Everyday Life in Australia*. Sydney, Australia: Sydney University Press.

Bucher, Taina. 2018. *If . . . Then: Algorithmic Power and Politics*. Oxford: Oxford University Press.

Butler, Judith. 2019. "The Backlash against 'Gender Ideology' Must Stop." *New Statesman*, January 21, 2019. https://www.newstatesman.com/2019/01/judith-butler-backlash-against-gender-ideology-must-stop.

Butler, Judith. 2020. *The Force of Nonviolence: The Ethical in the Political*. London: Verso.

Calhoun, Craig. 1991. "Indirect Relationships and Imagined Communities: Large Scale Social Integration and the Transformation of Everyday Life." In *Social Theory for a Changing Society*. London: Westview.

Calhoun, Craig. 1998. "Community without Propinquity Revisited: Communications Technology and the Transformation of the Urban Public Sphere." *Sociological Inquiry* 68 (3): 373–97. https://doi.org/10.1111/j.1475-682X.1998.tb00474.x.

Calhoun, Craig. 2016. "The Importance of Imagined Communities—and Benedict Anderson." In "Imagined Communities in the 21st Century: A Homage to Benedict Anderson." Special issue, *Debats* 1: 11.

Callison, William Andrew. 2019. "Political Deficits: The Dawn of Neoliberal Rationality and the Eclipse of Critical Theory." PhD diss., University of California, Berkeley.

Callison, William. 2020. "The Political Theory of Neoliberalism." *Contemporary Political Theory*, 1–5.

Callison, William, and Zachary Manfredi, eds. 2020. *Mutant Neoliberalism: Market Rule and Political Rupture*. New York: Fordham University Press.

Carter, Julia, and Lorena Arocha. 2020. *Romantic Relationships in a Time of "Cold Intimacies."* London: Palgrave Macmillan.

Castells, Manuel. 2009. *The Rise of the Network Society.* 2nd ed. Malden, MA: Wiley-Blackwell.

Castells, Manuel. 2012. *Networks of Outrage and Hope: Social Movements in the Internet Age.* Cambridge, UK: Polity.

Castoriadis, Cornelius. 1975. *The Imaginary Institution of Society.* Translated by K. Blarney. Cambridge, MA: MIT Press; Oxford: Polity.

Castoriadis, Cornelius. 1984. *Crossroads in the Labyrinth.* Brighton, UK: Harvester.

Castoriadis, Cornelius. 1997a. *World in Fragments: Writings on Politics, Society, Psychoanalysis and the Imagination.* Translated by David Ames Curtis. Stanford, CA: Stanford University Press.

Castoriadis, Cornelius. 1997b. "Anthropology, Philosophy, Politics." *Thesis Eleven* 49 (1): 99–116.

Cevolini, Alberto, and Elena Esposito. 2020. "From Pool to Profile: Social Consequences of Algorithmic Prediction in Insurance." *Big Data and Society* 7 (2). https://doi.org/10.1177/2053951720939228.

Chakrabarty, Dipesh. 2009. *Provincializing Europe Postcolonial Thought and Historical Difference.* Princeton, NJ: Princeton University Press.

Chamorel, Patrick. 2019. "Macron versus the Yellow Vests." *Journal of Democracy* 30 (4): 48–62.

Chatterjee, Partha. 1991. "Whose Imagined Community?" *Millennium* 20 (3): 521–25.

Chatterjee, Partha. 2004. *The Politics of the Governed: Reflections on Popular Politics in Most of the World.* New York: Columbia University Press.

Chayka, Kyle. 2019. "Does Monoculture Still Exist on the Internet?" *Vox*, December 17, 2019. https://www.vox.com/the-goods/2019/12/17/21024439/monoculture-algorithm-netflix-spotify.

Chesnais, François. 1996. "Mondialisation du capital et régime d'accumulation à domination financière." *Agone* 16: 15–39.

Christophers, Brett. 2020. *Rentier Capitalism: Who Owns the Economy, and Who Pays for It?* New York: Verso.

Cochrane, Richard. 2017. "The Tape Readers: Financial Trading as a Visual Practice." *Philosophy of Photography* 8, nos. 1–2: 109–17.

Cooper, Melinda. 2017. *Family Values: Between Neoliberalism and the New Social Conservatism.* New York: Zone.

Cooper, Melinda. 2020. "Anti-austerity on the Far Right." In *Mutant Neoliberalism: Market Rule and Political Rupture*, 112–45. New York: Fordham University Press.

Cornwell, Benjamin. 2007. "The Protestant Sect Credit Machine: Social Capital and the Rise of Capitalism." *Journal of Classical Sociology* 7 (3): 267–90.

Cowing, Cedric B. 2015. *Populists, Plungers, and Progressives: A Social History of Stock and Commodity Speculation, 1868-1932.* Princeton, NJ: Princeton University Press.

Cronon, William. 2009. *Nature's Metropolis: Chicago and the Great West.* New York: W. W. Norton.

Crosthwaite, Paul. 2019. *The Market Logics of Contemporary Fiction.* Cambridge: Cambridge University Press.

Crosthwaite, Paul, Peter Knight, and Nicky Marsh, eds. 2014. *Show Me the Money: The Image of Finance, 1700 to the Present.* Manchester, UK: Manchester University Press.

Crosthwaite, Paul, Peter Knight, and Nicky Marsh. 2019. "The Economic Humanities and the History of Financial Advice." *American Literary History* 31 (4): 661–86.

Daniels, Jessie, and Karen Gregory, eds. 2016. *Digital Sociologies*. Cambridge, UK: Policy.

Dasgupta, Rohit K., and Debanuj Dasgupta. 2018. "Intimate Subjects and Virtual Spaces: Rethinking Sexuality as a Category for Intimate Ethnographies." *Sexualities* 21, nos. 5–6: 932–50.

David, Gaby, and Carolina Cambre. 2016. "Screened Intimacies: Tinder and the Swipe Logic." *Social Media + Society* 2 (2). https://doi.org/10.1177/2056305116641976.

Davies, William. 2018. *Nervous States: How Feeling Took Over the World*. London: Jonathan Cape.

Davies, William, and Linsey McGoey. 2012. "Rationalities of Ignorance: On Financial Crisis and the Ambivalence of Neo-liberal Epistemology." *Economy and Society* 41 (1): 64–83. https://doi.org/10.1080/03085147.2011.637331.

Day, Graham. 2006. *Community and Everyday Life*. London: Routledge.

Dean, Jodi. 2016. *Crowds and Party*. Brooklyn, NY: Verso.

Debord, Guy. (1968) 2002. *Society of the Spectacle*. Detroit, MI: Black and Red.

de Goede, Marieke. 2005. *Virtue, Fortune, and Faith: A Genealogy of Finance*. Minneapolis: University of Minnesota Press.

De Marchi, Neil, and Paul Harrison. 1994. "Trading 'in the Wind' and with Guile: The Troublesome Matter of the Short Selling of Shares in Seventeenth-Century Holland." *Higgling: Transactors and Their Markets in the History of Economics* 26, suppl. 1: 47–65. https://doi.org/10.1215/00182702-1994-suppl_1008.

Donner, Henrike, and Goncalo Santos. 2016. "Love, Marriage, and Intimate Citizenship in Contemporary China and India: An Introduction." *Modern Asian Studies* 50 (4): 1123–46.

Donovan, Joan. 2017. "From Social Movements to Social Surveillance." *XRDS: Crossroads* 23 (3): 24–27. https://doi.org/10.1145/3055151.

Elfving-Hwang, Joanna. 2018. "K-pop Idols, Artificial Beauty and Affective Fan Relationships in South Korea." In *Routledge Handbook of Celebrity Studies*. Routledge Handbooks Online. https://doi.org/10.4324/9781315776774-12.

Essig, Laurie. 2019. *Love Inc.: Dating Apps, the Big White Wedding, and Chasing the Happily Neverafter*. Oakland: University of California Press.

Ewald, François. 1986. *L'Etat providence*. Paris: B. Grasset.

Fabian, Ann. 1999. *Card Sharps and Bucket Shops: Gambling in Nineteenth-Century America*. London: Psychology Press.

Faucher, Kane X. 2018. *Social Capital Online: Alienation and Accumulation*. London: University of Westminster Press.

Federici, Silvia. 2020. *Beyond the Periphery of the Skin*. Oakland, CA: PM Press.

Feher, Michel. 2018. *Rated Agency: Investee Politics in a Speculative Age*. Translated by Gregory Elliott. New York: Zone.

Fisher, Mark. 2009. *Capitalist Realism: Is There No Alternative?* Winchester, UK: Zero Books.

Fraser, Nancy. 2017. "A Triple Movement? Parsing the Politics of Crisis after Polanyi." In *Beyond Neoliberalism: Social Analysis after 1989*. Edited by Marian Burchardt and Gal Kirn, 29–42. Cham, Switz.: Springer International. https://doi.org/10.1007/978-3-319-45590-7_3.

Fraser, Nancy. 2019. *The Old Is Dying and the New Cannot Be Born: From Progressive Neoliberalism to Trump and Beyond*. London: Verso.

Fraser, Nancy, and Rahel Jaeggi. 2018. *Capitalism: A Conversation in Critical Theory.* Cambridge, UK: Polity.

Friedman, Walter. 2013. *Fortune Tellers: The Story of America's First Economic Forecasters.* Princeton, NJ: Princeton University Press.

Fuchs, Christian. 2017. "Reflections on Michael Hardt and Antonio Negri's Book *Assembly.*" *TripleC: Communication, Capitalism and Critique* 15 (2): 851–65. https://doi .org/10.31269/triplec.v15i2.931.

Fuchs, Christian. 2018. *Digital Demagogue: Authoritarian Capitalism in the Age of Trump and Twitter.* London: Pluto.

Gago, Verónica. 2017. *Neoliberalism from Below: Popular Pragmatics and Baroque Economies.* Durham, NC: Duke University Press.

Gaonkar, Dilip Parameshwar, ed. 2001. *Alternative Modernities.* 2nd ed. Durham, NC: Duke University Press.

Gerbaudo, Paolo. 2018. *The Digital Party: Political Organisation and Online Democracy.* London: Pluto.

Gerteis, Joseph, and Alyssa Goolsby. 2005. "Nationalism in America: The Case of the Populist Movement." *Theory and Society* 34 (2): 197–225.

Giddens, Anthony. 1993. *The Transformation of Intimacy: Love, Sexuality and Eroticism in Modern Societies.* Cambridge, UK: Polity.

Gilbert, Paul Robert. 2020. "Speculating on Sovereignty: 'Money Mining' and Corporate Foreign Policy at the Extractive Industry Frontier." *Economy and Society* 49 (1): 16–44. https://doi.org/10.1080/03085147.2019.1690255.

Gonzalez-Vicente, Ruben, and Toby Carroll. 2017. "Politics after National Development: Explaining the Populist Rise under Late Capitalism." *Globalizations* 14 (6): 991–1013.

Goodwin, Geoff. 2018. "Rethinking the Double Movement: Expanding the Frontiers of Polanyian Analysis in the Global South." *Development and Change* 49 (5): 1268–90. https://doi.org/10.1111/dech.12419.

Goodwyn, Lawrence. 1978. *The Populist Moment: A Short History of the Agrarian Revolt in America.* New York: Oxford University Press.

Goswami, Omkar. 1991. *Industry, Trade, and Peasant Society: The Jute Economy of Eastern India, 1900–1947.* Delhi: Oxford University Press.

Graeber, David. 2014. *Debt, Updated and Expanded: The First 5,000 Years.* Rev. ed. Brooklyn, NY: Melville House.

Gross, Matthias, and Linsey McGoey, eds. 2015. *Routledge International Handbook of Ignorance Studies.* London: Routledge.

Guha, Ranajit, and Gayatri Chakravorty Spivak, eds. 1988. *Selected Subaltern Studies.* New York: Oxford University Press.

Haiven, Max. 2011. "Finance as Capital's Imagination? Reimagining Value and Culture in an Age of Fictitious Capital and Crisis." *Social Text* 29 (3 [108]): 93–124.

Haiven, Max. 2020. *Revenge Capitalism: The Ghosts of Empire, the Demons of Capital, and the Settling of Unpayable Debts.* London: Pluto.

Haiven, Max, and Aris Komporozos-Athanasiou. 2019. "From Anxiety to Revolt? Against the Financialized University." *ROAR*, October 15. https://roarmag.org /essays/from-anxiety-to-revolt-against-the-financialized-university/.

Hardt, Michael, and Antonio Negri. 2017. *Assembly.* Oxford: Oxford University Press.

Harris, E. 1970. "History of the Chicago Mercantile Exchange." *Futures Trading in Livestock—Origins and Concepts*, 49–54. Chicago: Chicago Mercantile Exchange.

Harris, Robert. 2012. *The Fear Index*. Repr. New York: Vintage.

Harvey, David. 2000. *Spaces of Hope*. Berkeley: University of California Press.

Hicks, John Donald. 1931. *The Populist Revolt: A History of the Farmers' Alliance and the People's Party*. Minneapolis: University of Minnesota Press.

Hirschman, Albert O. 2013. *The Passions and the Interests: Political Arguments for Capitalism before Its Triumph*. Rev. ed. Princeton, NJ: Princeton University Press.

Ho, Karen Zouwen. 2009. *Liquidated: An Ethnography of Wall Street*. Durham, NC: Duke University Press.

Hoang, Kimberly Kay. 2015. *Dealing in Desire: Asian Ascendancy, Western Decline, and the Hidden Currencies of Global Sex Work*. Oakland: University of California Press.

Hobbes, Thomas. (1651) 2017. *Leviathan*. Edited by Christopher Brooke. Harmonds worth, UK: Penguin Classics.

Hochfelder, David. 2006. "'Where the Common People Could Speculate': The Ticker, Bucket Shops, and the Origins of Popular Participation in Financial Markets, 1880–1920." *Journal of American History* 93 (2): 335–58. https://doi.org/10.2307/4486233.

Hochman, Nadav. 2014. "The Social Media Image." *Big Data and Society* 1 (2): https://doi.org/10.1177/2053951714546645.

Hochschild, Arlie Russell. 2003. *The Commercialization of Intimate Life: Notes from Home and Work*. Berkeley: University of California Press.

Hochschild, Arlie Russell. 2016. *Strangers in Their Own Land: Anger and Mourning on the American Right*. Illustrated edition. New York: The New Press.

Hofstadter, Richard. 1956. *The Age of Reform: Form Bryan to FDR*. New York: Alfred A. Knopf.

Hogan, Bernie. 2010. "The Presentation of Self in the Age of Social Media: Distinguishing Performances and Exhibitions Online." *Bulletin of Science, Technology and Society* 30 (6): 377–86.

Holmes, David. 2005. *Communication Theory: Media, Technology and Society*. Thousand Oaks, CA: Sage.

Hooff, Jenny van. 2020. "Swipe Right? Tinder, Commitment and the Commercialisation of Intimate Life." In *Romantic Relationships in a Time of "Cold Intimacies."* Edited by Julia Carter and Lorena Arocha, 109–27. London: Palgrave Macmillan.

Hopkin, Jonathan. 2017. "When Polanyi Met Farage: Market Fundamentalism, Economic Nationalism, and Britain's Exit from the European Union." *British Journal of Politics and International Relations* 19 (3): 465–78. https://doi.org/10.1177/136 9148117710894.

Horton, Donald, and R. Richard Wohl. 1956. "Mass Communication and Para-Social Interaction: Observations on Intimacy at a Distance." *Psychiatry* 19 (3): 215–29.

Illouz, Eva. 1997. *Consuming the Romantic Utopia: Love and the Cultural Contradictions of Capitalism*. Berkeley: University of California Press.

Illouz, Eva. 2007. *Cold Intimacies: The Making of Emotional Capitalism*. Cambridge, UK: Polity.

Illouz, Eva. 2013. *Why Love Hurts: A Sociological Explanation*. Cambridge, UK: Polity.

Illouz, Eva. 2019. *The End of Love: A Sociology of Negative Relations*. New York: Oxford University Press.

Jamieson, Lynn. 1998. *Intimacy: Personal Relationships in Modern Societies*. Cambridge, UK: Polity.

Jamieson, Lynn. 1999. "Intimacy Transformed? A Critical Look at the 'Pure Relationship.'" *Sociology* 33 (3): 477–94.

Joseph, Miranda. 2002. *Against the Romance of Community*. Minneapolis: University of Minnesota Press.

Juhel, Jean-Claude, and Dominique Dufour. 2010. "A Discussion of Stock Market Speculation by Pierre-Joseph Proudhon." *Twelfth World Congress of Accounting Historians.*

Kelton, Stephanie. 2020. *The Deficit Myth: Modern Monetary Theory and the Birth of the People's Economy*. New York: PublicAffairs.

Keynes, John Maynard. 1936. *The General Theory of Employment Interest and Money*. Whitefish, MT: Kessinger.

Kim, Suk-Young. 2018. *K-pop Live: Fans, Idols, and Multimedia Performance*. Stanford, CA: Stanford University Press.

King-O'Riain, Rebecca Chiyoko. 2020. "'They Were Having So Much Fun, So Genuinely . . .': K-pop Fan Online Affect and Corroborated Authenticity." *New Media and Society*, July 8. https://doi.org/10.1177/1461444820941194.

Knight, Frank Hyneman. 1999. *Selected Essays: "What Is Truth" in Economics?* Chicago: University of Chicago Press.

Knight, Peter. 2016. *Reading the Market: Genres of Financial Capitalism in Gilded Age America*. Baltimore: Johns Hopkins University Press.

Komporozos-Athanasiou, Aris. 2020. "Re-imagining the Future in Finance Capitalism." *Journal of Cultural Economy* 13 (3): 261–64.

Komporozos-Athanasiou, Aris, and Marianna Fotaki. 2015. "A Theory of Imagination for Organization Studies Using the Work of Cornelius Castoriadis." *Organization Studies* 36 (3): 321–42.

Komporozos-Athanasiou, Aris, and Marianna Fotaki. 2020. "The Imaginary Constitution of Financial Crises." *Sociological Review* 68 (5): 932–47. https://doi.org/10.1177/0038026119899350.

Konings, Martijn. 2015. *The Emotional Logic of Capitalism: What Progressives Have Missed*. Stanford, CA: Stanford University Press.

Konings, Martijn. 2018. *Capital and Time: For a New Critique of Neoliberal Reason*. Stanford, CA: Stanford University Press.

Kotsko, Adam. 2018. *Neoliberalism's Demons: On the Political Theology of Late Capital*. Stanford, CA: Stanford University Press.

Krippner, Greta R. 2017. "Democracy of Credit: Ownership and the Politics of Credit Access in Late Twentieth-Century America." *American Journal of Sociology* 123 (1): 1–47.

Krüger, Steffen, and Charlotte Ane Spilde. 2019. "Judging Books by Their Covers—Tinder Interface, Usage and Sociocultural Implications." *Information, Communication and Society*, 23 (10): 1–16.

La Berge, Leigh Claire. 2014. *Scandals and Abstraction: Financial Fiction of the Long 1980s*. New York: Oxford University Press.

Laclau, Ernesto. 2007. *On Populist Reason*. Repr. London: Verso.

Lambert, Emily. 2010. *The Futures: The Rise of the Speculator and the Origins of the World's Biggest Markets*. New York: Basic Books.

Lapavitsas, Costas. 2013. "The Financialization of Capitalism: 'Profiting without Producing.'" *City* 17 (6): 792–805. https://doi.org/10.1080/13604813.2013.853865.

Lazzarato, Maurizio. 2015. *Governing by Debt*. Translated by Joshua David Jordan. South Pasadena, CA: Semiotext.

Leins, Stefan. 2018. *Stories of Capitalism: Inside the Role of Financial Analysts*. Chicago: University of Chicago Press.

Levy, Jonathan Ira. 2006. "Contemplating Delivery: Futures Trading and the Problem of Commodity Exchange in the United States, 1875–1905." *American Historical Review* 111 (2): 307–35. https://doi.org/10.1086/ahr.111.2.307.

Levy, Jonathan. 2012. *Freaks of Fortune: The Emerging World of Capitalism and Risk in America*. Cambridge, MA: Harvard University Press.

LiPuma, Edward. 2017. *The Social Life of Financial Derivatives: Markets, Risk, and Time*. Durham, NC: Duke University Press.

LiPuma, Edward, and Benjamin Lee. 2004. *Financial Derivatives and the Globalization of Risk*. Durham, NC: Duke University Press.

LiPuma, Edward, and Benjamin Lee. 2012. "A Social Approach to the Financial Derivatives Markets." *South Atlantic Quarterly* 111 (2): 289–316.

Lovink, Geert. 2019. *Sad by Design: On Platform Nihilism*. London: Pluto.

Luckhurst, Roger. 2011. Introduction to Bram Stoker's *Dracula*. Oxford: Oxford University Press.

MacKenzie, Donald, and Yuval Millo. 2003. "Constructing a Market, Performing Theory: The Historical Sociology of a Financial Derivatives Exchange." *American Journal of Sociology* 109 (1): 107–45.

Mannheim, Karl. 1966. *Ideology and Utopia: An Introduction to the Sociology of Knowledge*. London: Routledge and Kegan Paul.

Martin, Randy. 2015. *Knowledge LTD: Toward a Social Logic of the Derivative*. Philadelphia: Temple University Press.

Marx, Karl. 1843. *1975. On the Jewish Question*. Vol. 211241.

Marx, Karl. 1887. *Capital: A Critique of Political Economy*. Moscow: Progress Publishers.

Marx, Karl, and Friedrich Engels. 2015. *The Communist Manifesto*. Penguin Classics.

Massumi, Brian. 2018. *99 Theses on the Revaluation of Value: A Postcapitalist Manifesto*. Minneapolis: University of Minnesota Press.

Masur, Louis P. 1991. "A Bettor Nation." Review of *Card Sharps, Dream Books, and Bucket Shops: Gambling in 19th-Century America*, by Ann Fabian. *Reviews in American History* 19 (4): 505–10. https://doi.org/10.2307/2703289.

Mazzucato, Mariana. 2018. *The Value of Everything: Making and Taking in the Global Economy*. London: Penguin UK.

Mbembe, Achille. 2003. "Necropolitics." *Public Culture* 15 (1): 11–40.

Mbembe, Achille. 2017. *Critique of Black Reason*. Translated by Laurent Dubois. Durham, NC: Duke University Press.

McFall, Liz. 2019. "Personalizing Solidarity? The Role of Self-Tracking in Health Insurance Pricing." *Economy and Society* 48 (1): 52–76. https://doi.org/10.1080/03085147.2019.1570707.

McGoey, Linsey. 2012. "The Logic of Strategic Ignorance." *British Journal of Sociology* 63 (3): 533–76. https://doi.org/10.1111/j.1468-4446.2012.01424.x.

McGoey, Linsey. 2019. *The Unknowers: How Strategic Ignorance Rules the World*. London: Zed.

Mills, C. Wright. 2014. "The Protestant Sects and the Spirit of Capitalism." In *From Max Weber: Essays in Sociology*, 314–34. London: Routledge.

Mills, Charles W. 1997. *The Racial Contract*. Ithaca, NY: Cornell University Press.

Mills, Charles W. 2017. *Black Rights/White Wrongs: The Critique of Racial Liberalism*. New York: Oxford University Press.

Mische, Ann. 2014. "Measuring Futures in Action: Projective Grammars in the Rio+20 Debates." *Theory and Society* 43 (3–4): 437–64.

Miyazaki, Hirokazu. 2013. *Arbitraging Japan: Dreams of Capitalism at the End of Finance.* Berkeley: University of California Press.

Molnár, Virág. 2016. "Civil Society, Radicalism and the Rediscovery of Mythic Nationalism." *Nations and Nationalism* 22 (1): 165–85.

Montgomerie, Johnna, and Daniela Tepe-Belfrage. 2019. "Spaces of Debt Resistance and the Contemporary Politics of Financialised Capitalism." *Geoforum* 98: 309–17.

Morozov, Evgeny. 2019. "Capitalism's New Clothes." *Baffler*, February 4.

Mounk, Yascha. 2018. *The People vs. Democracy: Why Our Freedom Is in Danger and How to Save It.* Cambridge, MA: Harvard University Press.

Murawski, Michał. 2020. "Mutations of Publicness: From the Social Condenser to Social Distancing." *Tank Magazine* 84 (Fall-Winter): 216–25.

Murawski, Michał. 2021. "Falshfasad: Disavowed Infrastructure and Everyday Marxism in Putin's PPParadise." Unpublished manuscript.

Murray, Douglas. 2019. *The Madness of Crowds: Gender, Race and Identity.* London: Bloomsbury Continuum.

Nussbaum, Martha C. 2001. *The Fragility of Goodness: Luck and Ethics in Greek Tragedy and Philosophy.* 2nd ed. Cambridge: Cambridge University Press.

Olson, Kevin. 2016. *Imagined Sovereignties: The Power of the People and Other Myths of the Modern Age.* New York: Cambridge University Press.

Ong, Jonathan Corpus, and Jason Vincent A. Cabañes. 2018. "Architects of Networked Disinformation: Behind the Scenes of Troll Accounts and Fake News Production in the Philippines." Communication Department Faculty Publication Series 74. University of Massachusetts Amherst.

Ott, Julia C. 2011. *When Wall Street Met Main Street.* Cambridge, MA: Harvard University Press.

Pascal, Blaise. 2008. *Pensées and Other Writings.* Edited by Anthony Levi. Translated by Honor Levi. Oxford: Oxford University Press.

Pasquale, Frank. 2015. *The Black Box Society: The Secret Algorithms That Control Money and Information.* Cambridge, MA: Harvard University Press.

Peck, Jamie. 2013. "Disembedding Polanyi: Exploring Polanyian Economic Geographies." *Environment and Planning A* 45 (7): 1536–44.

Pietruska, Jamie L. 2017. *Looking Forward: Prediction and Uncertainty in Modern America.* Chicago: University of Chicago Press.

Pinker, Steven. 2018. *Enlightenment Now: The Case for Reason, Science, Humanism, and Progress.* New York: Viking.

Polanyi, Karl. 1944. *The Great Transformation: The Political and Economic Origins of Our Time.* Boston: Beacon.

Pomerantsev, Peter. 2017. *Nothing Is True and Everything Is Possible: Adventures in Modern Russia.* London: Faber and Faber.

Pomerantsev, Peter. 2019. "'Take Back Control.'" *London Review of Books* (blog). October 15. https://www.lrb.co.uk/blog/2019/october/take-back-control.

Postel, Charles. 2007. *The Populist Vision.* Oxford: Oxford University Press.

Preda, Alex. 2009. *Framing Finance: The Boundaries of Markets and Modern Capitalism.* Chicago: University of Chicago Press.

Preda, Alex. 2017. *Noise: Living and Trading in Electronic Finance.* Illustrated edition. Chicago: University of Chicago Press.

Proudhon, Pierre-Joseph. 1857. *Manuel du spéculateur à la Bourse* . . . 5th ed. Paris: Garnier Frères.

Pryke, Michael. 2010. "Money's Eyes: The Visual Preparation of Financial Markets." *Economy and Society* 39 (4): 427–59.

Quinn, Sarah L. 2019. *American Bonds: How Credit Markets Shaped a Nation*. Princeton, NJ: Princeton University Press.

Ricoeur, Paul. 1985. *Lectures on Ideology and Utopia*. Edited and translated by George H. Taylor. New York: Columbia University Press.

Riemen, Rob. 2018. *To Fight against This Age: On Fascism and Humanism*. New York: W. W. Norton.

Riley, Dylan. 2017. "American Brumaire?" *New Left Review* 103: 21–32.

Riley, Dylan. 2018. "What Is Trump?" *New Left Review* 114: 5–31.

Rodríguez-Muñiz, Michael. 2021. *Figures of the Future: Latino Civil Rights and the Politics of Demographic Change*. Princeton, NJ: Princeton University Press.

Ronell, Avital. 1989. *The Telephone Book: Technology, Schizophrenia, Electric Speech*. Rev. ed. Lincoln: University of Nebraska Press.

Rosa, Hartmut. 2019. *Resonance: A Sociology of Our Relationship to the World*. Translated by James Wagner. Medford, MA: Polity.

Rosamond, E. (2020). "From Reputation Capital to Reputation Warfare: Online Ratings, Trolling, and the Logic of Volatility." *Theory, Culture & Society* 37 (2): 105–29.

Rosenfeld, Michael J., Reuben J. Thomas, and Sonia Hausen. 2019. "Disintermediating Your Friends: How Online Dating in the United States Displaces Other Ways of Meeting." *Proceedings of the National Academy of Sciences* 116 (36): 17753–58.

Salecl, Renata. 2020. *A Passion for Ignorance: What We Choose Not to Know and Why*. New edition. Princeton, NJ: Princeton University Press.

Samman, Amin. 2019. *History in Financial Times*. Stanford, CA: Stanford University Press.

Sandel, Michael J. 2013. *What Money Can't Buy: The Moral Limits of Markets*. 1st edition. London: Penguin.

Sapien, B. "Financial Weapons of Mass Destruction: From Bucket Shops to Credit Default Swaps." *Southern California Interdisciplinary Law Journal* 19: 411.

Sayer, Derek. 1990. *Capitalism and Modernity: An Excursus on Marx and Weber*. London: Routledge.

Seaver, N. 2018. "Captivating Algorithms: Recommender Systems as Traps." *Journal of Material Culture* 1: 16.

Sennett, Richard. 1992. *The Fall of Public Man*. Reissue. New York: W. W. Norton.

Shiller, Robert J. 2015. *Irrational Exuberance*. 3rd ed., rev. and expanded. Princeton, NJ: Princeton University Press.

Sica, Alan. 1988. *Weber, Irrationality, and Social Order*. Berkeley: University of California Press.

Skocpol, Theda, and Vanessa Williamson. 2016. *The Tea Party and the Remaking of Republican Conservatism*. Updated ed. New York: Oxford University Press.

Smallwood, Christine. 2019. "Astrology in the Age of Uncertainty." *New Yorker*, October 21, 2019. https://www.newyorker.com/magazine/2019/10/28/astrology-in-the -age-of-uncertainty.

Spieker, Jörg. 2013. "Defending the Open Society: Foucault, Hayek, and the Problem of Biopolitical Order." *Economy and Society* 42 (2): 304–21.

Stäheli, Urs. 2013. *Spectacular Speculation: Thrills, the Economy, and Popular Discourse.* Stanford, CA: Stanford University Press.

Stetler, Harrison. 2020. "'Collapsologie': Constructing an Idea of How Things Fall Apart." *New York Review of Books*, January 21. https://www.nybooks.com/daily /2020/01/21/collapsologie-constructing-an-idea-of-how-things-fall-apart/.

Steyerl, Hito. 2009. "In Defense of the Poor Image." *E-Flux Journal* 10 (11).

Stimilli, Elettra. 2017. *The Debt of the Living: Ascesis and Capitalism.* Translated by Arianna Bove. Albany: State University of New York Press.

Straus, Murray A. 1962. "Deferred Gratification, Social Class, and the Achievement Syndrome." *American Sociological Review* 27 (3): 326–35.

Streeck, Wolfgang. 2014. "How Will Capitalism End?" *New Left Review* 87: 35–64.

Szelenyi, Iván. 2016. "Weber's Theory of Domination and Post-communist Capitalisms." *Theory and Society* 45 (1): 1–24.

Tett, Gillian. 2018. "Gillian Tett Asks If Banking Culture Has Really Changed." *Financial Times*, August 27. https://www.ft.com/video/0e20f113-f559-4f8e-85b3-6773 e96c75b0.

Thomasberger, Claus. 2005. "Human Freedom and the 'Reality of Society.'" *History of Economic Thought* 47 (2): 1–14.

Thwaites, Rachel. 2020. "Intimate Relationships and Choice in a Time of 'Cold Intimacies': Examining Illouz." In *Romantic Relationships in a Time of "Cold Intimacies."* Edited by Julia Carter and Lorena Arocha, 17–35. London: Palgrave Macmillan.

Toscano, Alberto, and Jeff Kinkle. 2015. *Cartographies of the Absolute.* Winchester, UK: Zero Books.

Turner, James. 1980. "Understanding the Populists." *Journal of American History* 67 (2): 354–73. https://doi.org/10.2307/1890413.

Ullock, Christopher J. 1996. "Imagining Community: A Metaphysics of Being or Becoming?" *Millennium* 25 (2): 425–41.

Uncertain Commons. 2013. *Speculate This!* Durham, NC: Duke University Press.

Upadhya, Carol. 2020. "Assembling Amaravati: Speculative Accumulation in a New Indian City." *Economy and Society* 49 (1): 141–69. https://doi.org/10.1080/03085 147.2019.1690257.

van der Zwan, Natascha. 2014. "Making Sense of Financialization." *Socio-economic Review* 12 (1): 99–129. https://doi.org/10.1093/ser/mwt020.

Vogel, Frank E., and Samuel L. Hayes. 1998. *Islamic Law and Finance: Religion, Risk, and Return.* The Hague, Neth.: Brill.

Vogl, Joseph. 2014. *The Specter of Capital.* Stanford, CA: Stanford University Press.

Wade, Lisa. 2017. *American Hookup: The New Culture of Sex on Campus.* New York: W. W. Norton.

Ward, Janelle. 2017. "What Are You Doing on Tinder? Impression Management on a Matchmaking Mobile App." *Information, Communication and Society* 20 (11): 1644–59.

Weber, Max. (1894) 2000. "Stock and Commodity Exchanges [*Die Börse* (1894)]." *Theory and Society* 29 (3): 305–38.

Weber, Max. 1978. *Economy and Society: An Outline of Interpretive Sociology.* Berkeley: University of California Press.

Weber, Max. 1992. *The Protestant Ethic and the Spirit of Capitalism*. Translated by Talcott Parsons. Introduction by Anthony Giddens. London: Routledge.

Woolf, Virginia. 1979. *The Diary of Virginia Woolf*. Vol. 1, *1915–1919*. New York: Mariner.

Wuthnow, Robert. 2018. *The Left Behind: Decline and Rage in Rural America*. Princeton, NJ: Princeton University Press.

Zaloom, Caitlin. 2006. *Out of the Pits: Traders and Technology from Chicago to London*. Chicago: University of Chicago Press.

Zeckhauser, Richard. 2014. "New Frontiers beyond Risk and Uncertainty: Ignorance, Group Decision, and Unanticipated Themes." *Handbook of the Economics of Risk and Uncertainty*. Oxford, UK: Elsevier.

Zelizer, Viviana A. Rotman. 1979. *Morals and Markets: The Development of Life Insurance in the United States*. New York: Columbia University Press.

Zelizer, Viviana A. 2007. *The Purchase of Intimacy*. Princeton, NJ: Princeton University Press.

Ziewitz, Malte. 2016. "Governing Algorithms: Myth, Mess, and Methods." *Science, Technology, and Human Values* 41 (1): 3–16.

Zuboff, Shoshana. 2019. *The Age of Surveillance Capitalism: The Fight for a Human Future at the New Frontier of Power*. London: Profile.

INDEX

experts *(cont.)*
    relationship of/conflict between, 20, 24,
    128; Trump's dismissal of, 116, 168n28
Extinction Rebellion movement, 134

Fabian, Ann, 47, 159n5, 159n7
Facebook: astrology apps and, 79;
    contradictory promises of, 73; Gilets
    Jaunes posts on, 134; as image-driven
    social networking platform, 65;
    perpetual scroll of, 2, 35; populist
    movements, role in, 67; regulation
    of posts on, 169n6; as a speculative
    technology, 66; "story" format that
    dominates on, 32; traditional posting
    structure of, 80
Facebook Timeline, 71
Farage, Nigel, 115
Faucher, Kane X., 163n21
Federici, Silvia, 141
Feher, Michel, 22, 75, 126
finance: dominance of based on its spec-
    ulative imagination, 144–46; history
    of, 4–5; neoliberalism and, escalating
    tension between, 22–25; political role
    of, 22 (*see also* neoliberals/neoliberal-
    ism); populism and, 98–100, 104–5,
    112–14, 117–18; power based on the
    imagination of, 6; re-imagining, impli-
    cations of, 3–4; society and, 1–3; states
    of (un)reality embedded in, 148
financial astrology, 77
financial crisis of 2008: breakdown of
    pre-2008 certainties, 33; derivatives
    and, 18; "fed-up-ness" following the,
    24; populist movement following
    (*see* neopopulists/neopopulism);
    public view of speculation follow-
    ing, 16; re-alignment of markets and
    politics following, 19–20; volatility
    and uncertainty following, 63
financialization: critiques of, 104; digi-
    talization and, convergence of, 66–67;
    emergence of in Chicago, 41–43;
    historical shift from *homo economicus*
    to *homo speculans* and, 4–6; paradox of
    neopopulism and, 100–102; paradox

of neopopulism and, explanations of,
    102–7; resistance to, 124–27; spectacle
    and, 74–75
Fisher, Mark, 140
Fordist model, 24, 87, 127
Foucault, Michel, 23
4chan, 71, 100, 165n5
France: Gilets Jaunes in, 11, 35, 96, 106,
    123, 171–72n21
Fraser, Nancy, 103, 167n17
futures exchanges: bucket shops
    (*see* bucket shops); exclusion and seg-
    regation in the history of, 42–43; grass-
    roots speculation distinguished from,
    45–48; moral legitimacy of, distinction
    between formal exchanges and infor-
    mal bucket shops and, 44–48; origins
    in Chicago, 41–43; the telegraph, ticker
    tapes, and the expansion of, 43–44

Gab, 71
Gago, Verónica, 5, 104, 130
gambling: anti-gambling movements,
    46–47; grassroots speculation deni-
    grated as, 45–47; as irrationality, 45;
    speculation, distinguished from, 16,
    45–48; speculative fever and, 40
Gann, W. D., 77, 79
Gerbaudo, Paolo, 167n24
German Romanticism, 55
Germany, 46
Gerteis, Joseph, 160n11
Gibson, William, 101
Giddens, Anthony, 88, 91
Gilets Jaunes, 35, 96, 106, 123, 133–36,
    139, 170–71n21
glass house metaphor, 36–37, 67–68,
    162n7
Glass-Steagall Act, 22
global injustice as spectacle, 75
globalized finance, alternative rationali-
    ties to, 3
Gonzalez-Vicente, Ruben, 166n9
Goodwin, Geoff, 166n7
Google, Artists Machine Intelligence
    Program, 79
Goolsby, Alyssa, 160n11